House of Odd

CREATED BY

DEAN KOONTZ

WRITTEN BY **LANDRY Q. WALKER** AND **DEAN KOONTZ**

ILLUSTRATIONS BY **QUEENIE CHAN**

BALLANTINE BOOKS
NEW YORK

House of Odd is a work of fiction. Names, characters, places, and incidents are the products of the author's imagination or are used fictitiously. Any resemblance to actual events, locales, or persons, living or dead, is entirely coincidental.

A Del Rey Books Trade Paperback Original

Published in the United States by Del Rey, an imprint of The Random House Publishing Group, a division of Random House, Inc., New York.

DEL REY is a registered trademark and the Del Rey colophon is a trademark of Random House, Inc.

ISBN 978-0-345-52545-1
eBook ISBN 978-0-345-53546-7

Printed in the United States of America

www.delreybooks.com

2 4 6 8 9 7 5 3 1

Cover Design—David Stevenson

Toning Assistant—Dee DuPuy

CONTENTS

Also by Dean Koontz

77 Shadow Street • What the Night Knows • Breathless • Relentless • Your Heart Belongs to Me • Odd Hours • The Darkest Evening of the Year • The Good Guy • Brother Odd • The Husband • Forever Odd • Velocity • Life Expectancy • The Taking • Odd Thomas • The Face • By the Light of the Moon • One Door Away from Heaven • From the Corner of His Eye • False Memory • Seize the Night • Fear Nothing • Mr. Murder • Dragon Tears • Hideaway • Cold Fire • The Bad Place • Midnight • Lightning • Watchers • Strangers • Twilight Eyes • Darkfall • Phantoms • Whispers • The Mask • The Vision • The Face of Fear • Night Chills • Shattered • The Voice of the Night • The Servants of Twilight • The House of Thunder • The Key to Midnight • The Eyes of Darkness • Shadowfires • Winter Moon • The Door to December • Dark Rivers of the Heart • Icebound • Strange Highways • Intensity • Sole Survivor • Ticktock • The Funhouse • Demon Seed

DEAN KOONTZ'S FRANKENSTEIN

Book One: Prodigal Son

Book Two: City of Night

Book Three: Dead and Alive

Book Four: Lost Souls

Book Five: The Dead Town

Also by Queenie Chan

The Dreaming, volumes 1-3

In Odd We Trust

Odd Is on Our Side

House of
of
Odd

Chapter 1

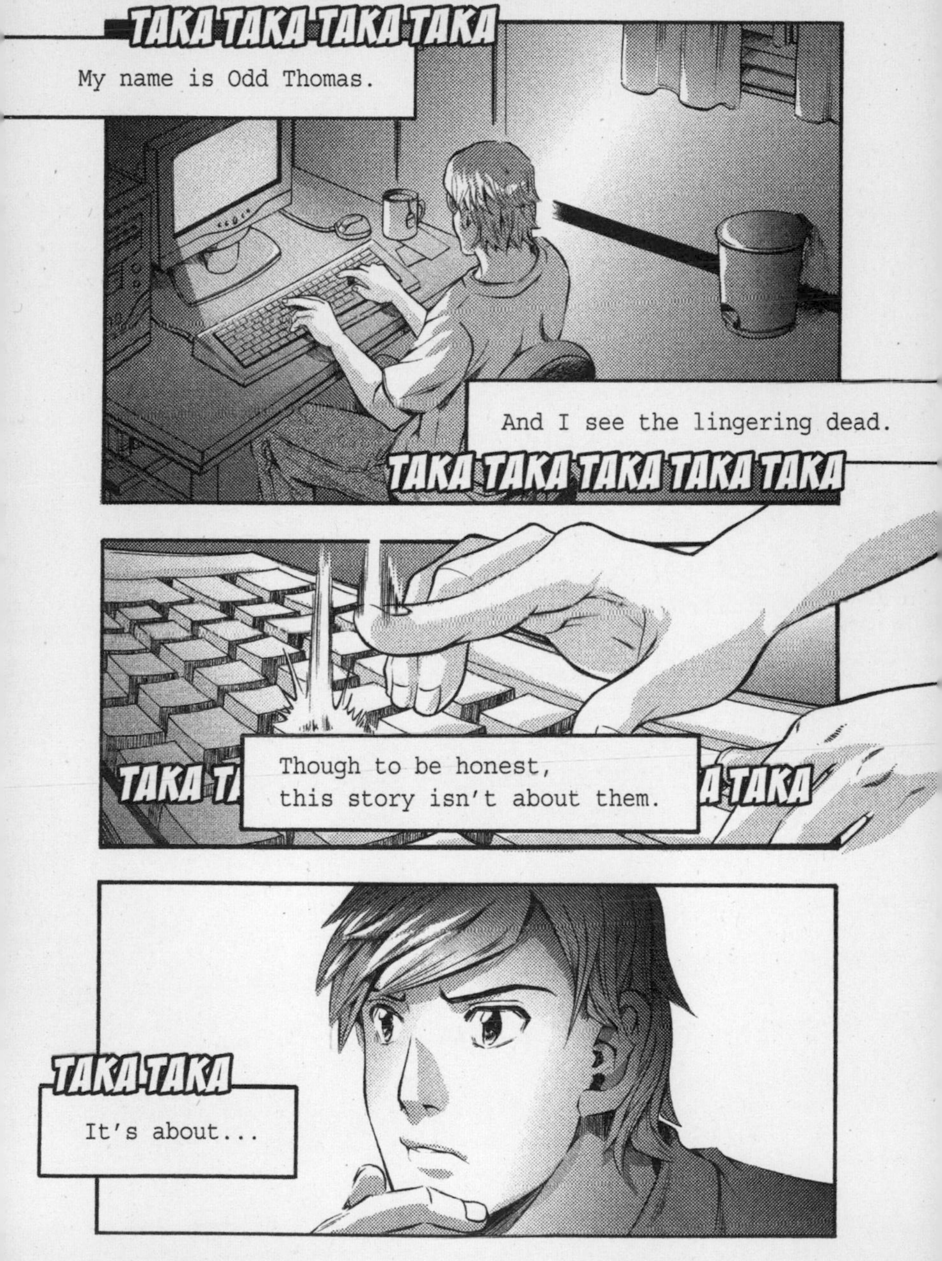
TAKA TAKA TAKA TAKA
My name is Odd Thomas.
And I see the lingering dead.
TAKA TAKA TAKA TAKA TAKA
TAKA
Though to be honest, this story isn't about them.
TAKA
TAKA TAKA
It's about...

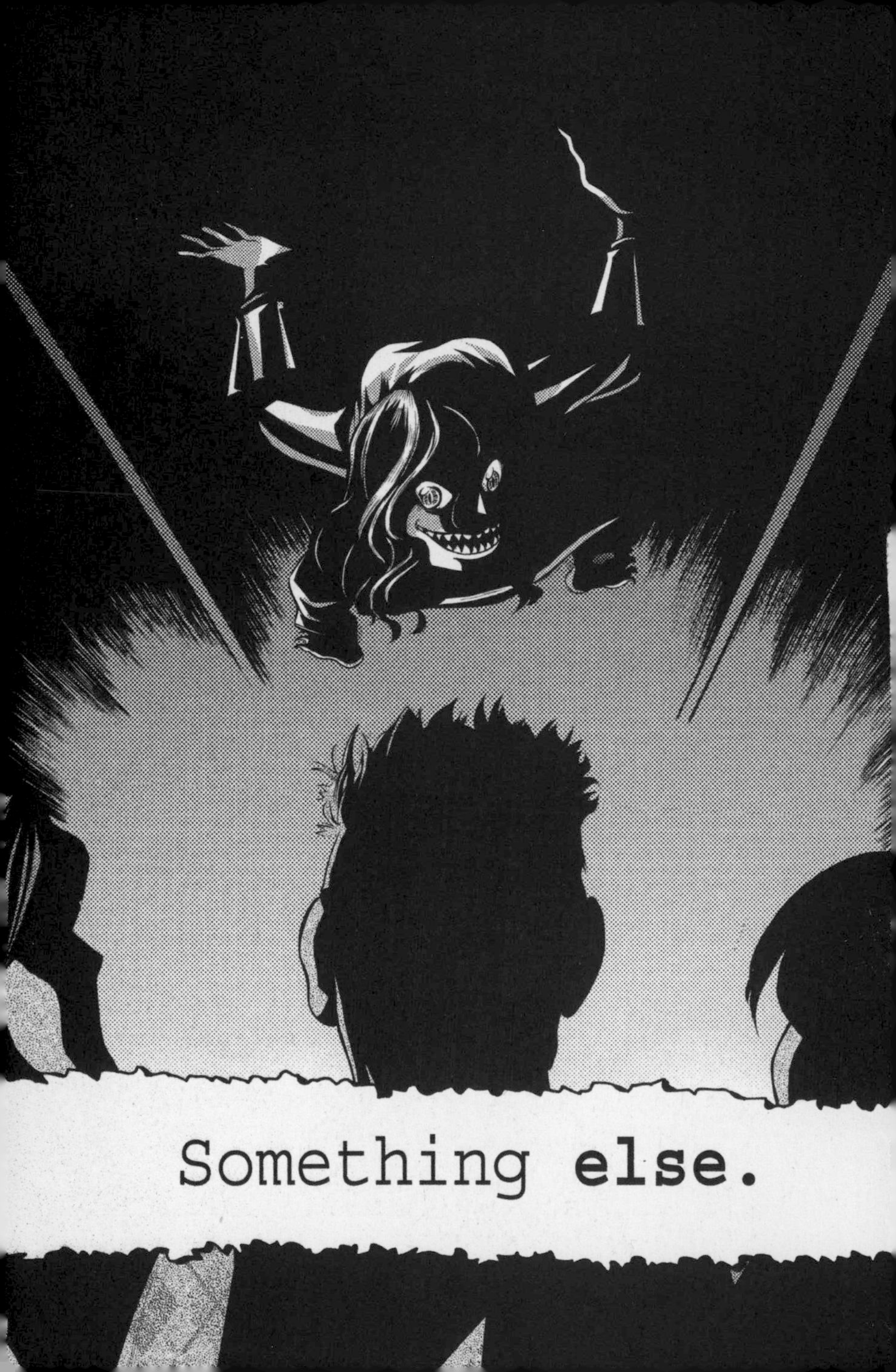
Something else.

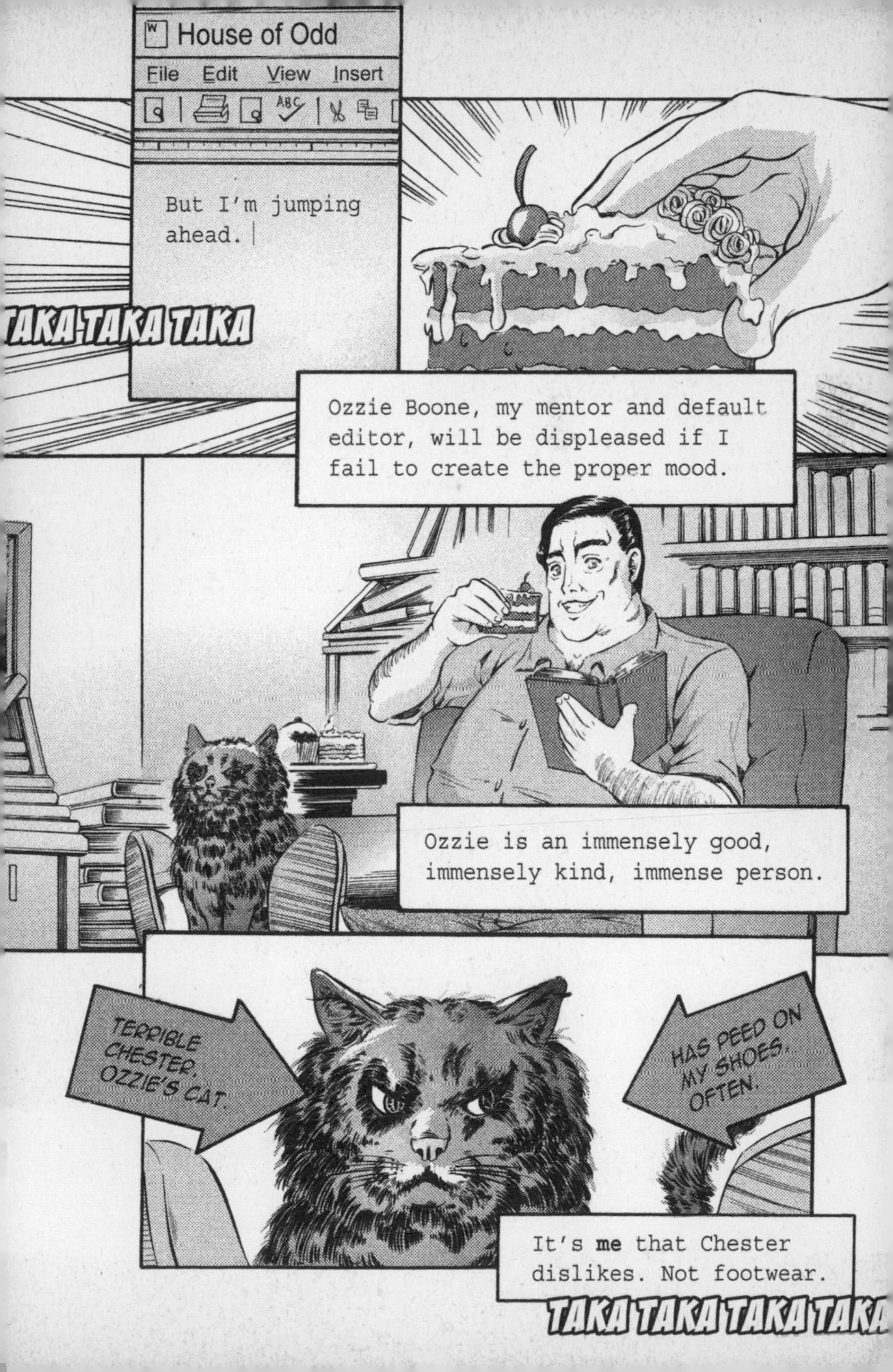
House of Odd
File Edit View Insert
But I'm jumping ahead.
TAKA TAKA TAKA
Ozzie Boone, my mentor and default editor, will be displeased if I fail to create the proper mood.
Ozzie is an immensely good, immensely kind, immense person.
TERRIBLE CHESTER, OZZIE'S CAT.
HAS PEED ON MY SHOES. OFTEN.
It's **me** that Chester dislikes. Not footwear.
TAKA TAKA TAKA TAKA

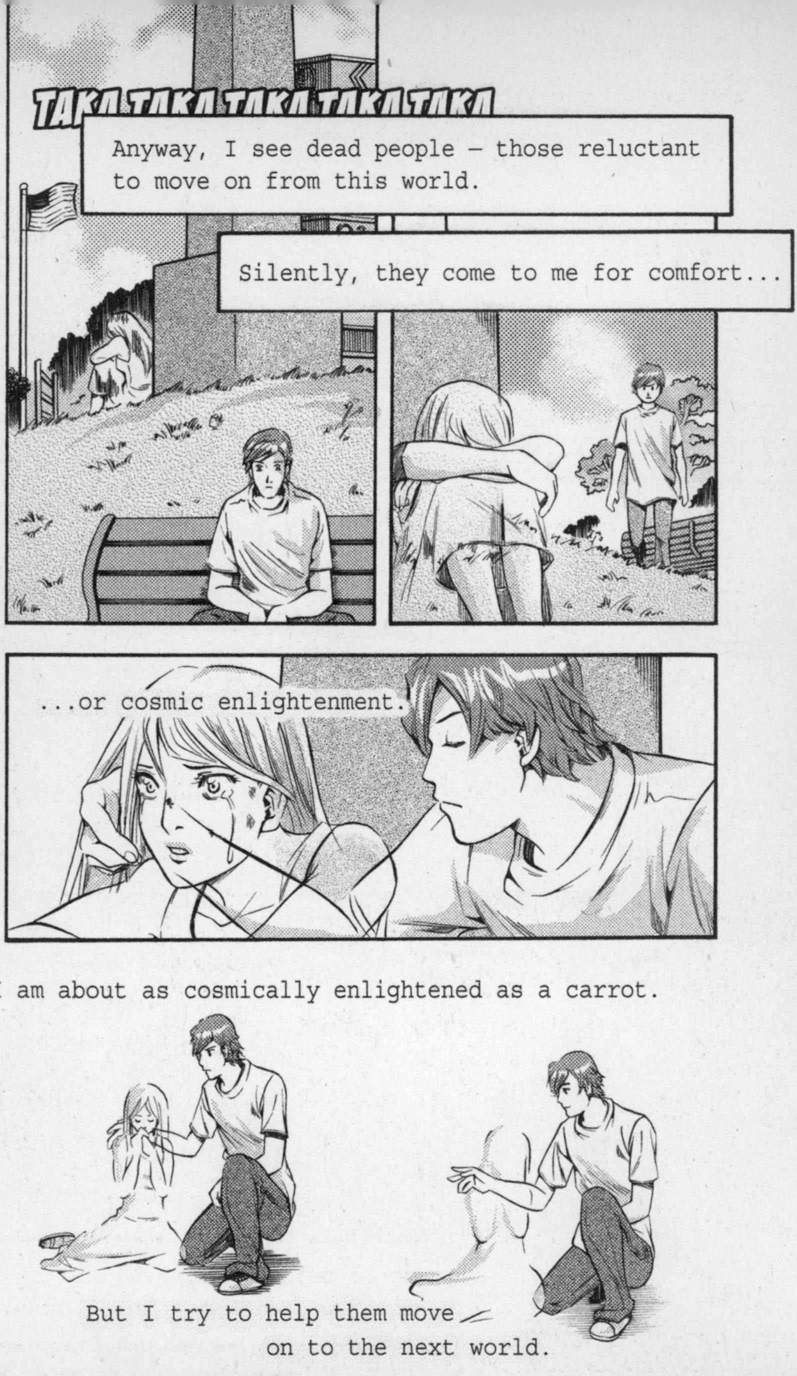
TAKA TAKA TAKA TAKA TAKA
Anyway, I see dead people – those reluctant to move on from this world.
Silently, they come to me for comfort...
...or cosmic enlightenment.
I am about as cosmically enlightened as a carrot.
But I try to help them move on to the next world.

At Ozzie's urging, I have already written several of these narratives.

My life is...**unusual**.
I've faced...

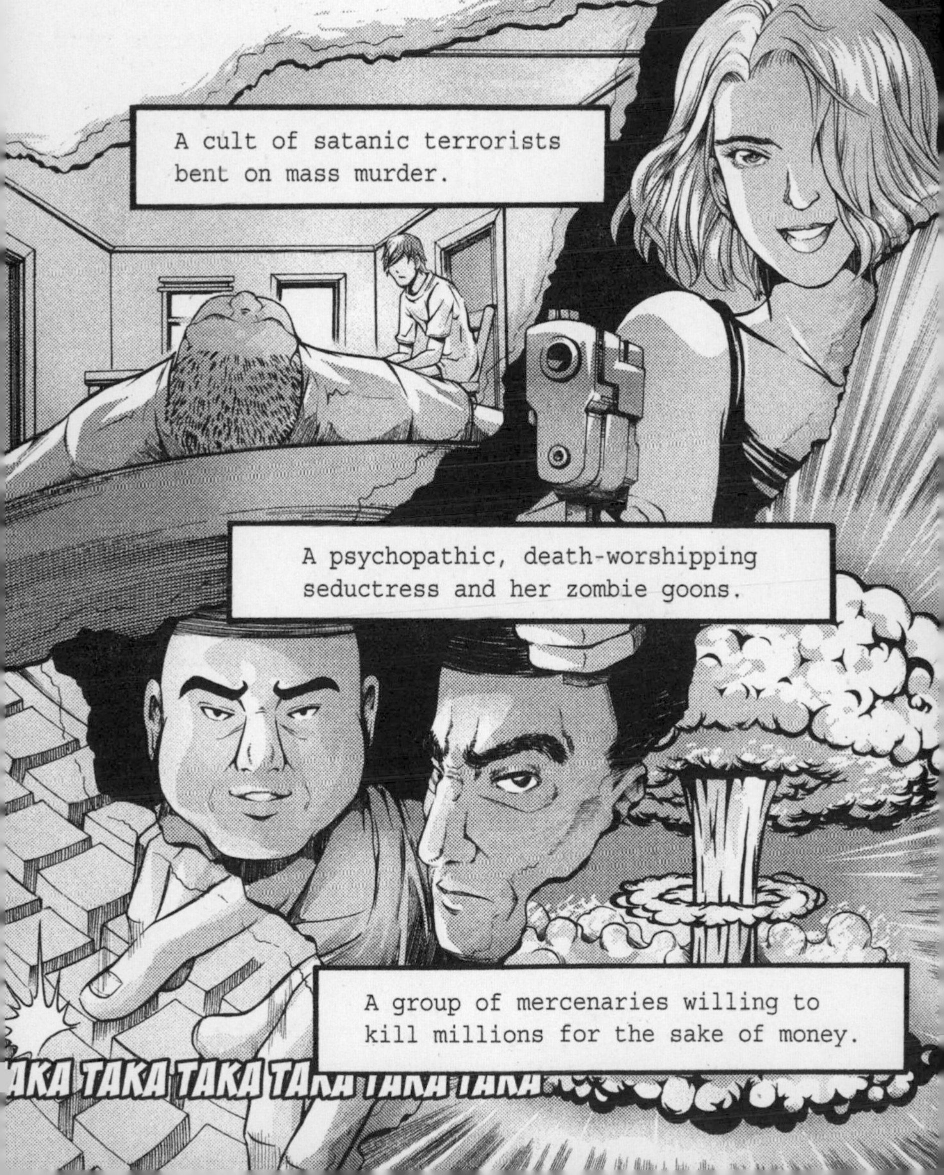
A cult of satanic terrorists bent on mass murder.
A psychopathic, death-worshipping seductress and her zombie goons.
A group of mercenaries willing to kill millions for the sake of money.
AKA TAKA TAKA TA

These things I have seen...
these **horrible** things.

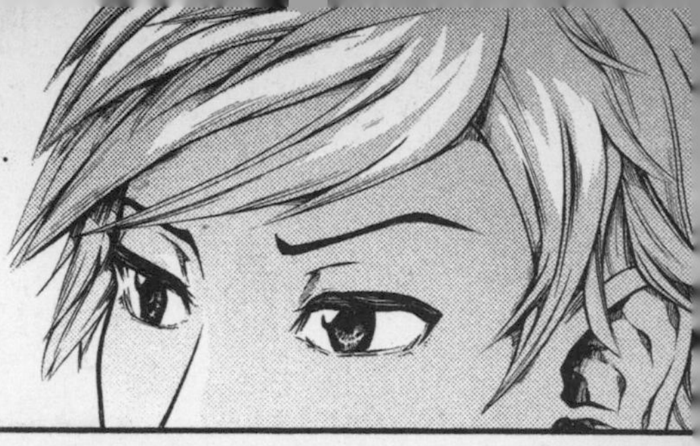

They are seldom
supernatural in origin.

Most evil is committed by the **living**
against the **living.**

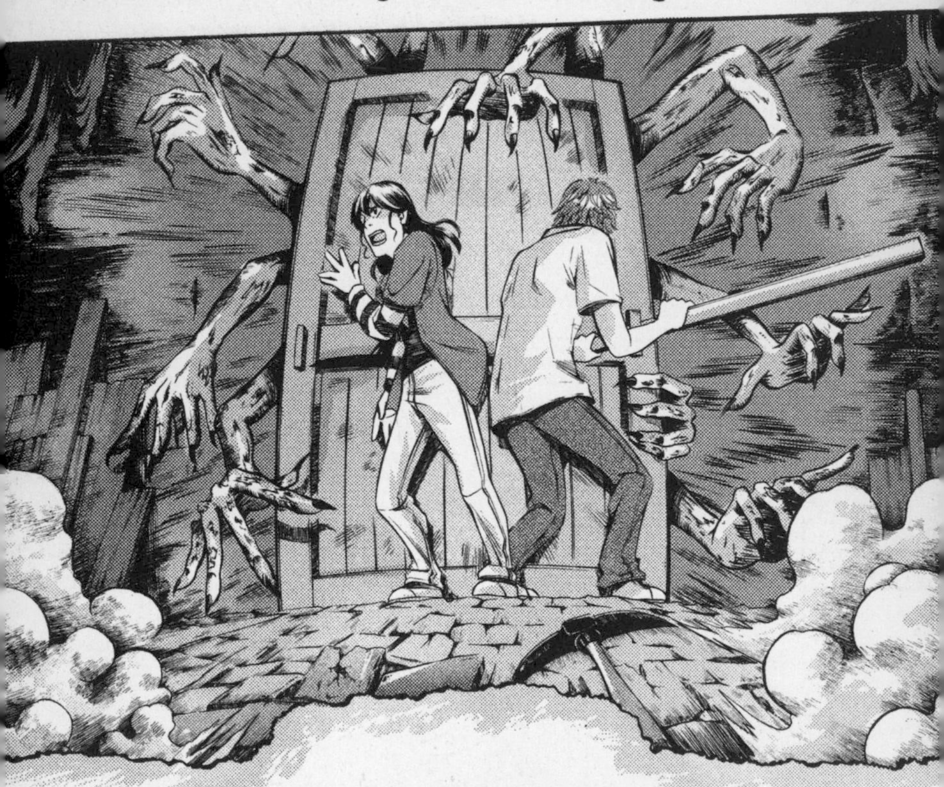

With an **occasional** exception.

I am writing this because Ozzie wants me to commit every one of my strange experiences to print.

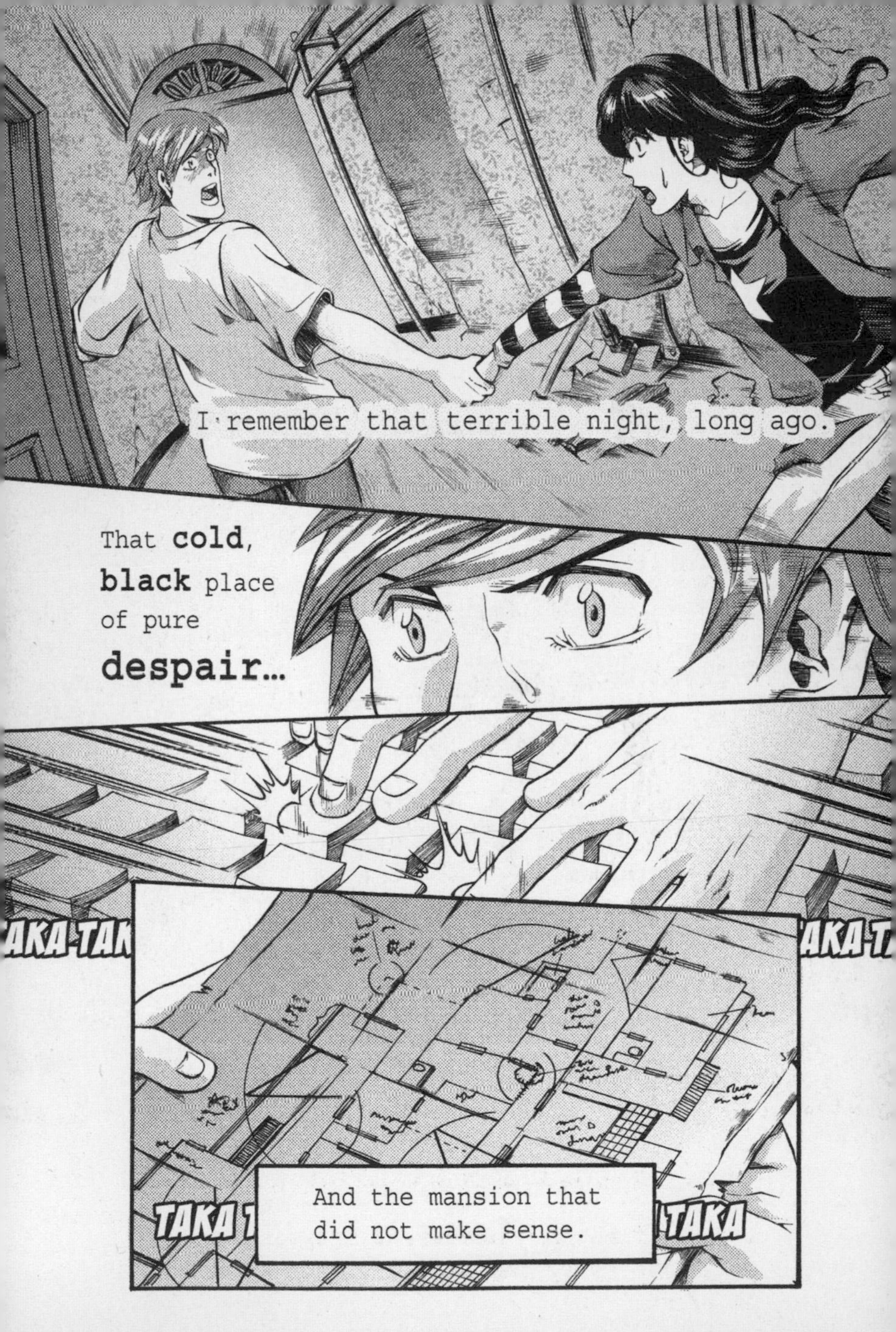
I remember that terrible night, long ago.
That **cold**, **black** place of pure **despair...**
AKA-TAK
AKA-T
TAKA T
TAKA
And the mansion that did not make sense.

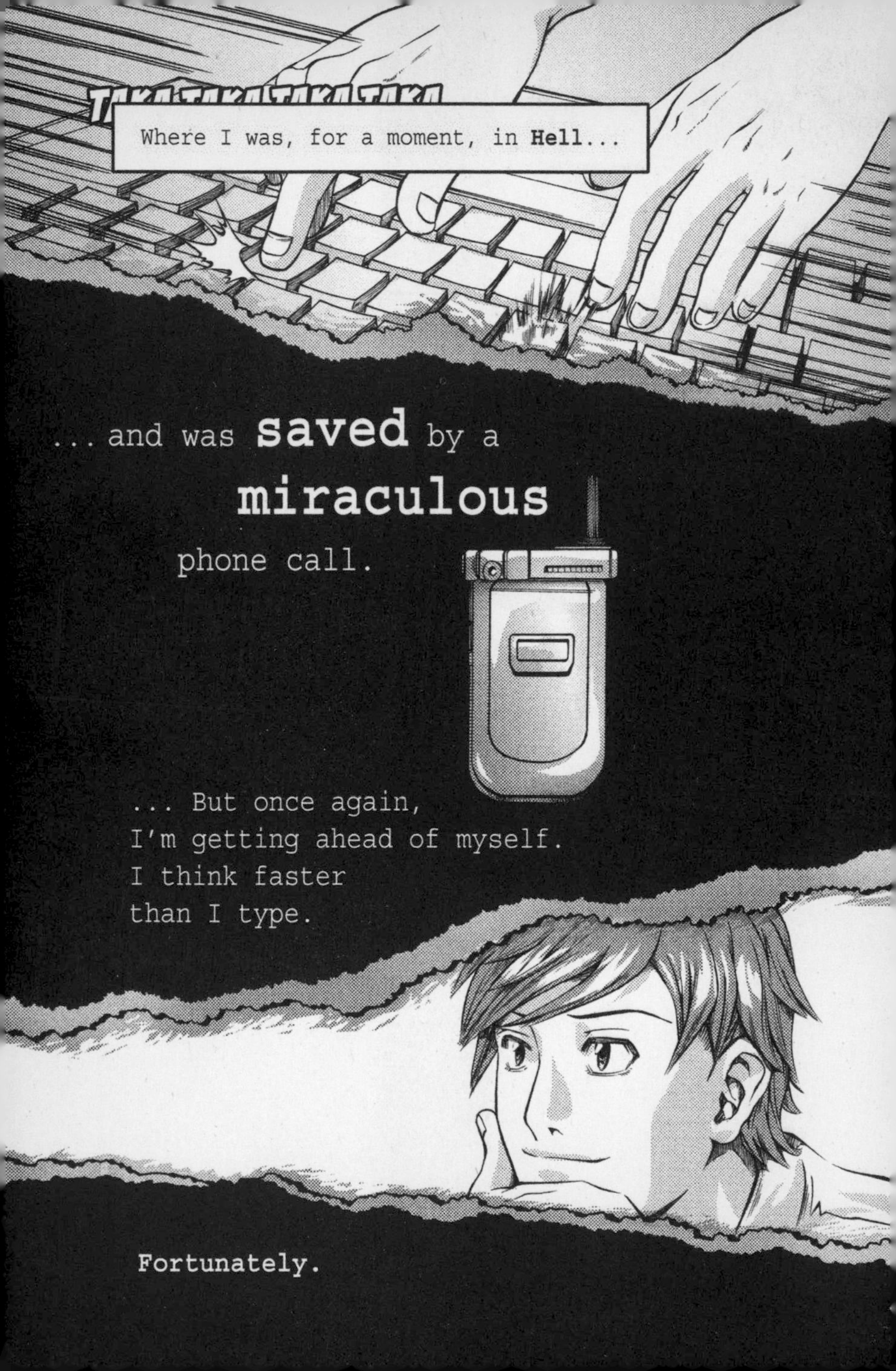
Where I was, for a moment, in **Hell**...
... and was **saved** by a **miraculous** phone call.
... But once again, I'm getting ahead of myself. I think faster than I type.
Fortunately.

Chapter 2

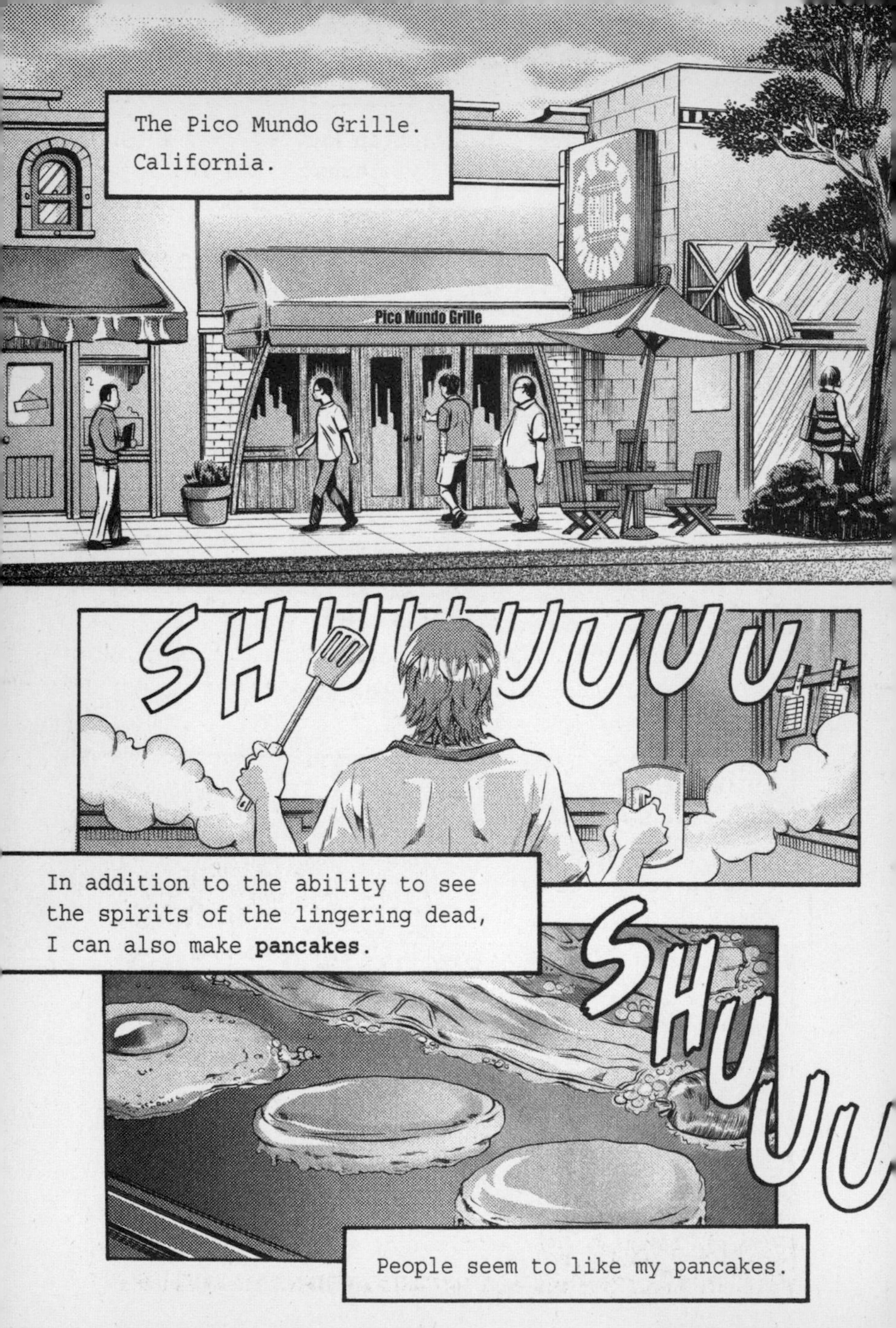

The Pico Mundo Grille.
California.
Pico Mundo Grille
SHUUUUUU
In addition to the ability to see the spirits of the lingering dead, I can also make **pancakes**.
SHUUU
People seem to like my pancakes.

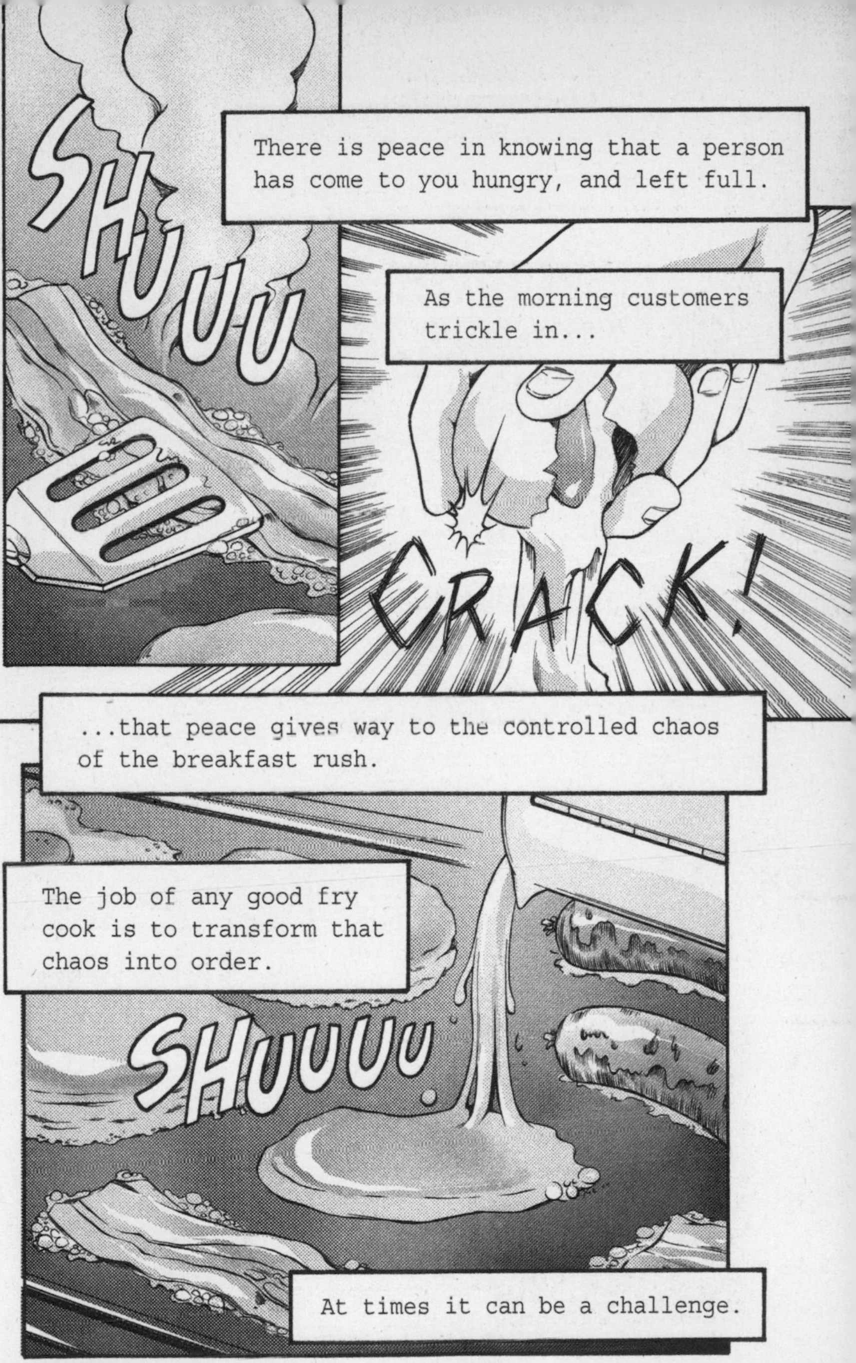
SHUUUU
There is peace in knowing that a person has come to you hungry, and left full.
As the morning customers trickle in...
CRACK!
...that peace gives way to the controlled chaos of the breakfast rush.
The job of any good fry cook is to transform that chaos into order.
SHUUUU
At times it can be a challenge.

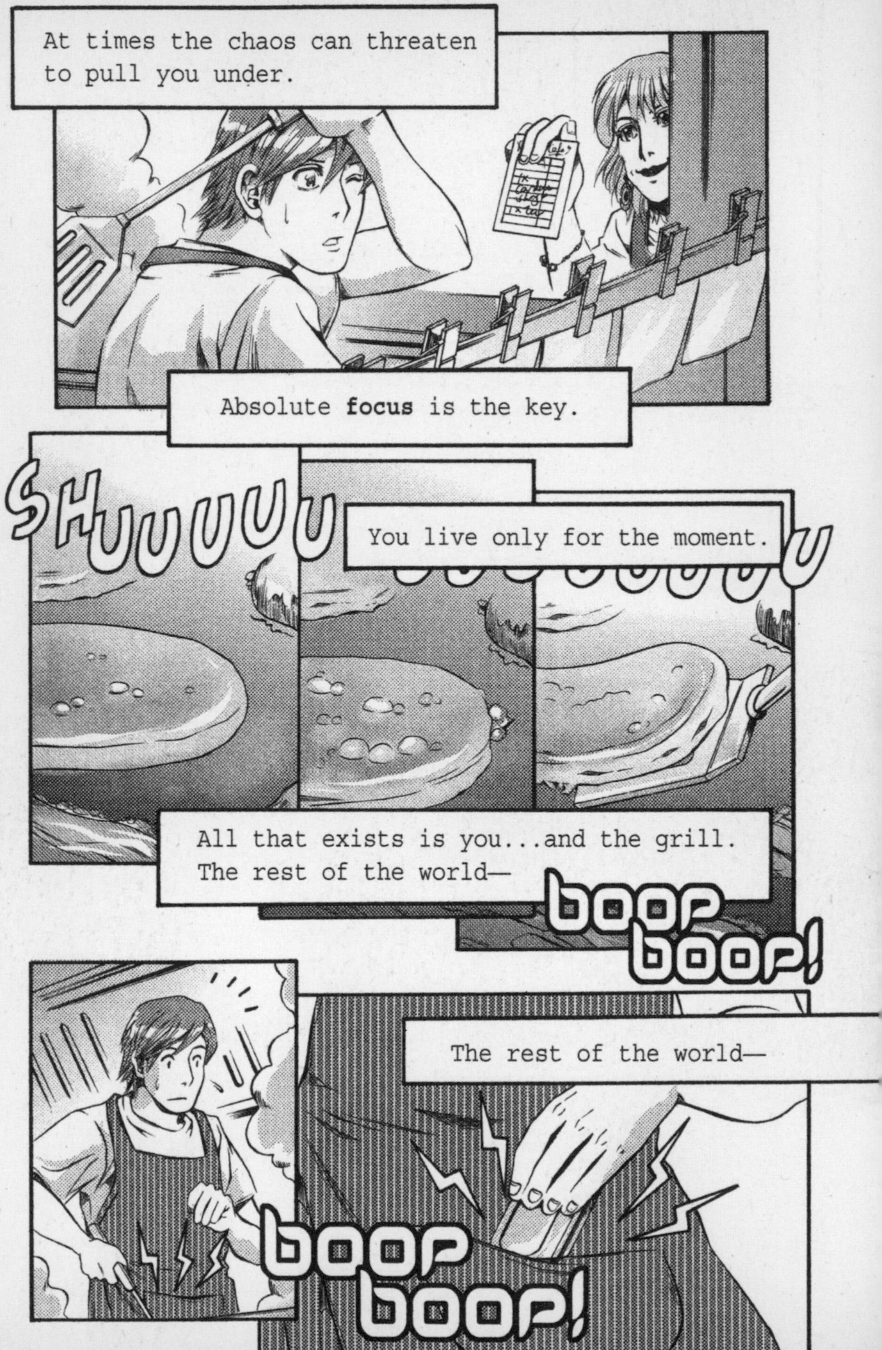
At times the chaos can threaten to pull you under.
Absolute focus is the key.
SHUUUUU
You live only for the moment.
All that exists is you...and the grill. The rest of the world—
boop boop!
The rest of the world—
boop boop!

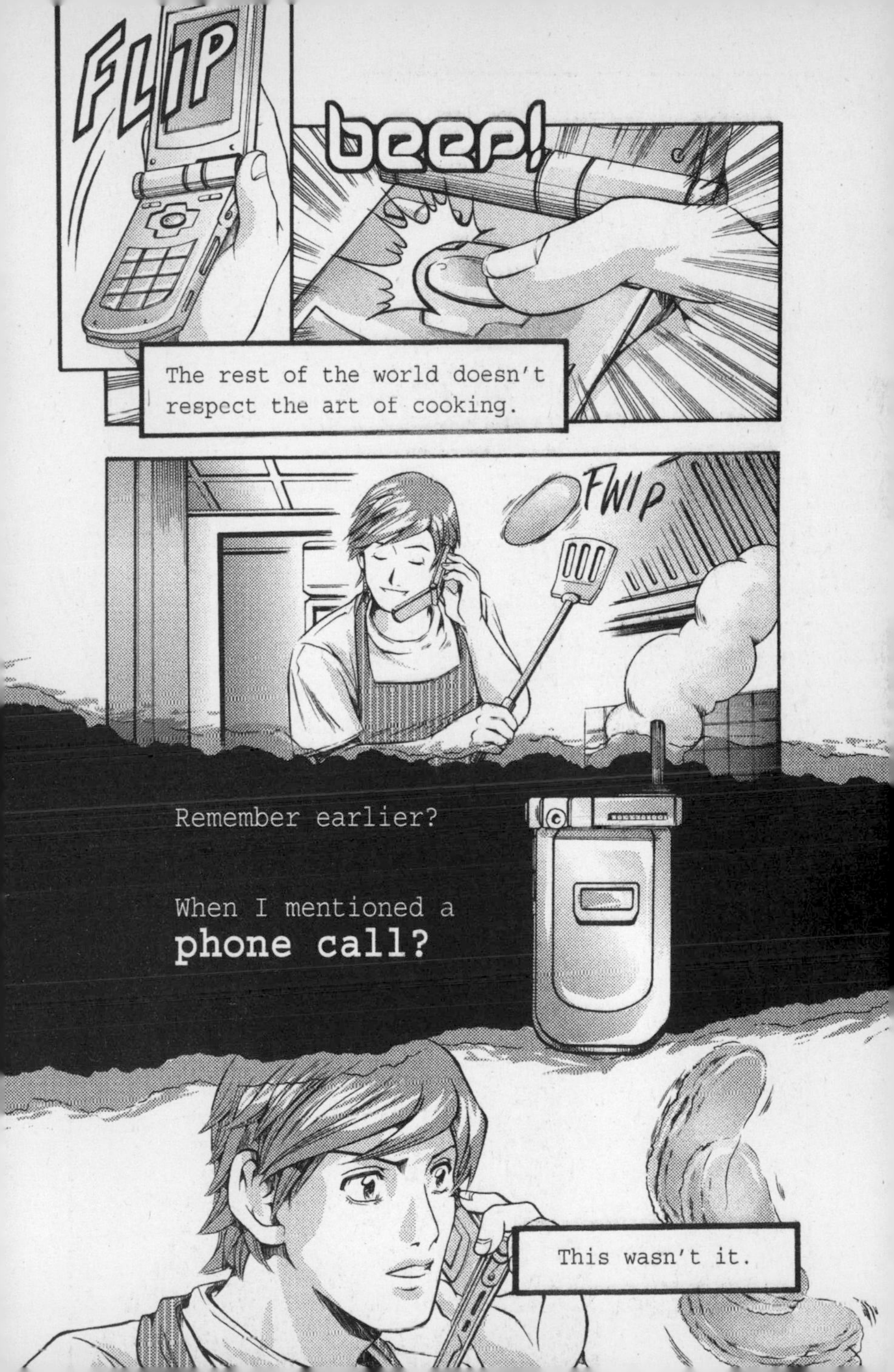
FLIP
beep!
The rest of the world doesn't respect the art of cooking.
FWIP
Remember earlier?
When I mentioned a **phone call?**
This wasn't it.

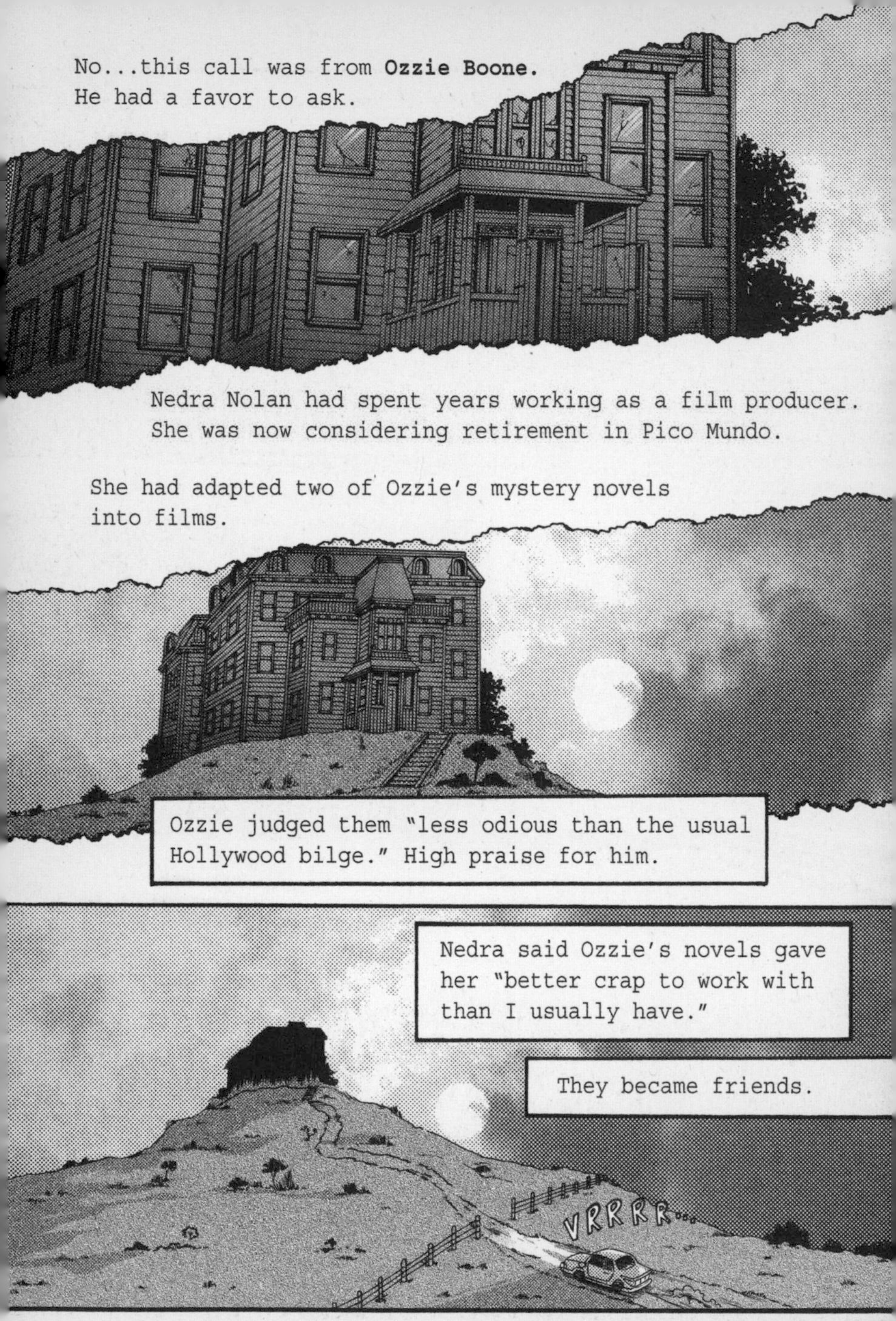
No...this call was from **Ozzie Boone.**
He had a favor to ask.
Nedra Nolan had spent years working as a film producer. She was now considering retirement in Pico Mundo.
She had adapted two of Ozzie's mystery novels into films.
Ozzie judged them "less odious than the usual Hollywood bilge." High praise for him.
Nedra said Ozzie's novels gave her "better crap to work with than I usually have."
They became friends.
VRRRR...

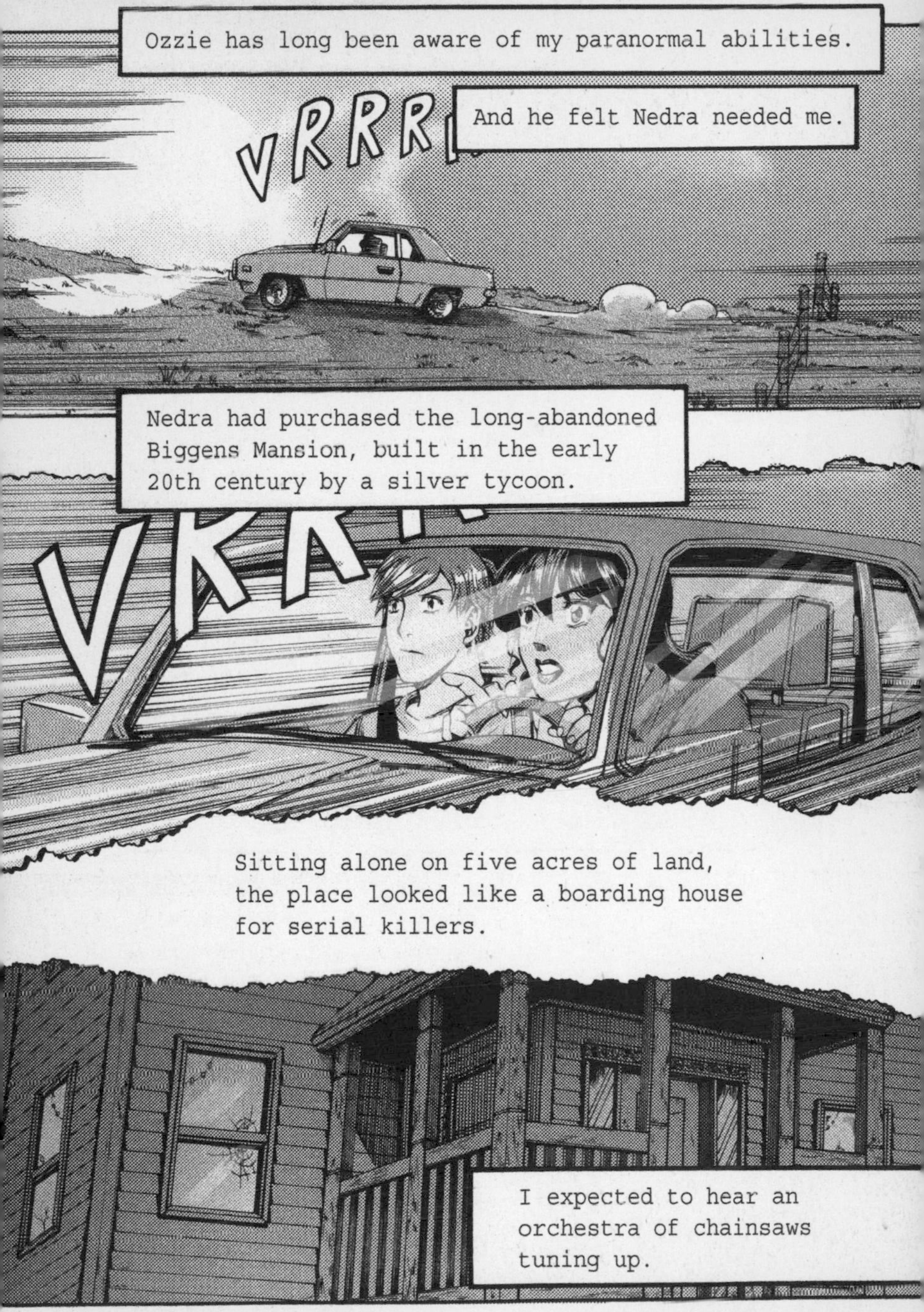
Ozzie has long been aware of my paranormal abilities.
VRRR
And he felt Nedra needed me.
Nedra had purchased the long-abandoned Biggens Mansion, built in the early 20th century by a silver tycoon.
Sitting alone on five acres of land, the place looked like a boarding house for serial killers.
I expected to hear an orchestra of chainsaws tuning up.

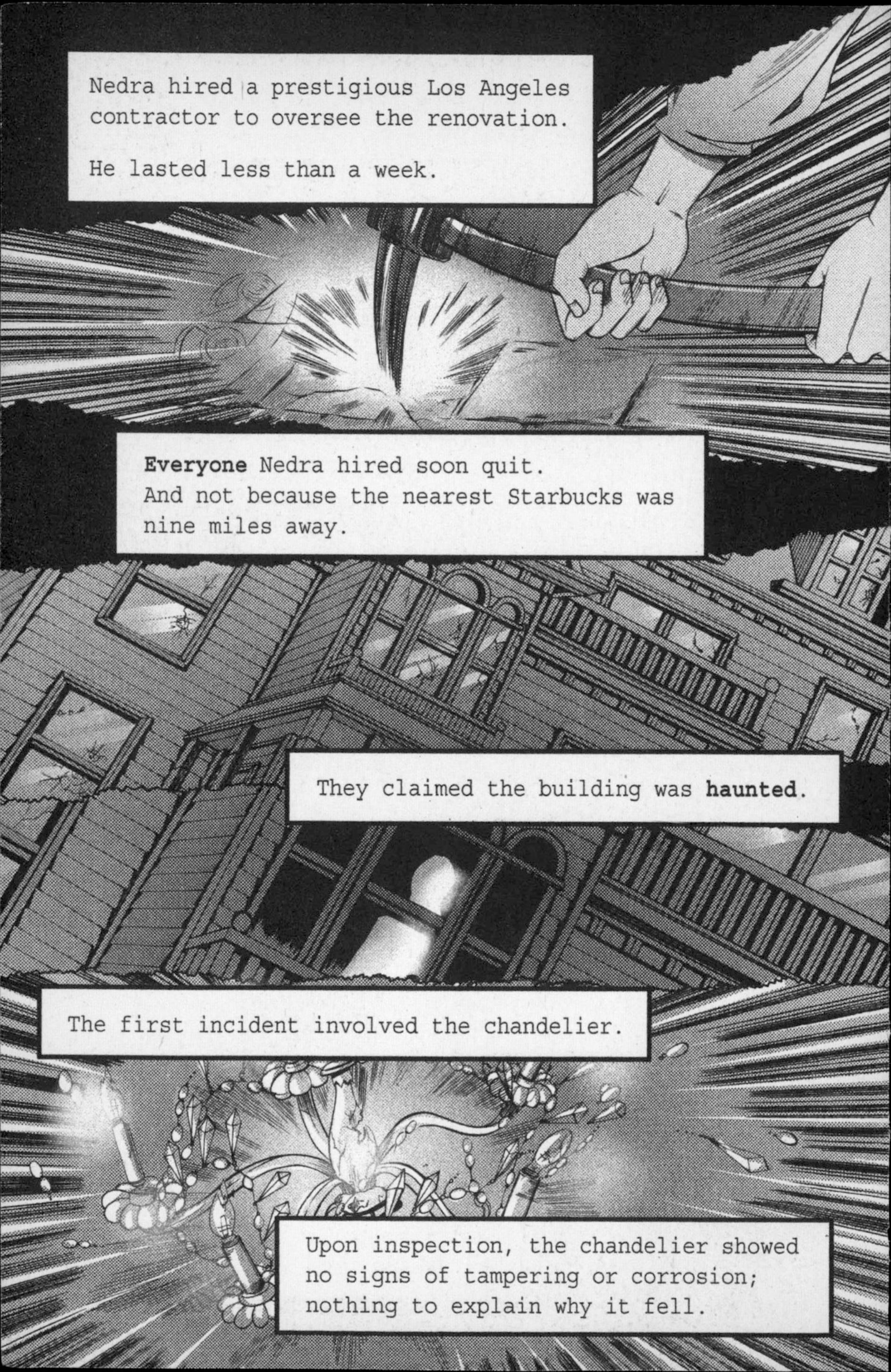
Nedra hired a prestigious Los Angeles contractor to oversee the renovation.
He lasted less than a week.
Everyone Nedra hired soon quit. And not because the nearest Starbucks was nine miles away.
They claimed the building was **haunted**.
The first incident involved the chandelier.
Upon inspection, the chandelier showed no signs of tampering or corrosion; nothing to explain why it fell.

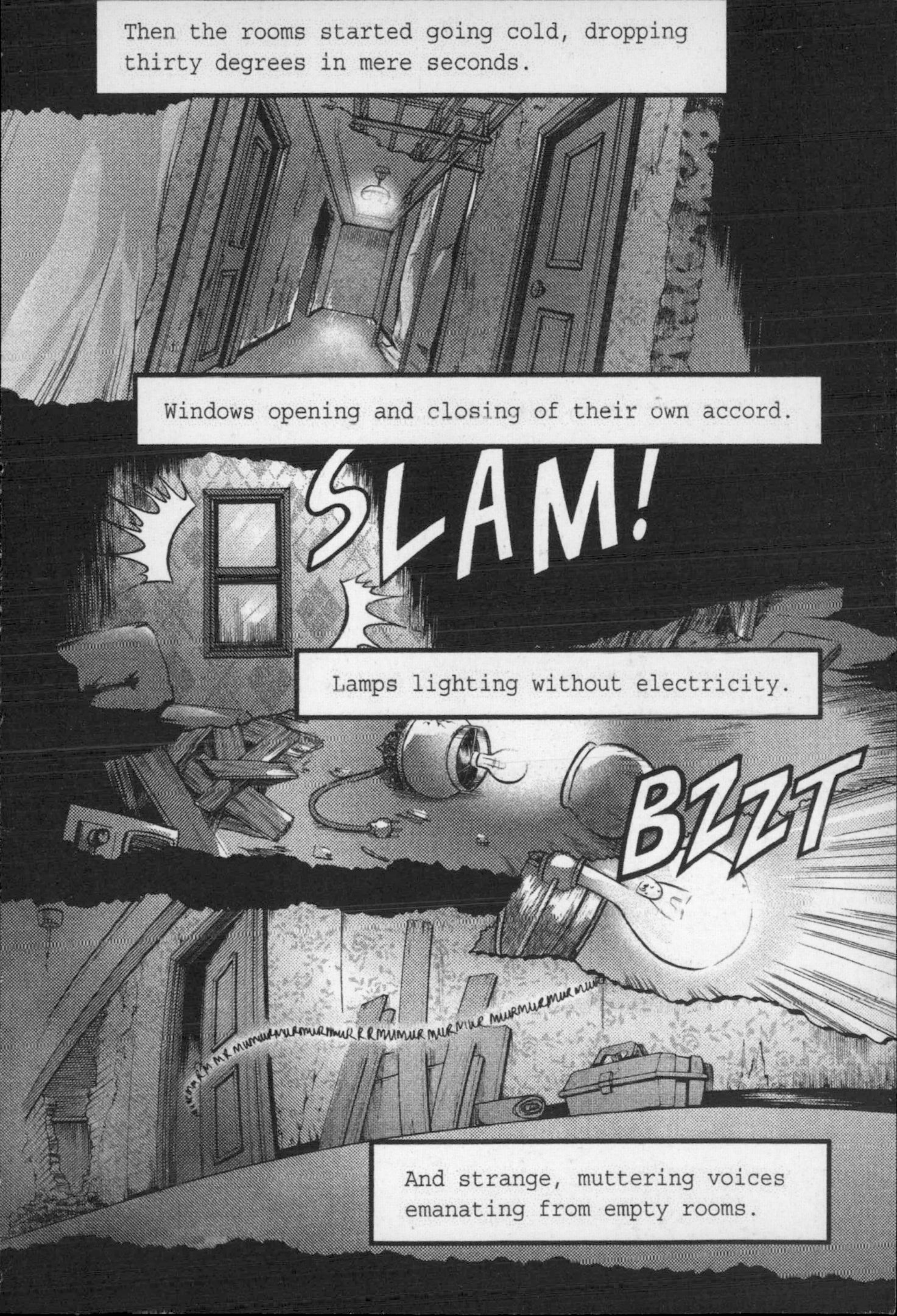
Then the rooms started going cold, dropping thirty degrees in mere seconds.
Windows opening and closing of their own accord.
SLAM!
Lamps lighting without electricity.
BZZT
And strange, muttering voices emanating from empty rooms.

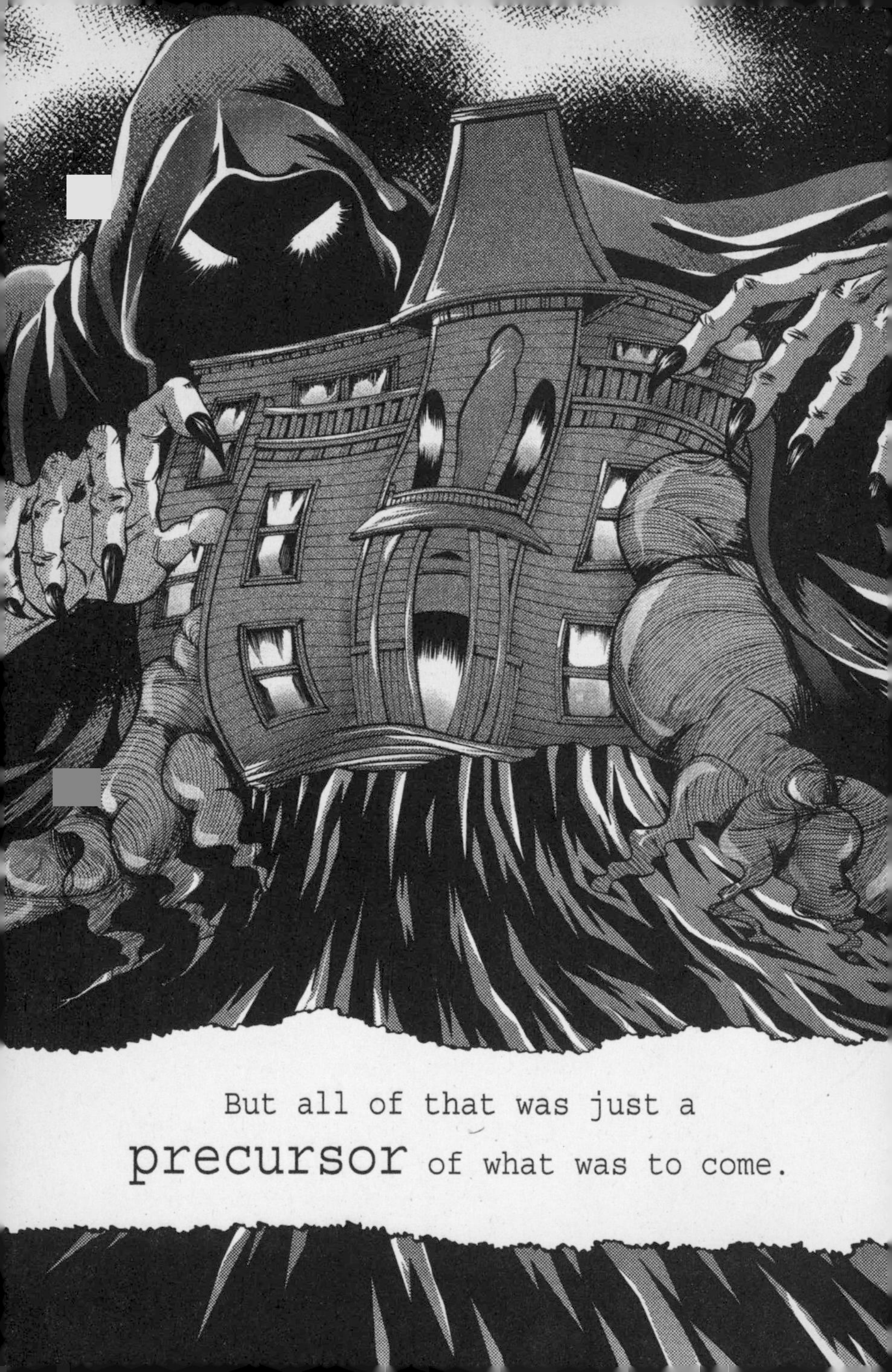
But all of that was just a
precursor of what was to come.

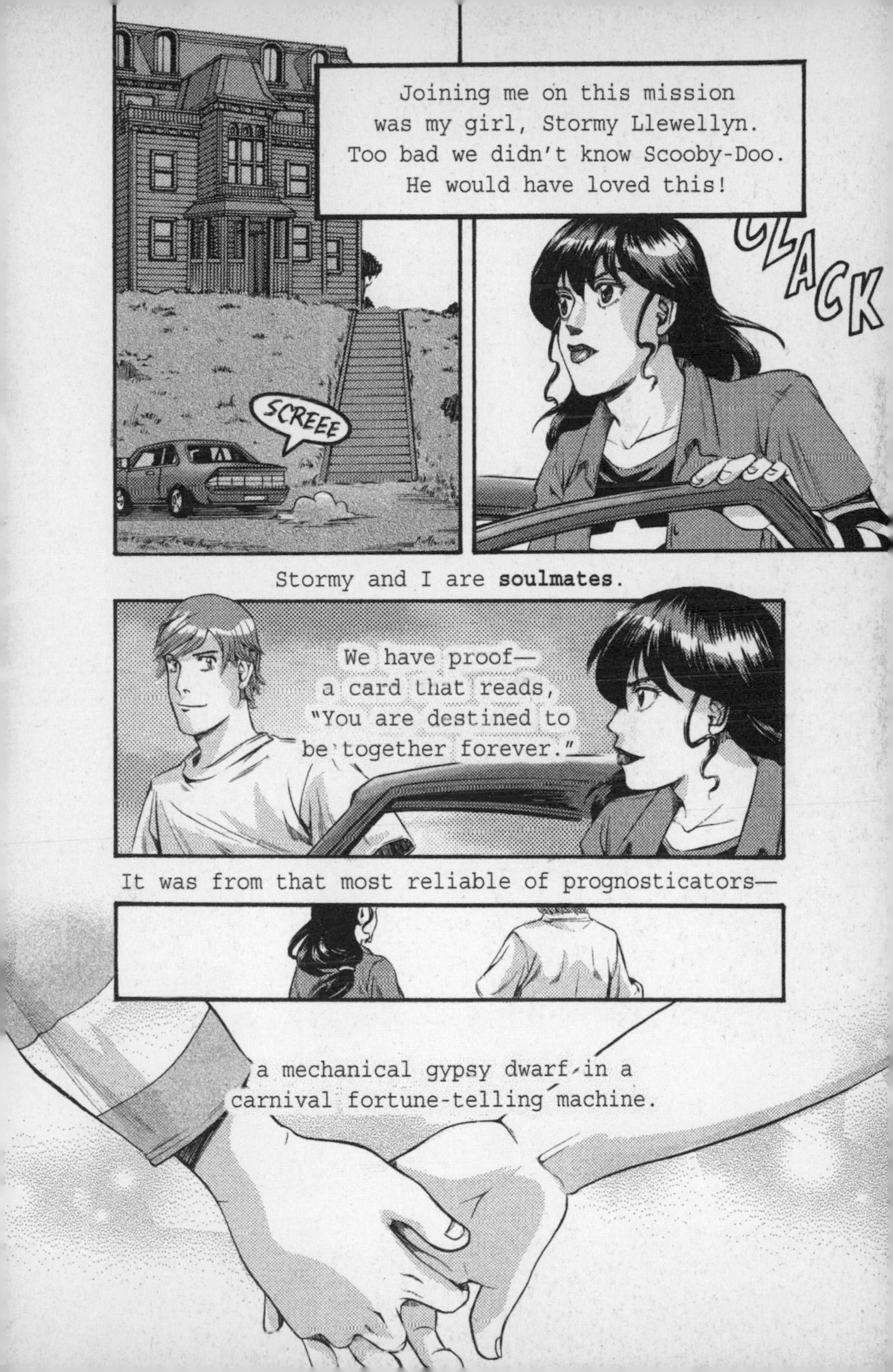
Joining me on this mission was my girl, Stormy Llewellyn. Too bad we didn't know Scooby-Doo. He would have loved this!
SCREEE
CLACK
Stormy and I are **soulmates**.
We have proof— a card that reads, "You are destined to be together forever."
It was from that most reliable of prognosticators—
a mechanical gypsy dwarf in a carnival fortune-telling machine.

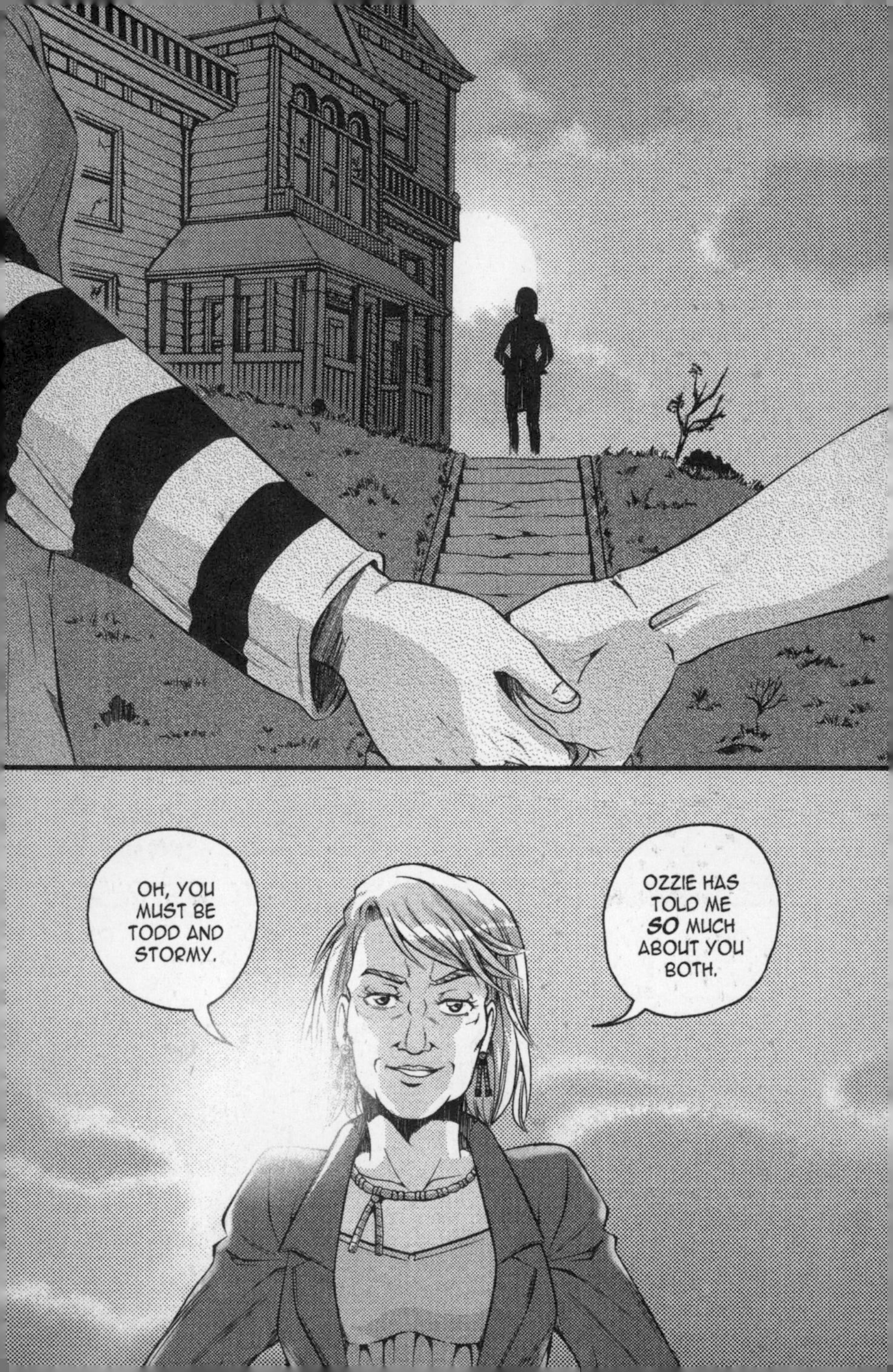
OH, YOU MUST BE TODD AND STORMY.
OZZIE HAS TOLD ME SO MUCH ABOUT YOU BOTH.

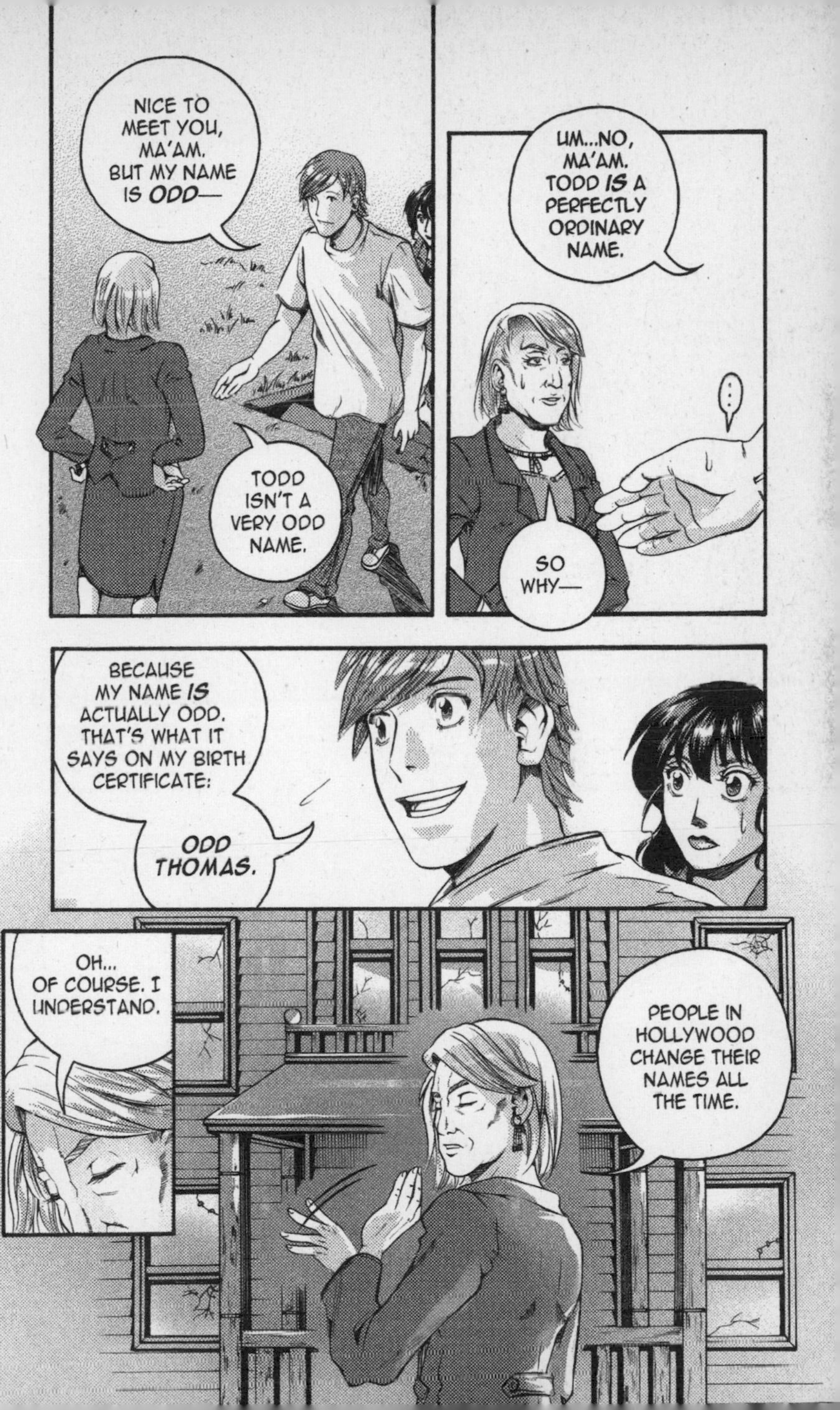
NICE TO MEET YOU, MA'AM. BUT MY NAME IS ODD—
TODD ISN'T A VERY ODD NAME.
UM...NO, MA'AM. TODD IS A PERFECTLY ORDINARY NAME.
SO WHY—
...
BECAUSE MY NAME IS ACTUALLY ODD. THAT'S WHAT IT SAYS ON MY BIRTH CERTIFICATE:
ODD THOMAS.
OH... OF COURSE. I UNDERSTAND.
PEOPLE IN HOLLYWOOD CHANGE THEIR NAMES ALL THE TIME.

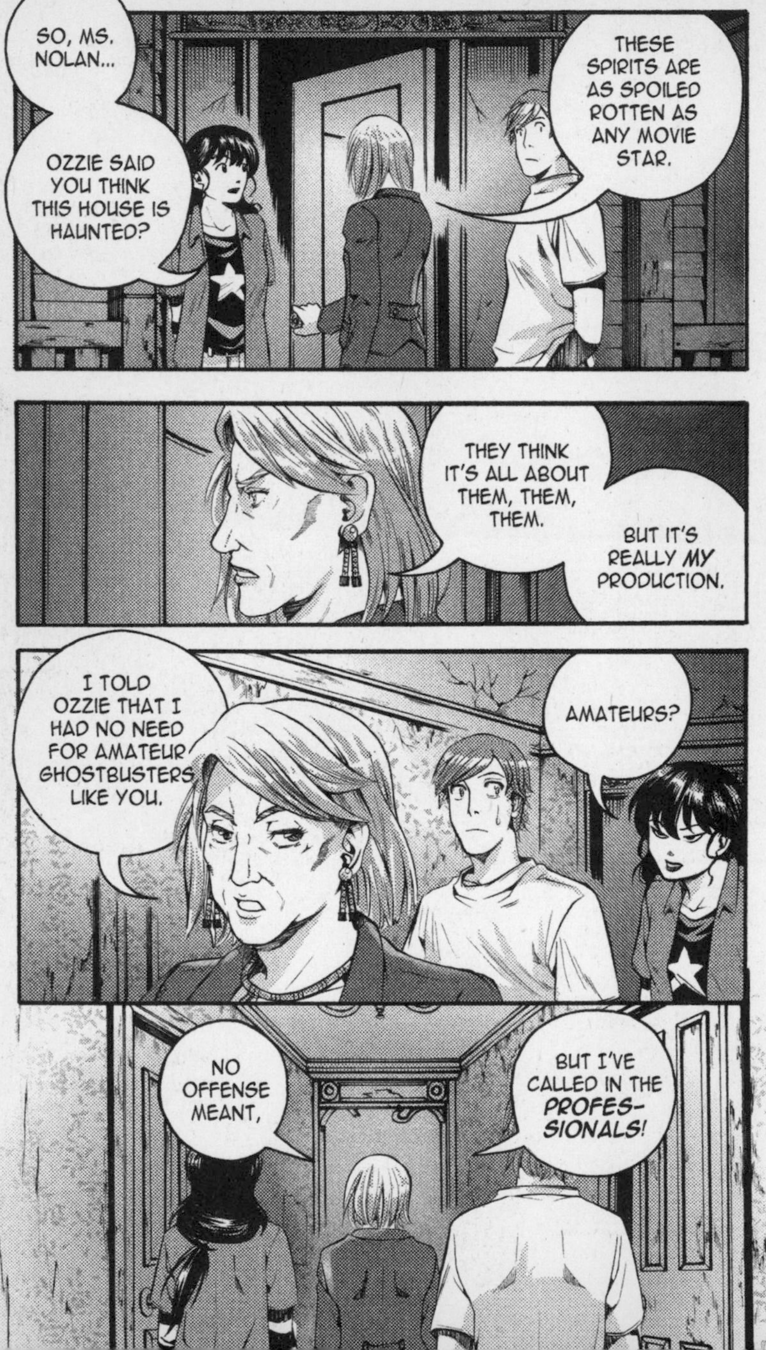
SO, MS. NOLAN...
OZZIE SAID YOU THINK THIS HOUSE IS HAUNTED?
THESE SPIRITS ARE AS SPOILED ROTTEN AS ANY MOVIE STAR.
THEY THINK IT'S ALL ABOUT THEM, THEM, THEM.
BUT IT'S REALLY *MY* PRODUCTION.
I TOLD OZZIE THAT I HAD NO NEED FOR AMATEUR GHOSTBUSTERS LIKE YOU.
AMATEURS?
NO OFFENSE MEANT,
BUT I'VE CALLED IN THE *PROFES-SIONALS!*

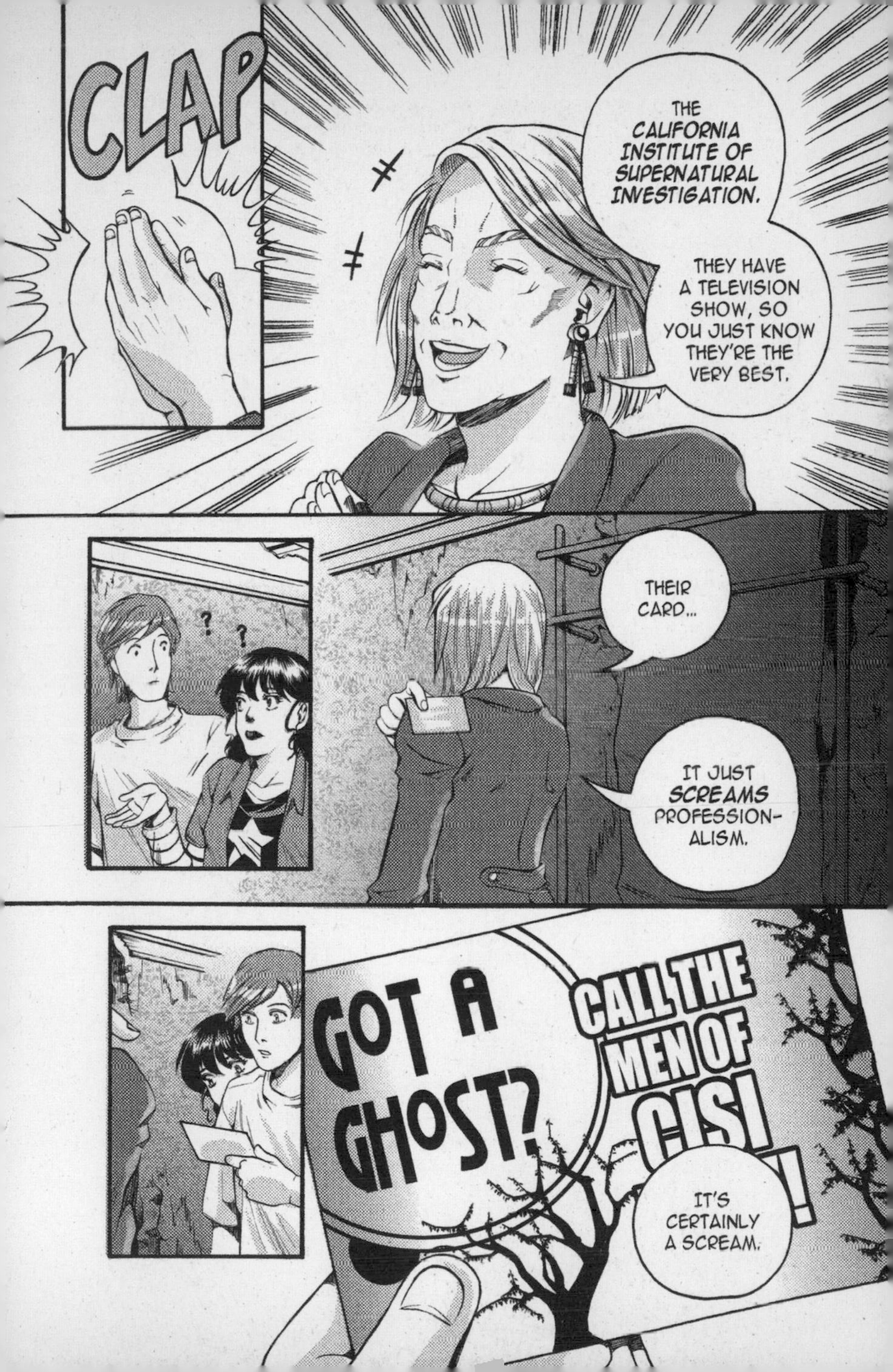
CLAP
THE CALIFORNIA INSTITUTE OF SUPERNATURAL INVESTIGATION.
THEY HAVE A TELEVISION SHOW, SO YOU JUST KNOW THEY'RE THE VERY BEST.
? ?
THEIR CARD...
IT JUST SCREAMS PROFESSION-ALISM.
GOT A GHOST?
CALL THE MEN OF CISI
IT'S CERTAINLY A SCREAM.

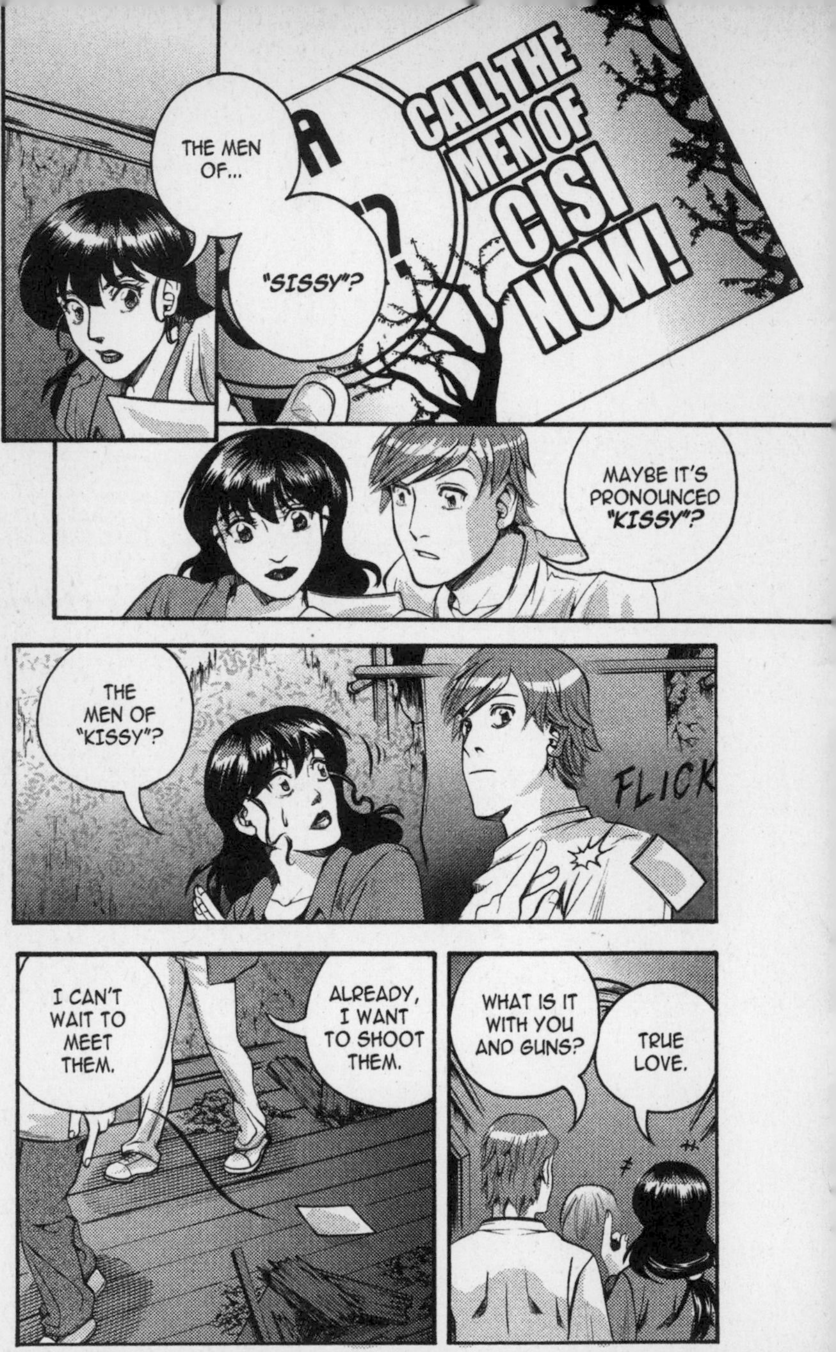
THE MEN OF...
"SISSY"?
CALL THE MEN OF CISI NOW!
MAYBE IT'S PRONOUNCED "KISSY"?
THE MEN OF "KISSY"?
FLICK
I CAN'T WAIT TO MEET THEM.
ALREADY, I WANT TO SHOOT THEM.
WHAT IS IT WITH YOU AND GUNS?
TRUE LOVE.

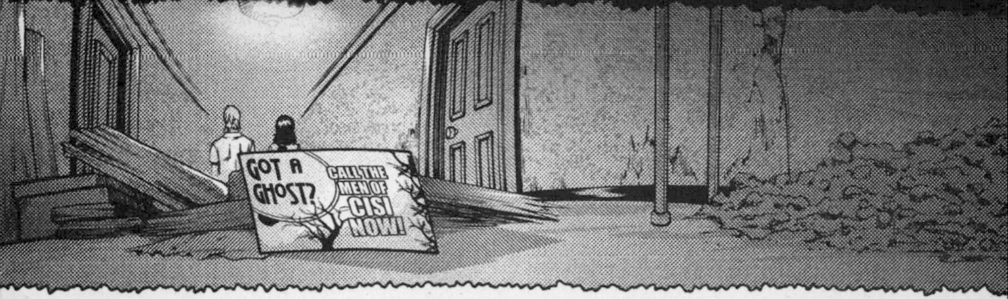
GOT A GHOST?
CALL THE MEN OF CISI NOW!

I felt a strange tingling. Faint. Short lived.

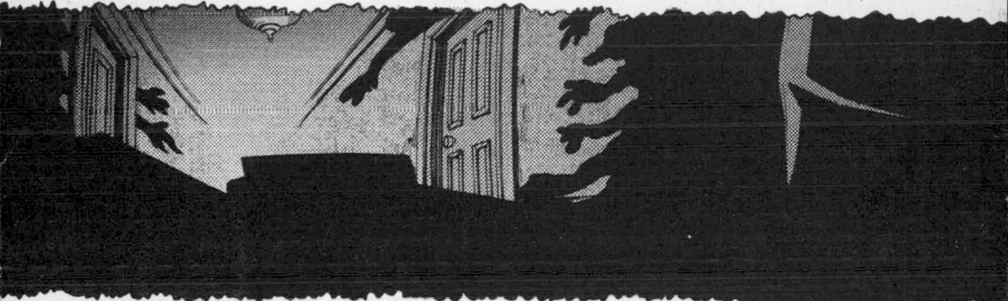

In hindsight, I know what that feeling meant.

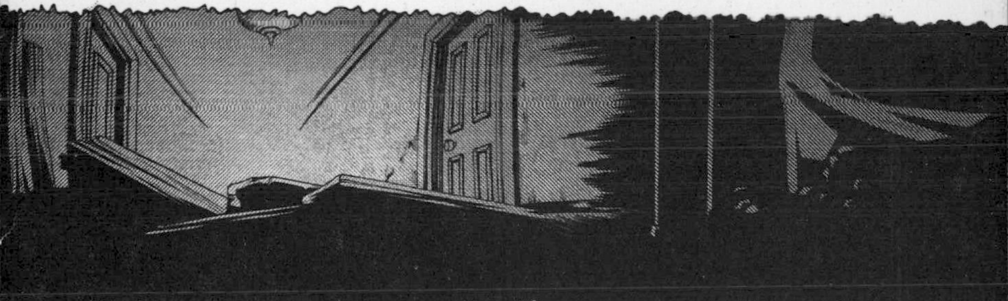

It meant, **"Leave now, Griddle Boy."**

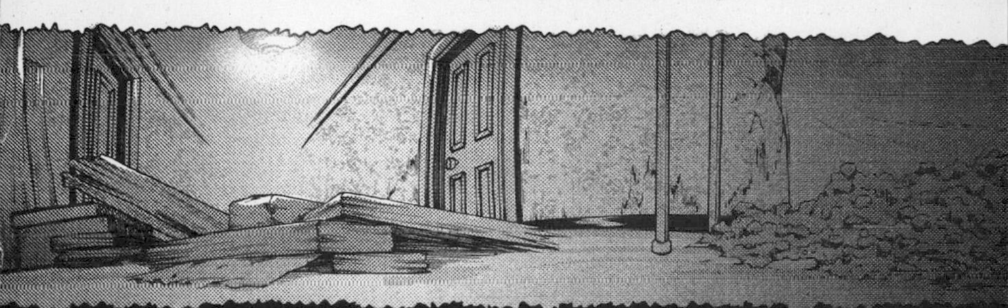

"And **Don't Come Back.**"

Chapter 3

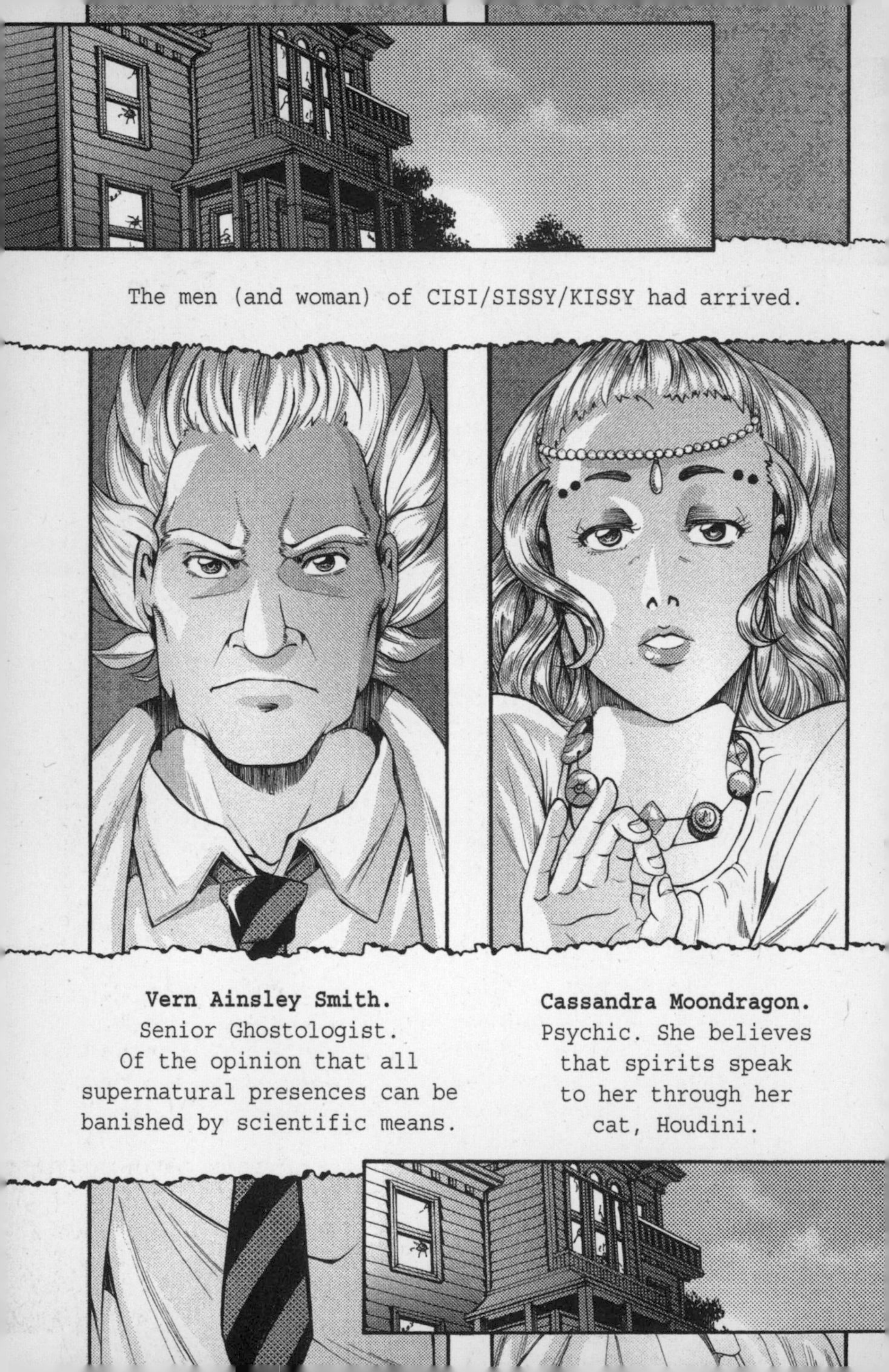
The men (and woman) of CISI/SISSY/KISSY had arrived.
Vern Ainsley Smith.
Senior Ghostologist.
Of the opinion that all supernatural presences can be banished by scientific means.
Cassandra Moondragon.
Psychic. She believes that spirits speak to her through her cat, Houdini.

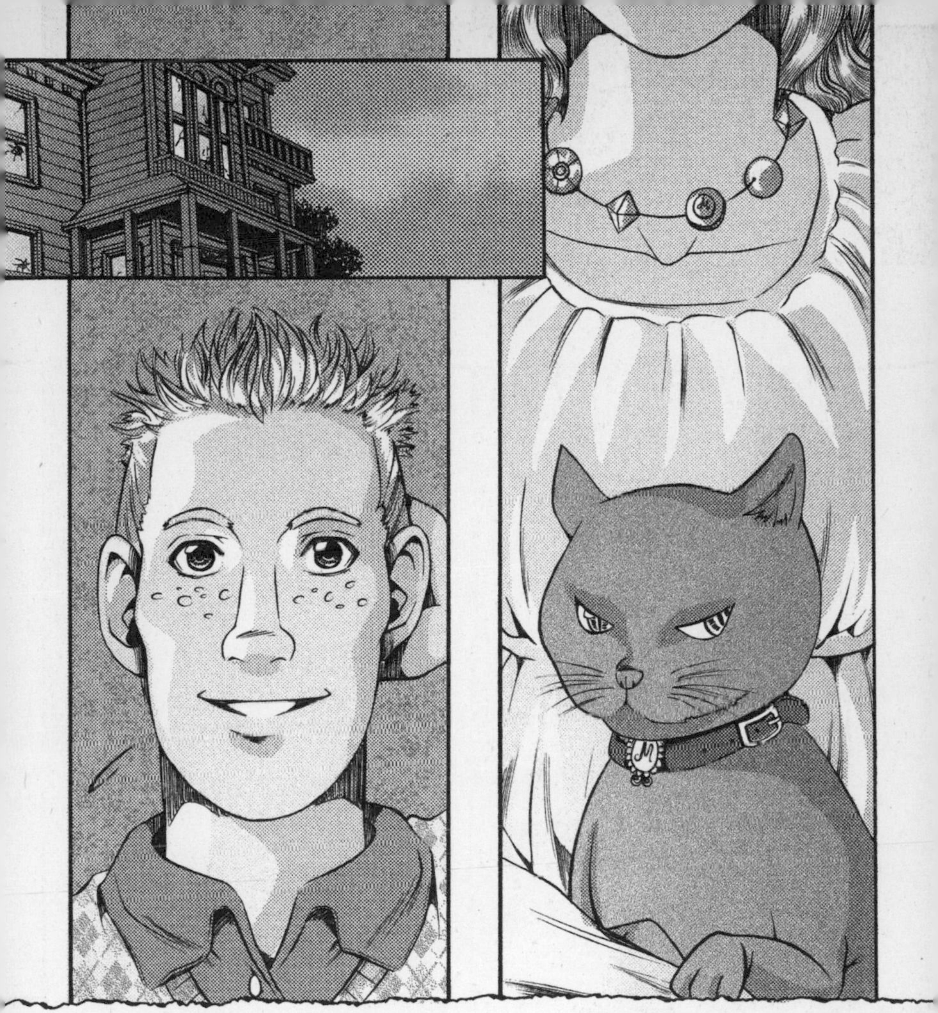

Kirk Adams.
Assistant Ghostologist.
Joined the field of psychic investigation after seeing Don Knotts in *The Ghost and Mr.Chicken*.

And... **Houdini.**
Somehow, I knew this cat was capable of a worse offense than peeing on my shoes.

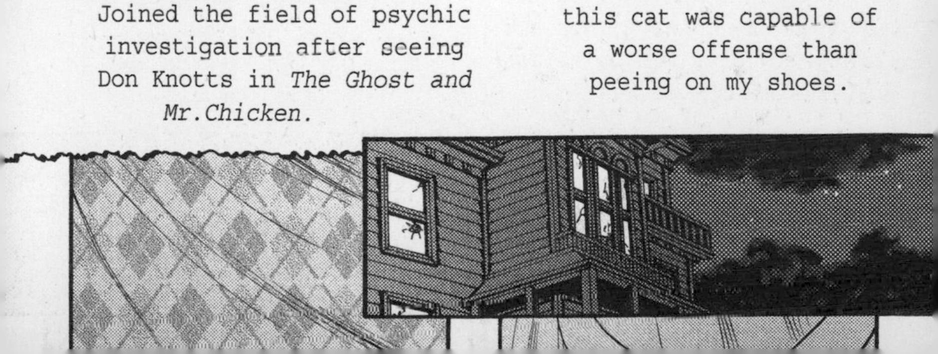

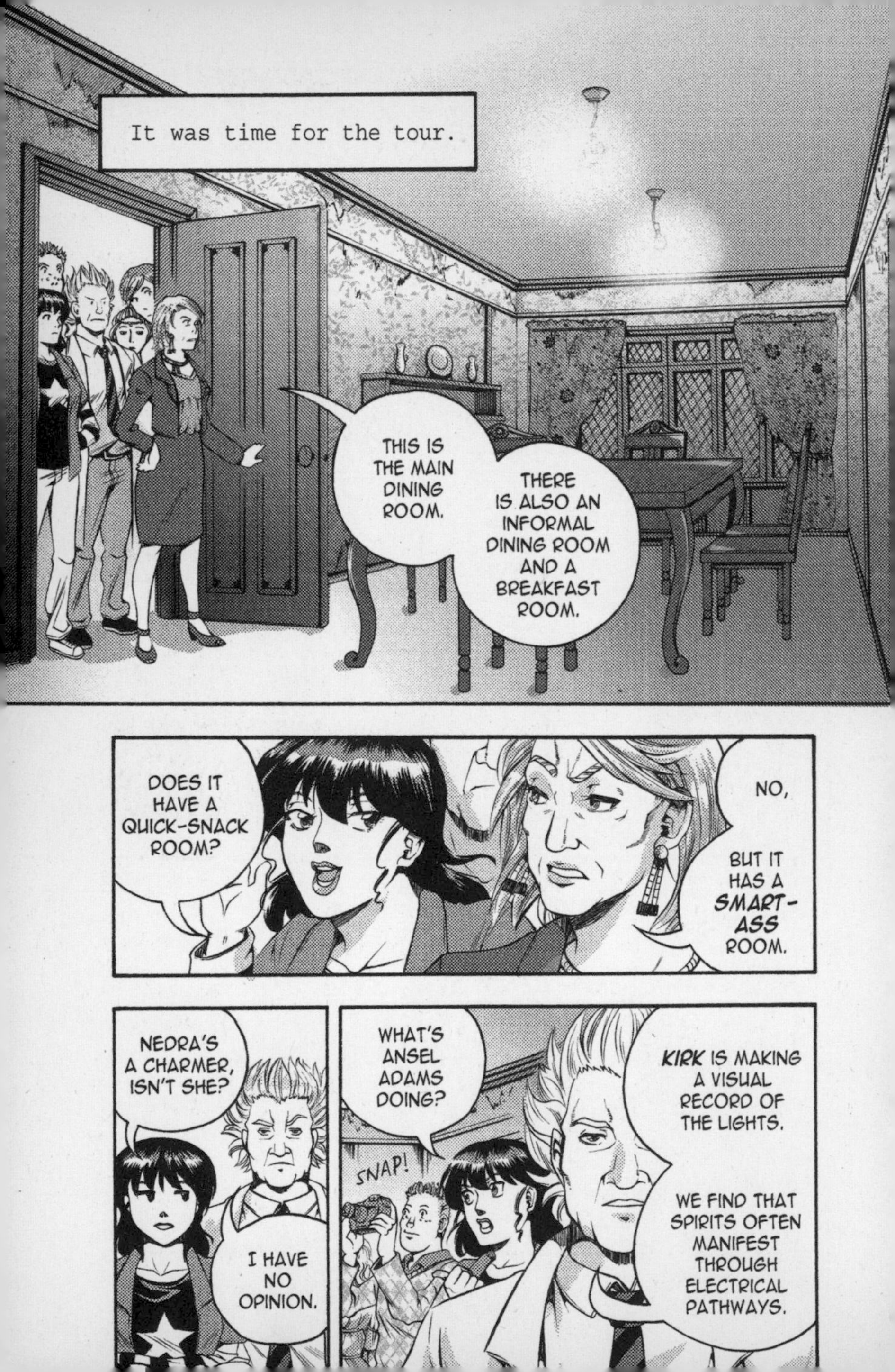
It was time for the tour.
THIS IS THE MAIN DINING ROOM.
THERE IS ALSO AN INFORMAL DINING ROOM AND A BREAKFAST ROOM.
DOES IT HAVE A QUICK-SNACK ROOM?
NO,
BUT IT HAS A SMART-ASS ROOM.
NEDRA'S A CHARMER, ISN'T SHE?
I HAVE NO OPINION.
WHAT'S ANSEL ADAMS DOING?
SNAP!
KIRK IS MAKING A VISUAL RECORD OF THE LIGHTS.
WE FIND THAT SPIRITS OFTEN MANIFEST THROUGH ELECTRICAL PATHWAYS.

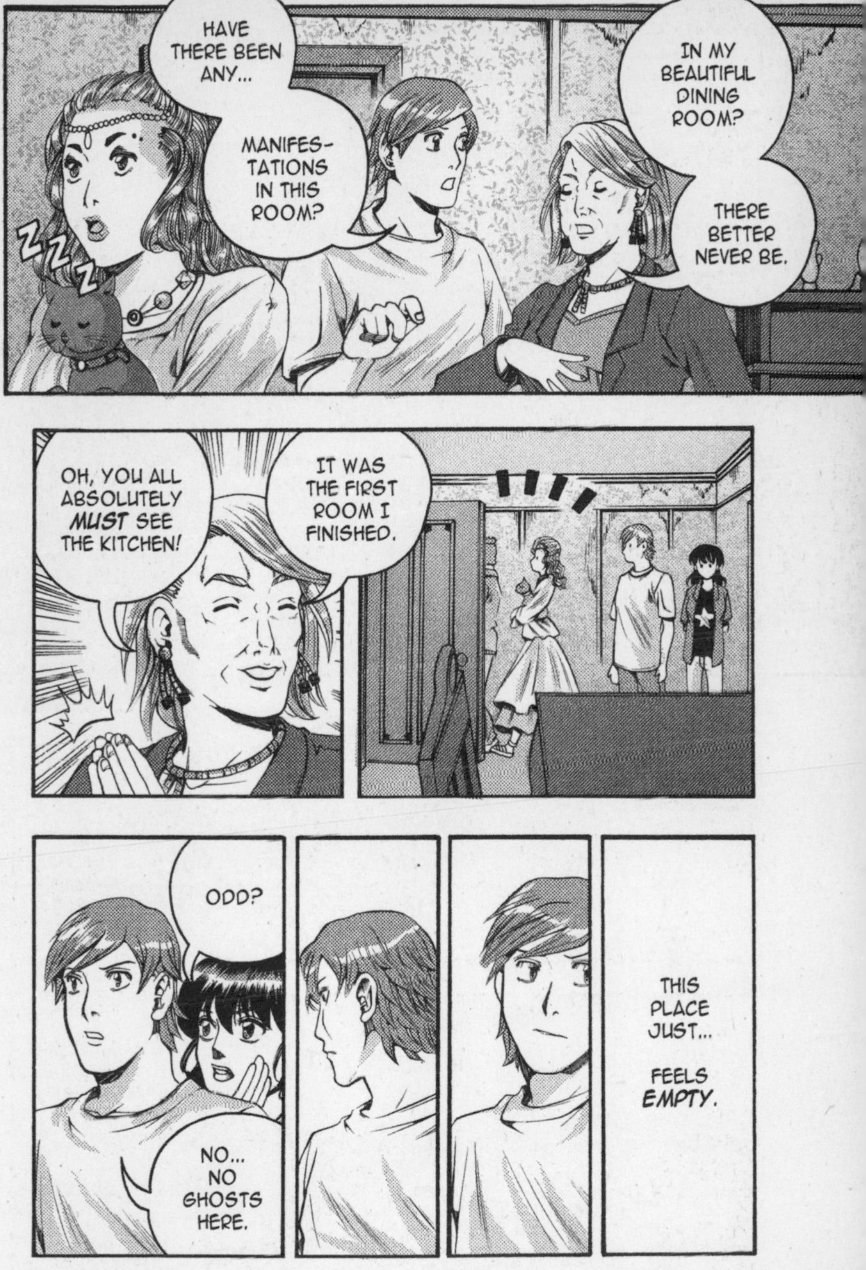
HAVE THERE BEEN ANY...
MANIFES-TATIONS IN THIS ROOM?
IN MY BEAUTIFUL DINING ROOM?
THERE BETTER NEVER BE.
OH, YOU ALL ABSOLUTELY *MUST* SEE THE KITCHEN!
IT WAS THE FIRST ROOM I FINISHED.
ODD?
NO... NO GHOSTS HERE.
THIS PLACE JUST...
FEELS *EMPTY*.

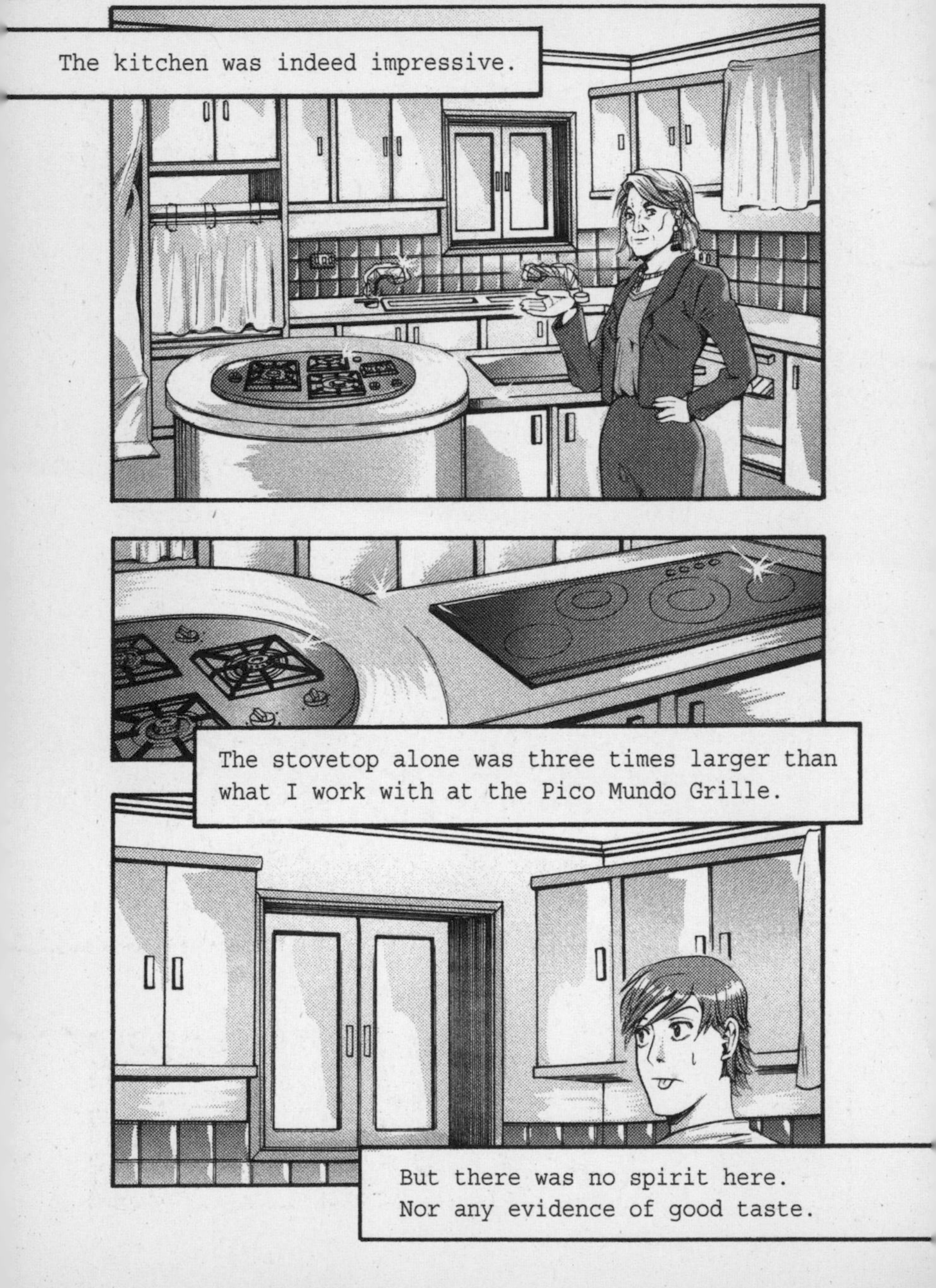
The kitchen was indeed impressive.
The stovetop alone was three times larger than what I work with at the Pico Mundo Grille.
But there was no spirit here. Nor any evidence of good taste.

We toured the first floor. Uncounted rooms, all connected by a series of mazelike hallways.

Second floor: bedrooms, libraries, and dressing rooms.

We toured the third floor.

And the fourth.

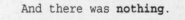

And there was **nothing**.

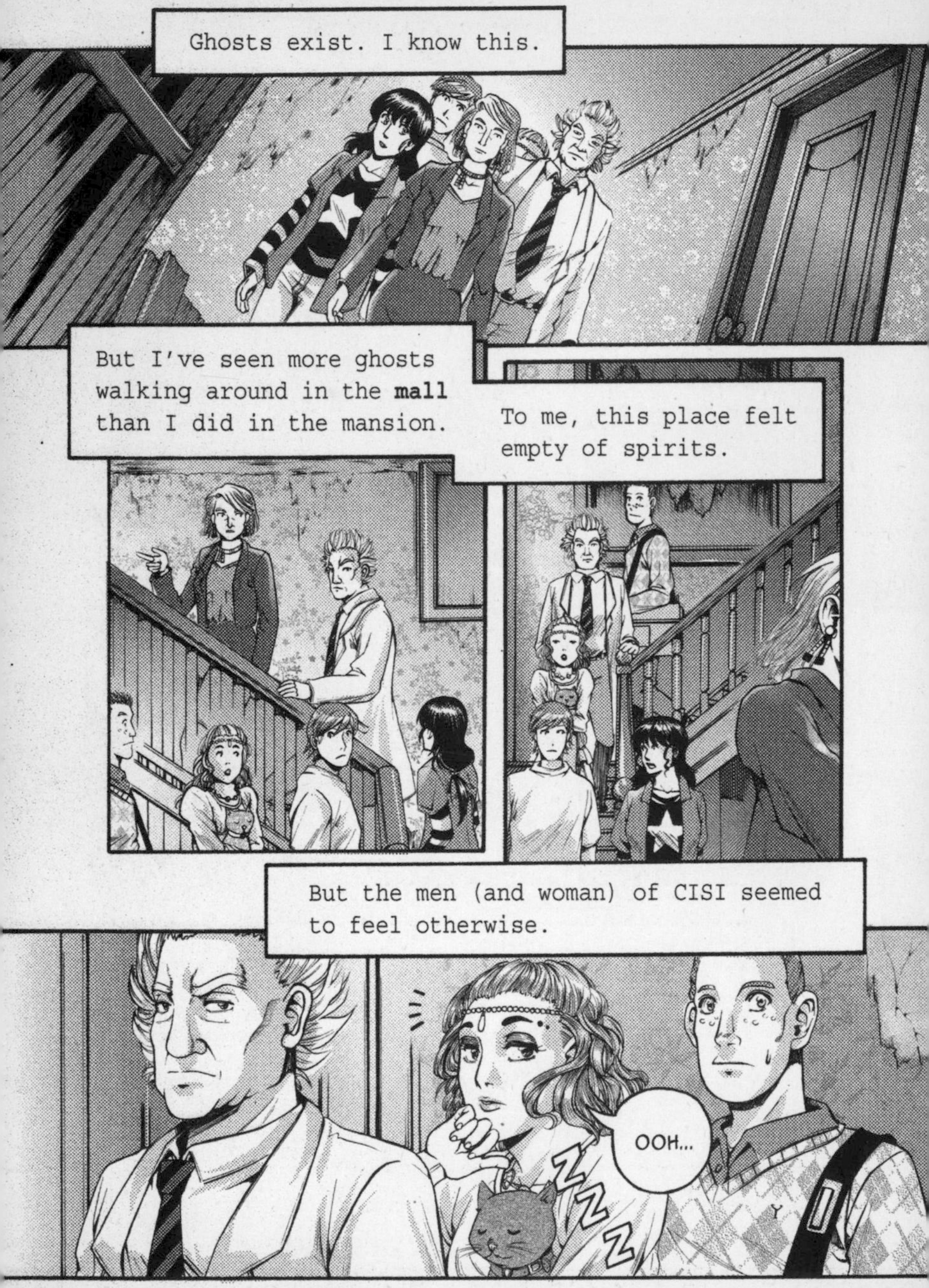
Ghosts exist. I know this.
But I've seen more ghosts walking around in the **mall** than I did in the mansion.
To me, this place felt empty of spirits.
But the men (and woman) of CISI seemed to feel otherwise.
OOH...

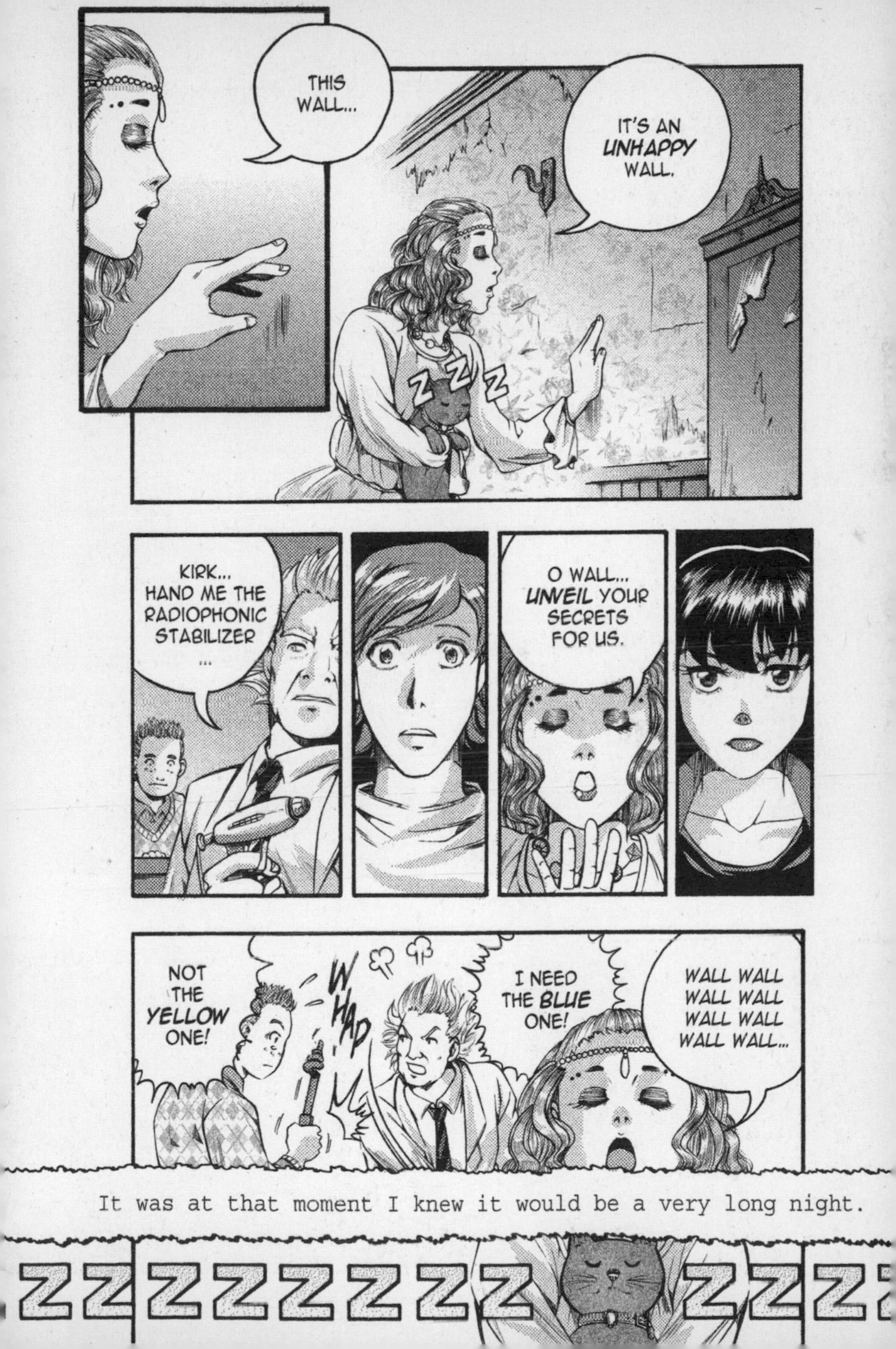
THIS WALL...
ZZZ
IT'S AN UNHAPPY WALL.
KIRK... HAND ME THE RADIOPHONIC STABILIZER ...
O WALL... UNVEIL YOUR SECRETS FOR US.
NOT THE YELLOW ONE!
WHAP
I NEED THE BLUE ONE!
WALL WALL WALL WALL WALL WALL WALL WALL...
It was at that moment I knew it would be a very long night.

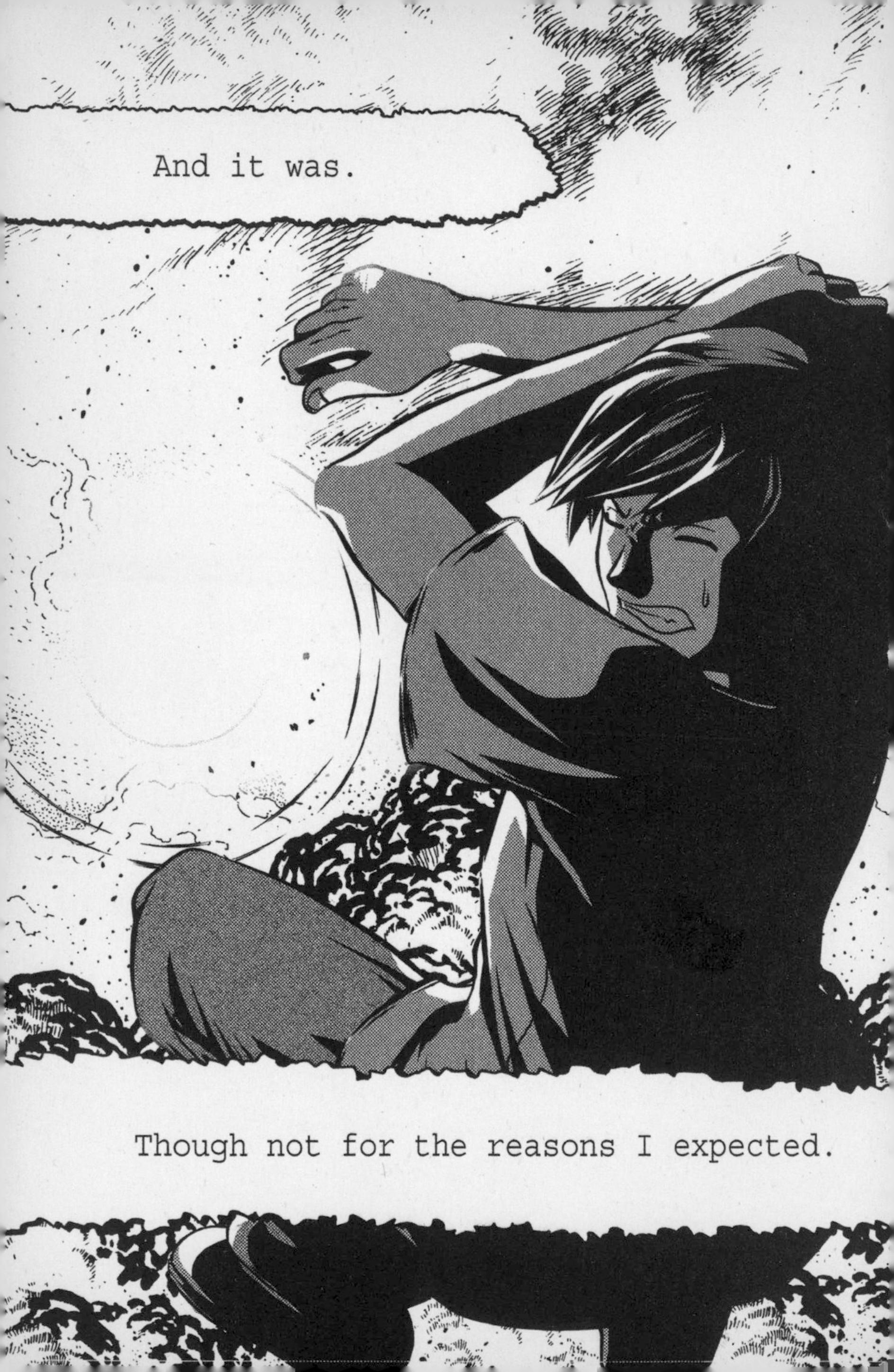
And it was.
Though not for the reasons I expected.

Chapter 4

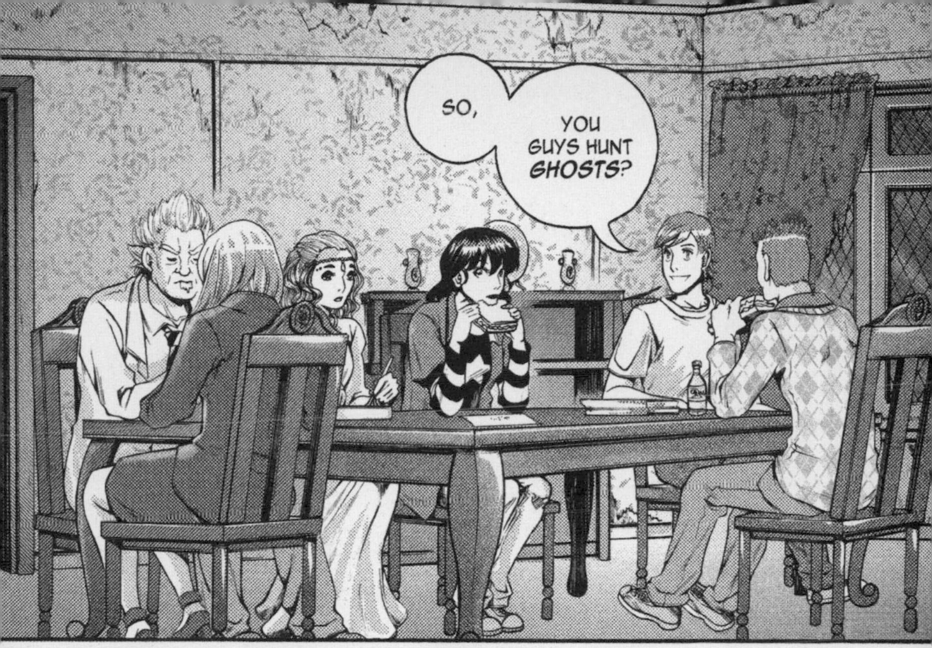
SO,
YOU GUYS HUNT GHOSTS?

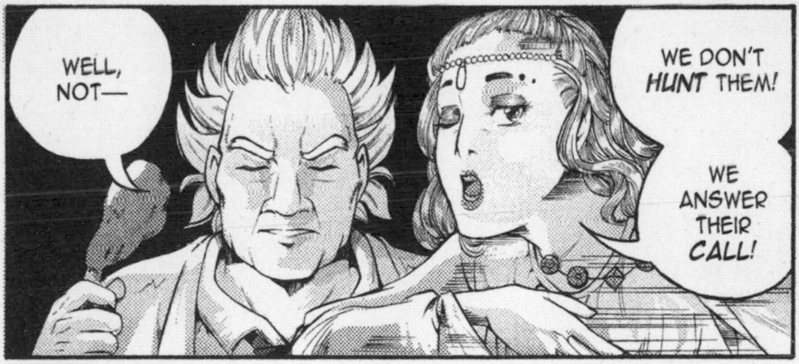
WELL, NOT—
WE DON'T HUNT THEM!
WE ANSWER THEIR CALL!

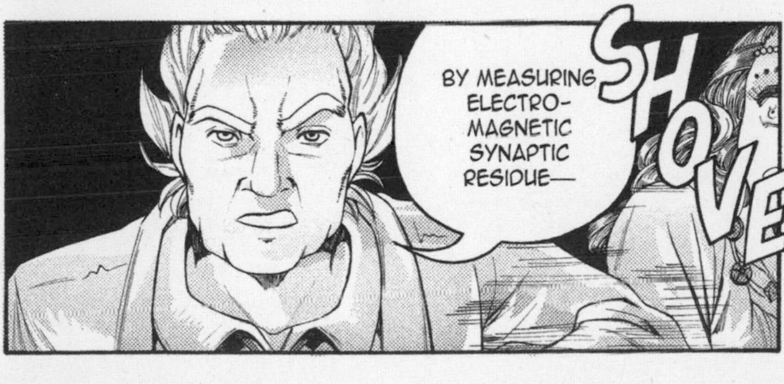
BY MEASURING ELECTRO-MAGNETIC SYNAPTIC RESIDUE—
SHOVE

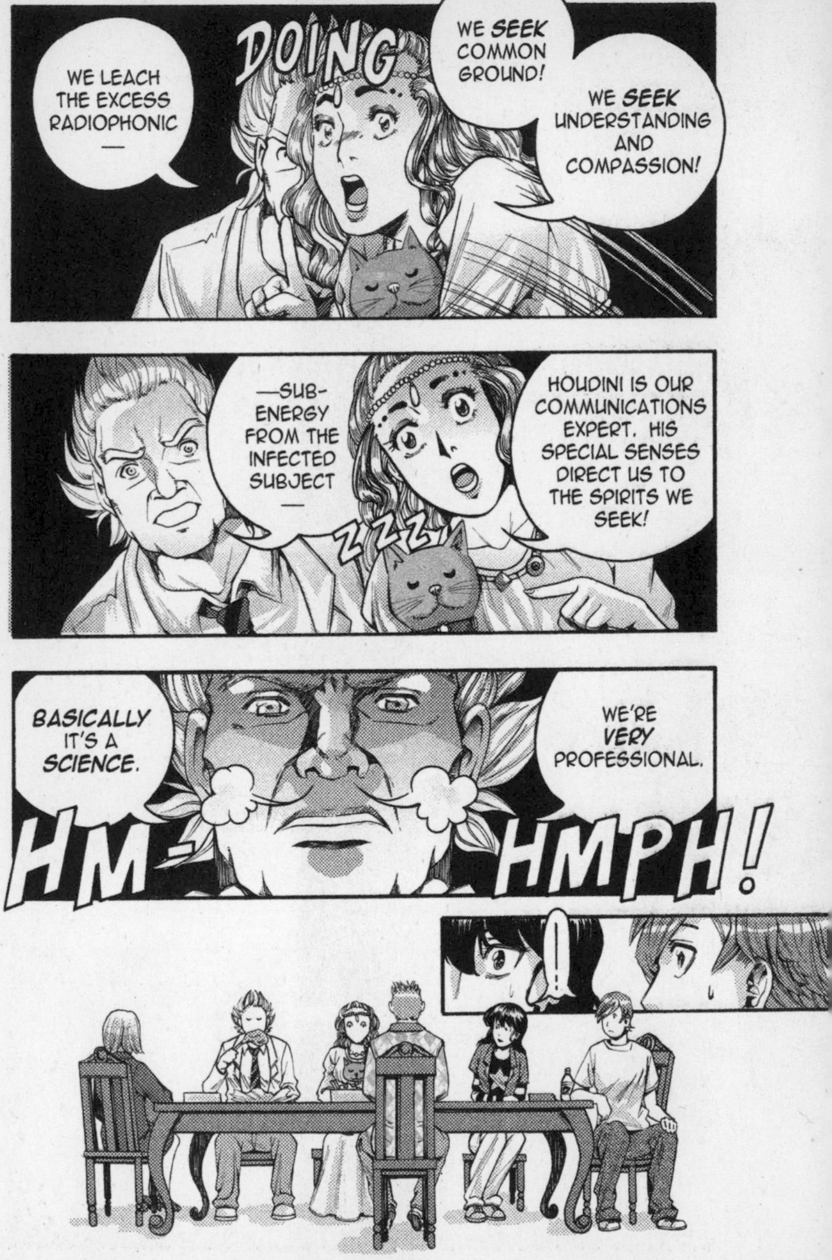
WE LEACH THE EXCESS RADIOPHONIC —
DOING
WE SEEK COMMON GROUND!
WE SEEK UNDERSTANDING AND COMPASSION!
—SUB-ENERGY FROM THE INFECTED SUBJECT —
ZZZ
HOUDINI IS OUR COMMUNICATIONS EXPERT. HIS SPECIAL SENSES DIRECT US TO THE SPIRITS WE SEEK!
BASICALLY IT'S A SCIENCE.
WE'RE VERY PROFESSIONAL.
HM-HMPH!
!

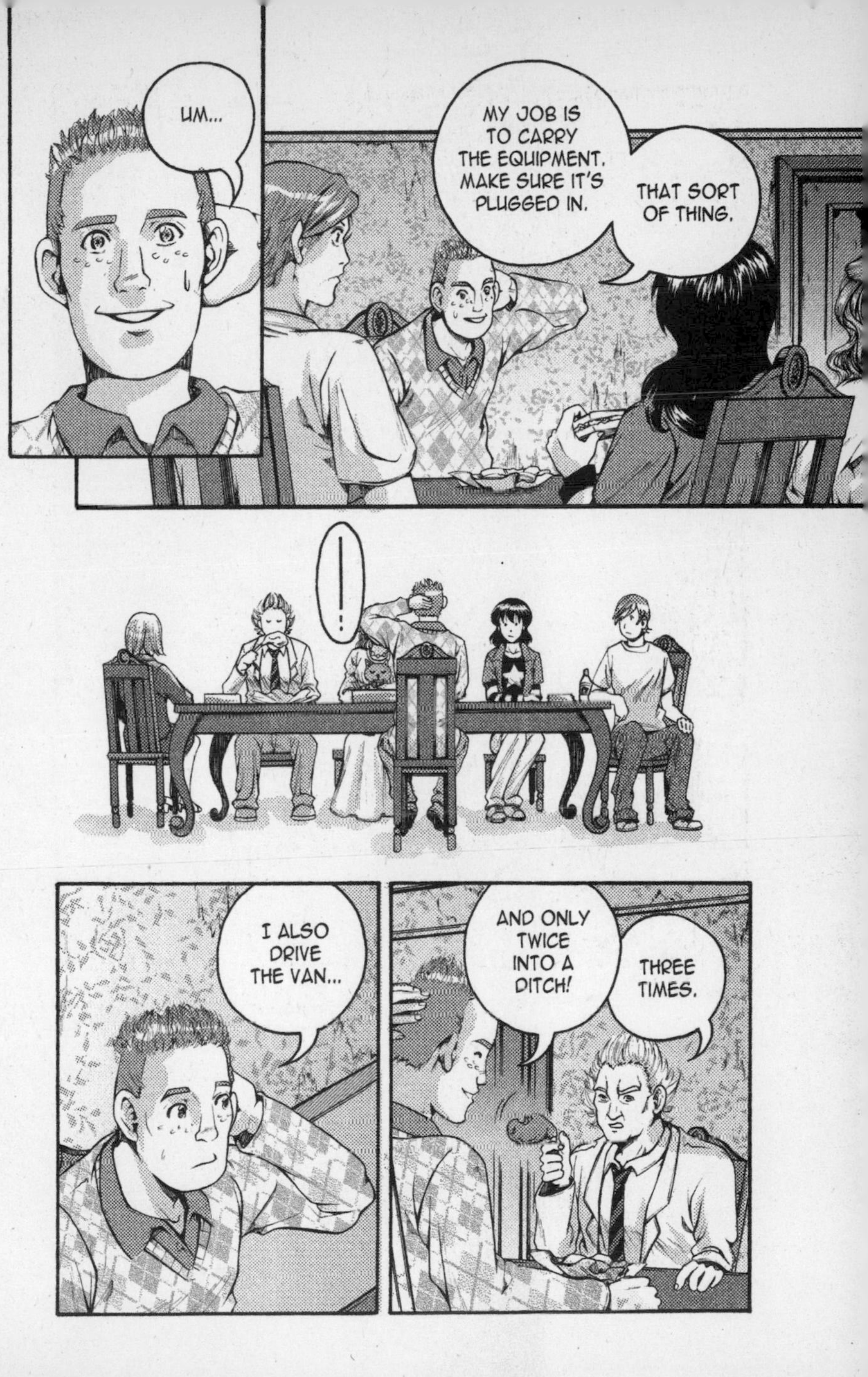
UM...
MY JOB IS TO CARRY THE EQUIPMENT. MAKE SURE IT'S PLUGGED IN.
THAT SORT OF THING.
!
I ALSO DRIVE THE VAN...
AND ONLY TWICE INTO A DITCH!
THREE TIMES.

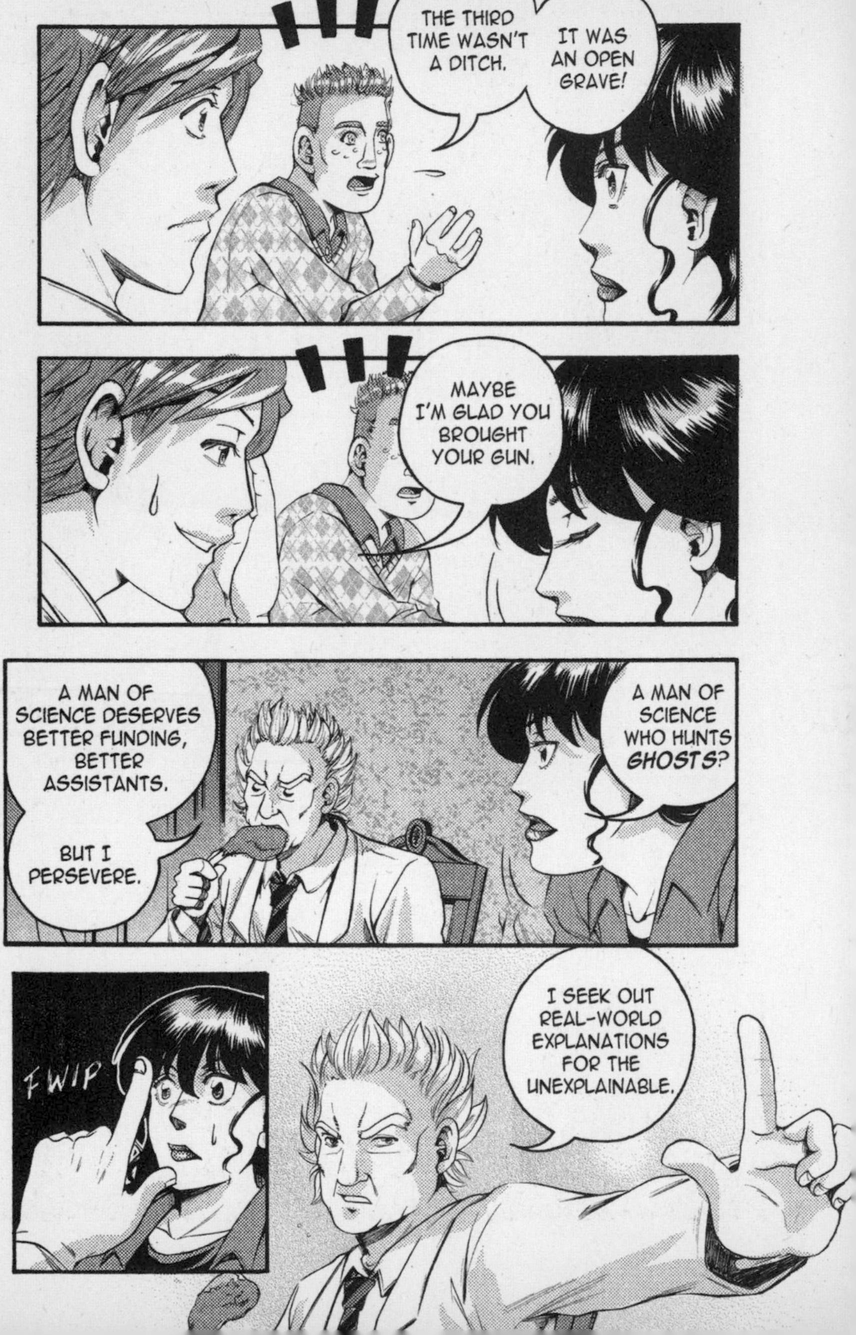
THE THIRD TIME WASN'T A DITCH.
IT WAS AN OPEN GRAVE!
MAYBE I'M GLAD YOU BROUGHT YOUR GUN.
A MAN OF SCIENCE WHO HUNTS GHOSTS?
A MAN OF SCIENCE DESERVES BETTER FUNDING, BETTER ASSISTANTS.
BUT I PERSEVERE.
FWIP
I SEEK OUT REAL-WORLD EXPLANATIONS FOR THE UNEXPLAINABLE.

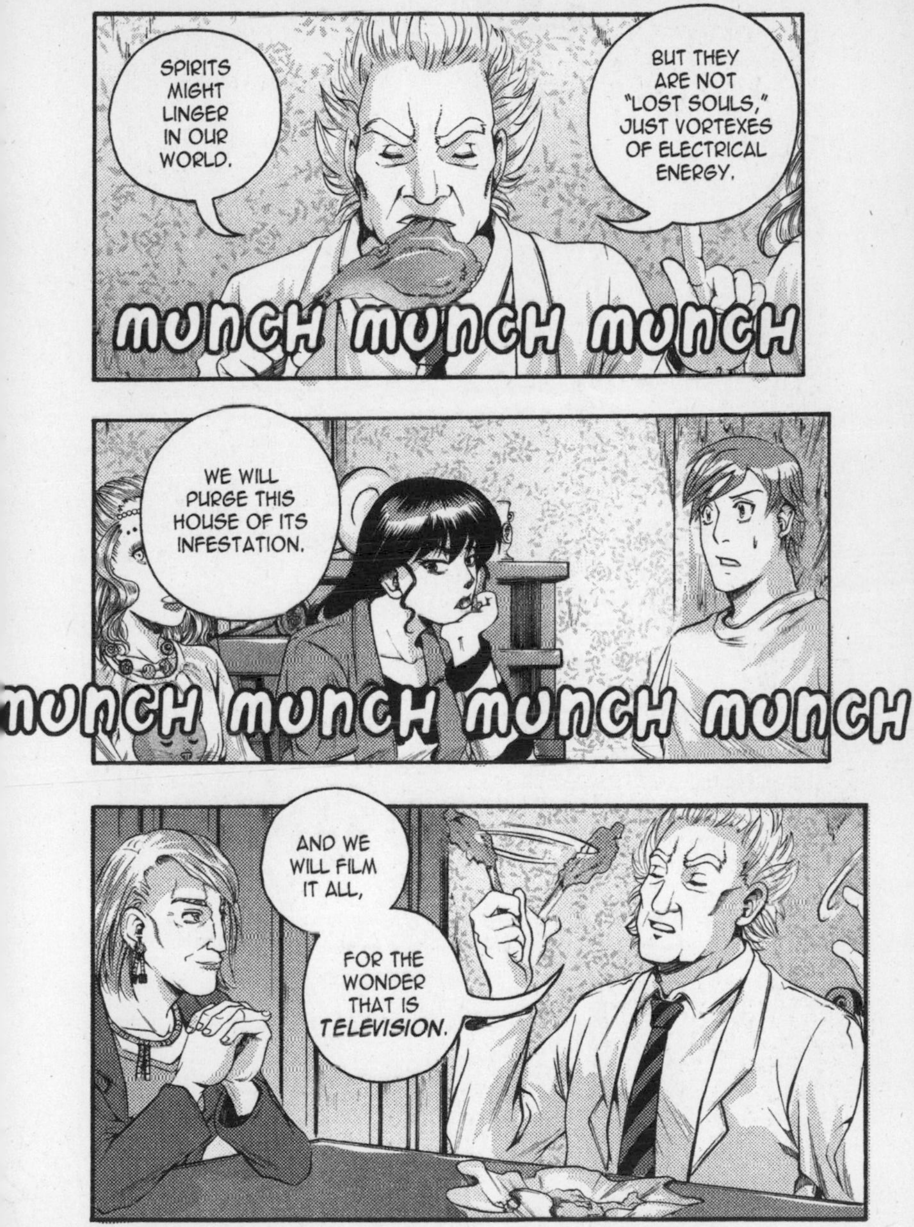
SPIRITS MIGHT LINGER IN OUR WORLD.
BUT THEY ARE NOT "LOST SOULS," JUST VORTEXES OF ELECTRICAL ENERGY.
MUNCH MUNCH MUNCH
WE WILL PURGE THIS HOUSE OF ITS INFESTATION.
MUNCH MUNCH MUNCH MUNCH
AND WE WILL FILM IT ALL,
FOR THE WONDER THAT IS *TELEVISION*.

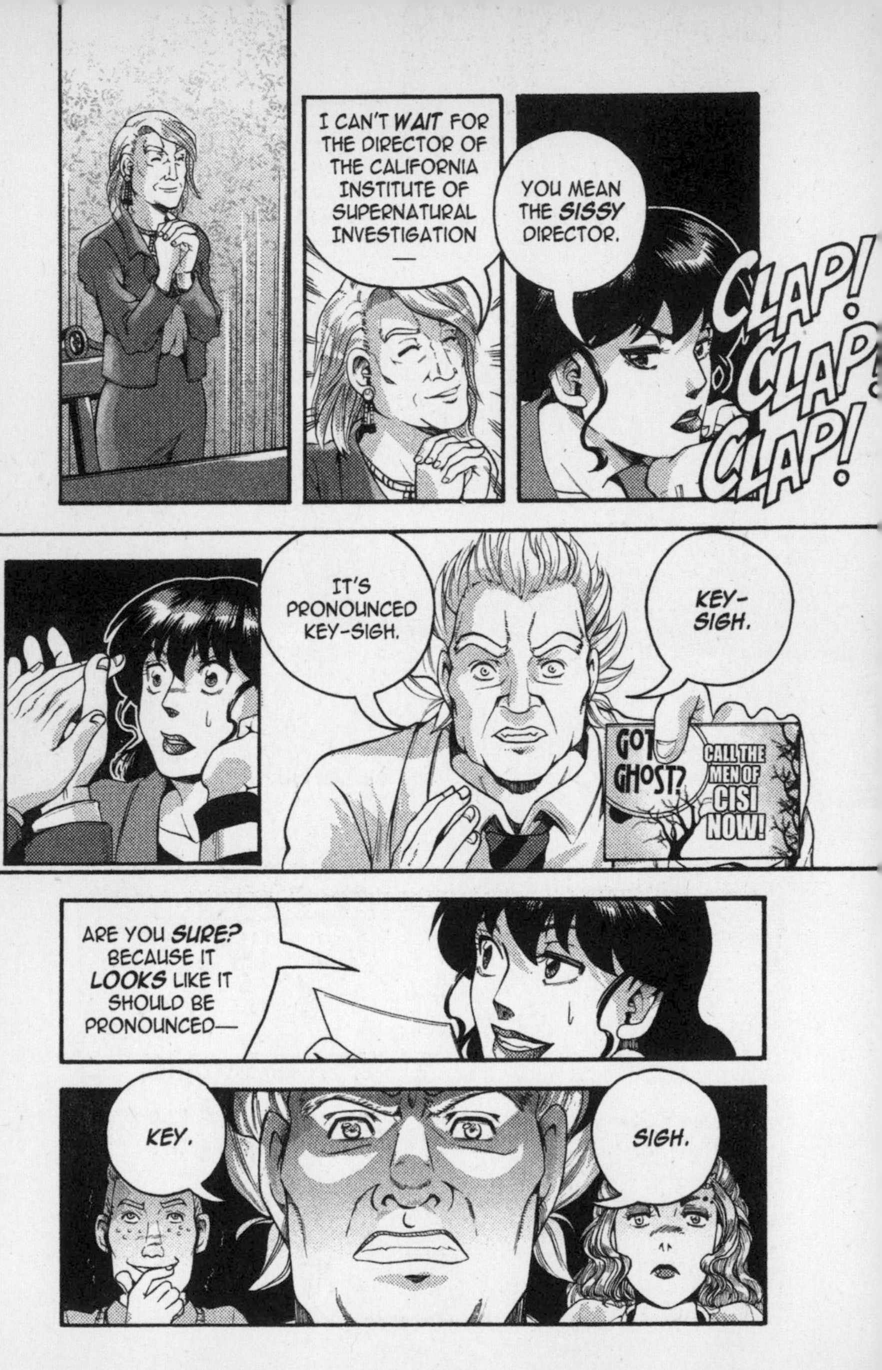
I CAN'T WAIT FOR THE DIRECTOR OF THE CALIFORNIA INSTITUTE OF SUPERNATURAL INVESTIGATION —
YOU MEAN THE SISSY DIRECTOR.
CLAP! CLAP! CLAP!
IT'S PRONOUNCED KEY-SIGH.
KEY-SIGH.
GOT GHOST? CALL THE MEN OF CISI NOW!
ARE YOU SURE? BECAUSE IT LOOKS LIKE IT SHOULD BE PRONOUNCED—
KEY.
SIGH.

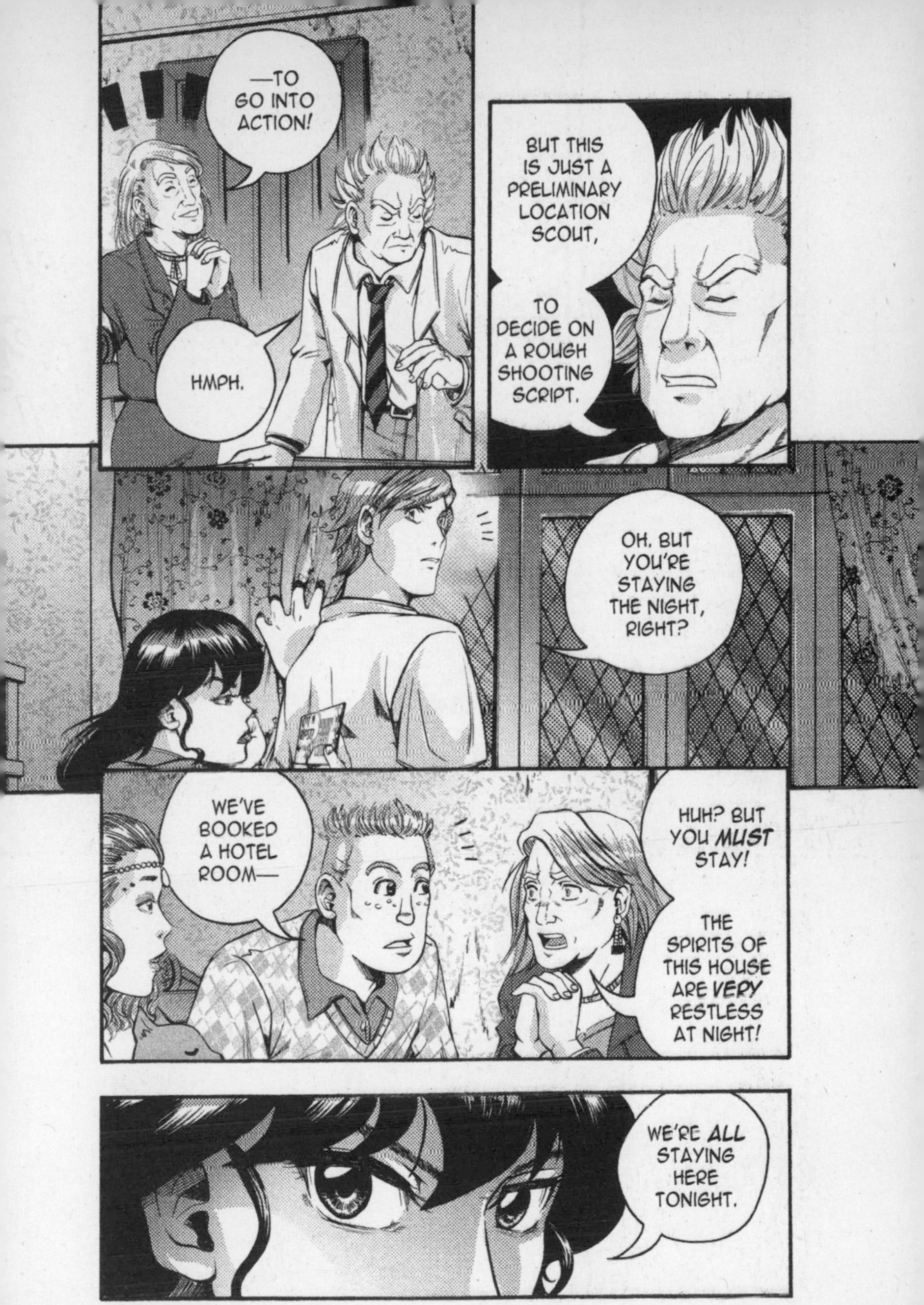
—TO GO INTO ACTION!
HMPH.
BUT THIS IS JUST A PRELIMINARY LOCATION SCOUT,
TO DECIDE ON A ROUGH SHOOTING SCRIPT.
OH. BUT YOU'RE STAYING THE NIGHT, RIGHT?
WE'VE BOOKED A HOTEL ROOM—
HUH? BUT YOU *MUST* STAY!
THE SPIRITS OF THIS HOUSE ARE *VERY* RESTLESS AT NIGHT!
WE'RE *ALL* STAYING HERE TONIGHT.

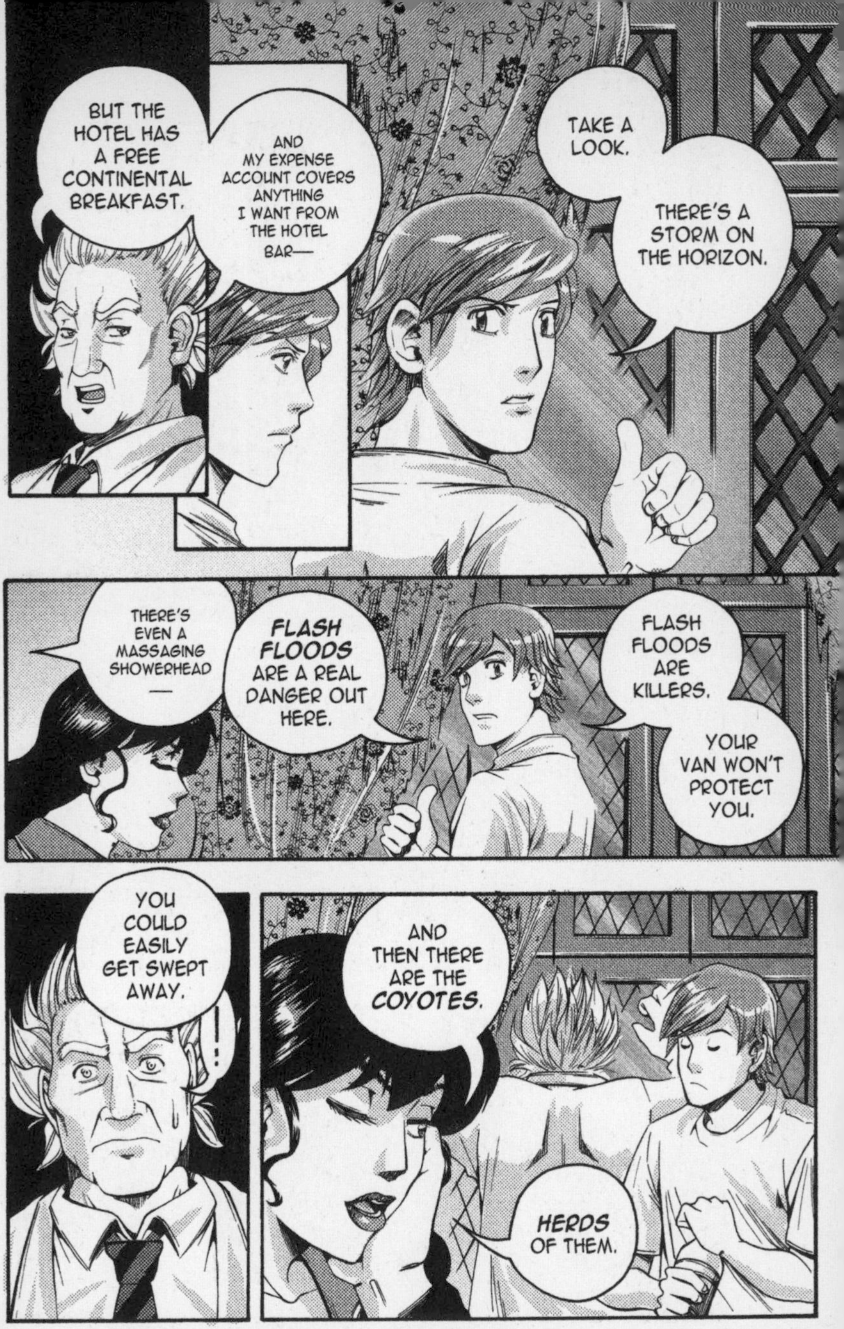
BUT THE HOTEL HAS A FREE CONTINENTAL BREAKFAST.
AND MY EXPENSE ACCOUNT COVERS ANYTHING I WANT FROM THE HOTEL BAR—
TAKE A LOOK.
THERE'S A STORM ON THE HORIZON.
THERE'S EVEN A MASSAGING SHOWERHEAD —
FLASH FLOODS ARE A REAL DANGER OUT HERE.
FLASH FLOODS ARE KILLERS.
YOUR VAN WON'T PROTECT YOU.
YOU COULD EASILY GET SWEPT AWAY.
!
AND THEN THERE ARE THE COYOTES.
HERDS OF THEM.

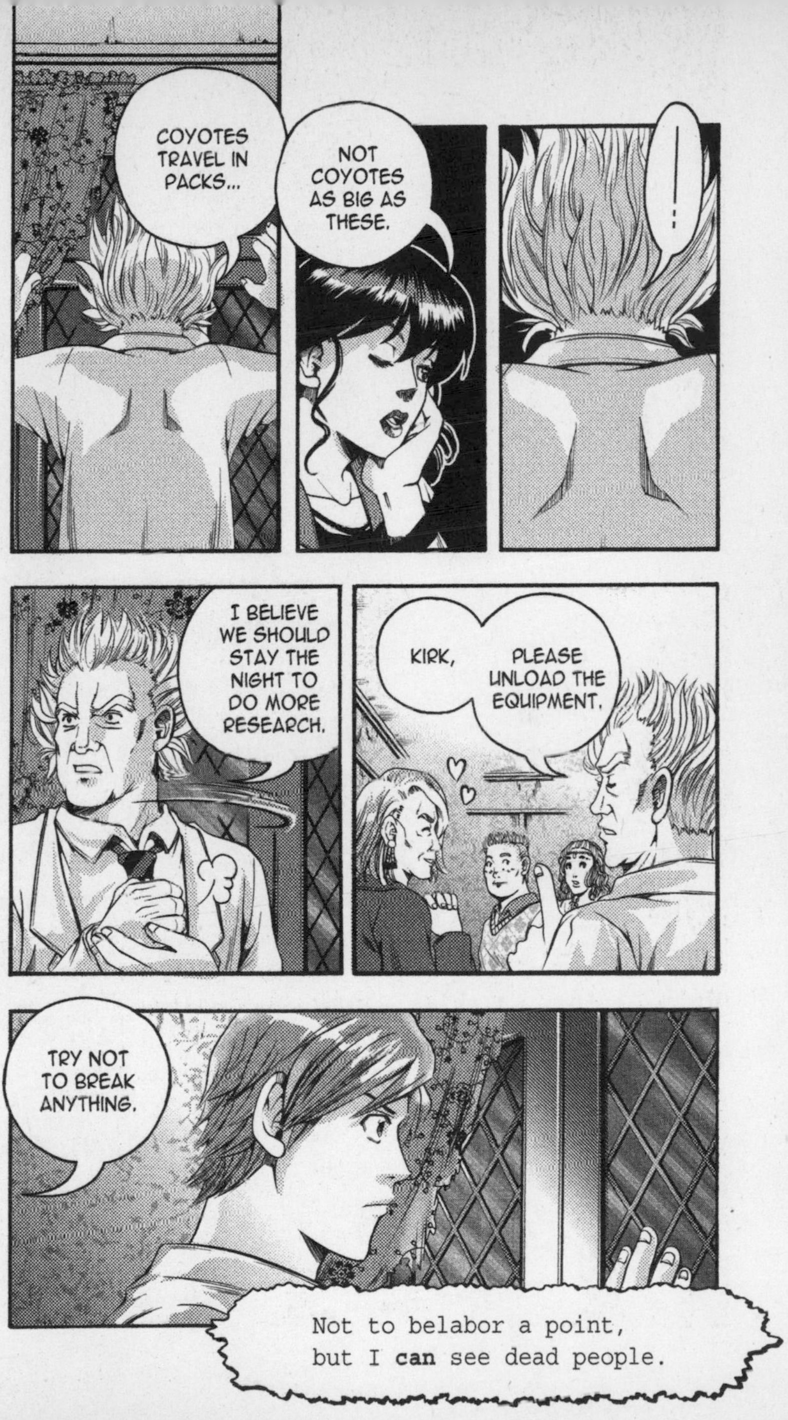
COYOTES TRAVEL IN PACKS...
NOT COYOTES AS BIG AS THESE.
!
I BELIEVE WE SHOULD STAY THE NIGHT TO DO MORE RESEARCH.
KIRK,
PLEASE UNLOAD THE EQUIPMENT.
TRY NOT TO BREAK ANYTHING.
Not to belabor a point, but I **can** see dead people.

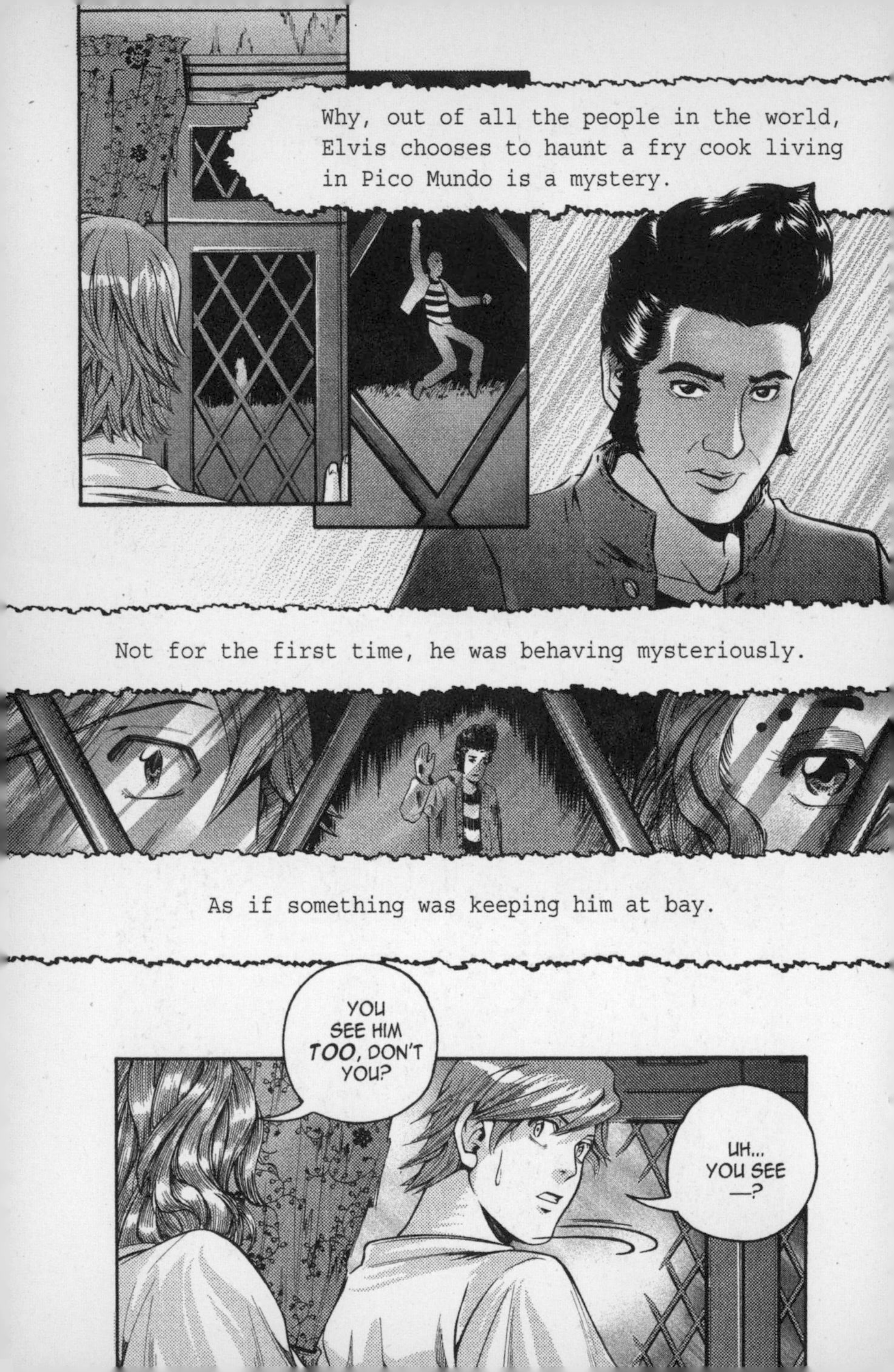
Why, out of all the people in the world, Elvis chooses to haunt a fry cook living in Pico Mundo is a mystery.
Not for the first time, he was behaving mysteriously.
As if something was keeping him at bay.
YOU SEE HIM *TOO*, DON'T YOU?
UH... YOU SEE —?

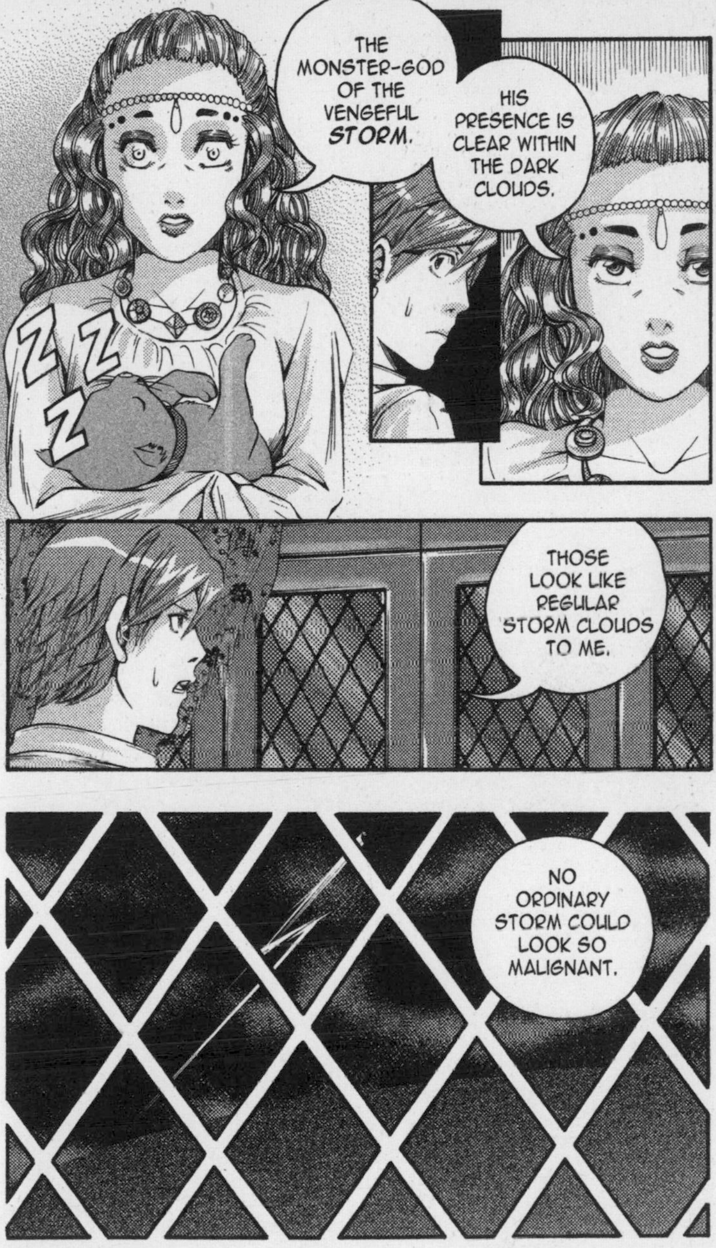
THE MONSTER-GOD OF THE VENGEFUL STORM.
HIS PRESENCE IS CLEAR WITHIN THE DARK CLOUDS.
Z Z Z
THOSE LOOK LIKE REGULAR STORM CLOUDS TO ME.
NO ORDINARY STORM COULD LOOK SO MALIGNANT.

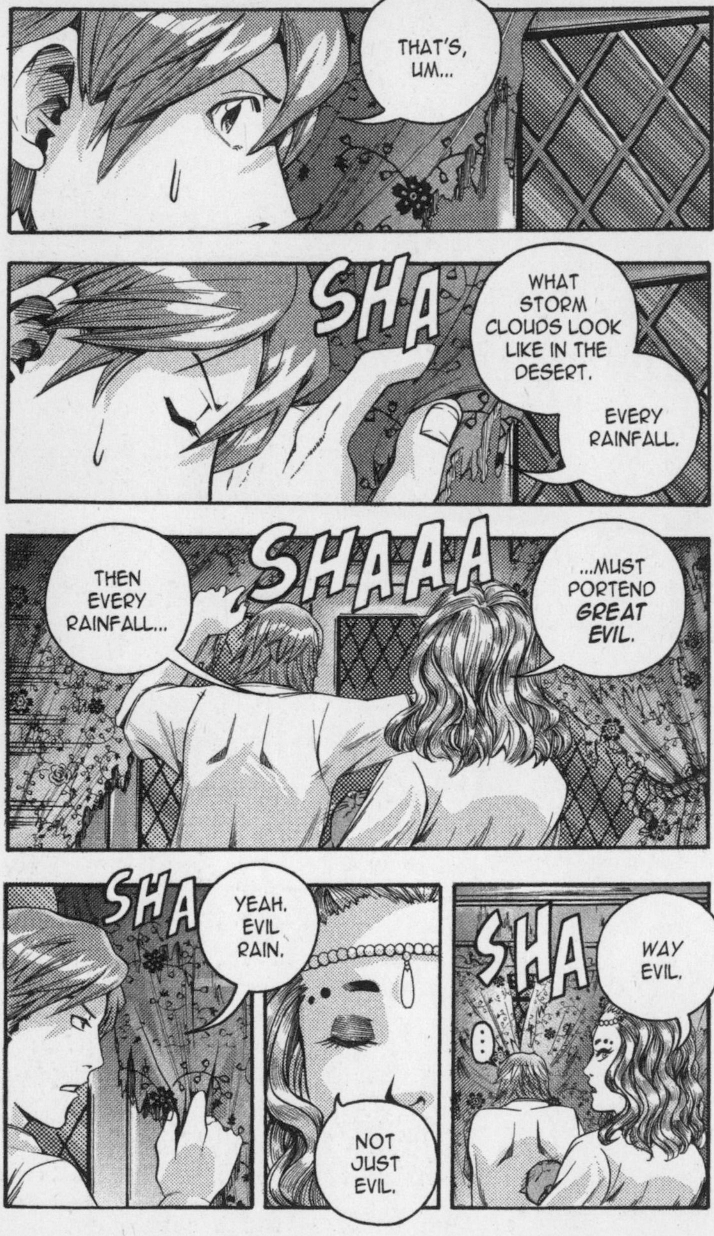
THAT'S, UM...
SHA
WHAT STORM CLOUDS LOOK LIKE IN THE DESERT.
EVERY RAINFALL.
SHAAA
THEN EVERY RAINFALL...
...MUST PORTEND GREAT EVIL.
SHA
YEAH. EVIL RAIN.
NOT JUST EVIL.
SHA
WAY EVIL.
...

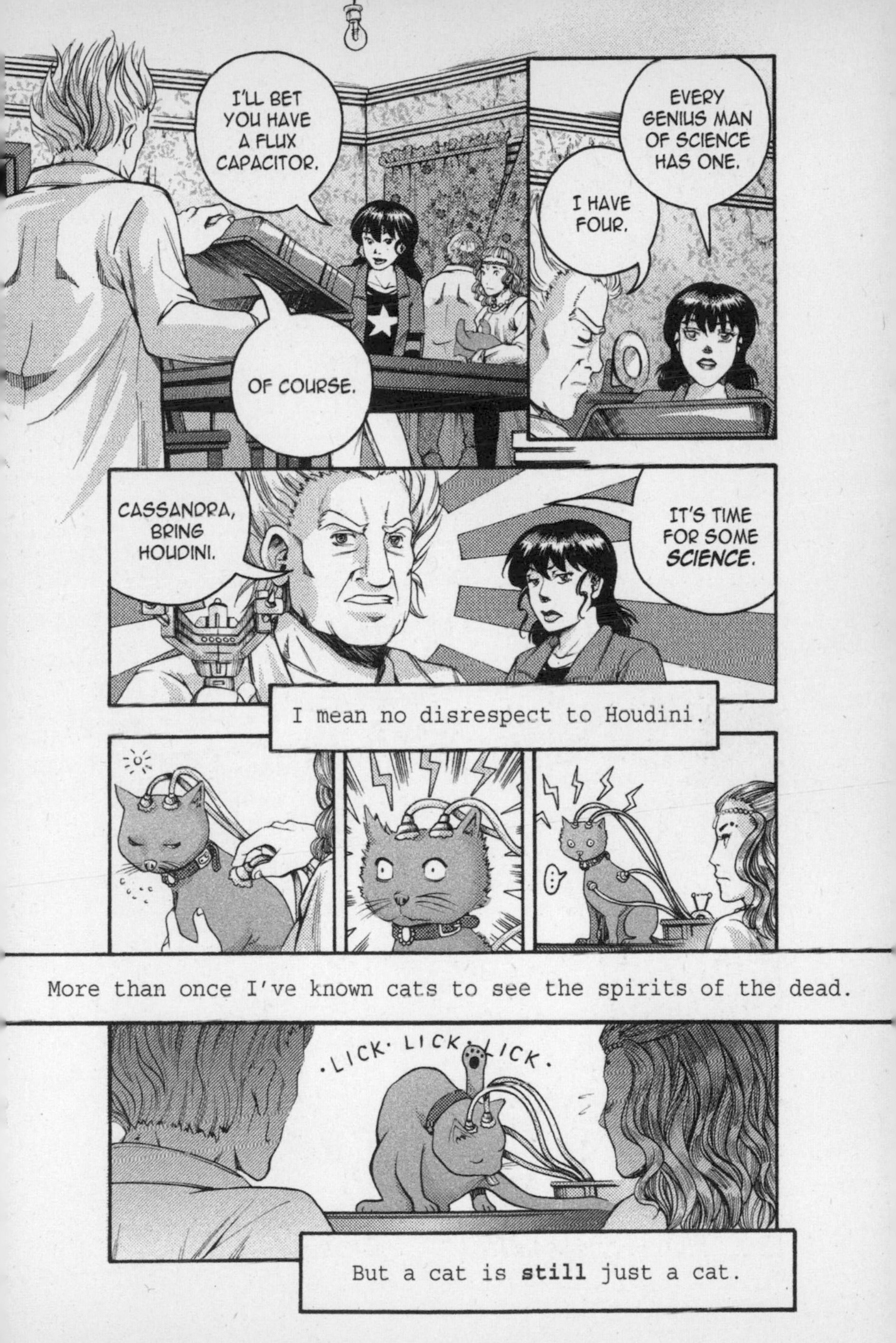
I'LL BET YOU HAVE A FLUX CAPACITOR.
OF COURSE.
EVERY GENIUS MAN OF SCIENCE HAS ONE.
I HAVE FOUR.
CASSANDRA, BRING HOUDINI.
IT'S TIME FOR SOME SCIENCE.
I mean no disrespect to Houdini.
More than once I've known cats to see the spirits of the dead.
·LICK· LICK·LICK·
But a cat is **still** just a cat.

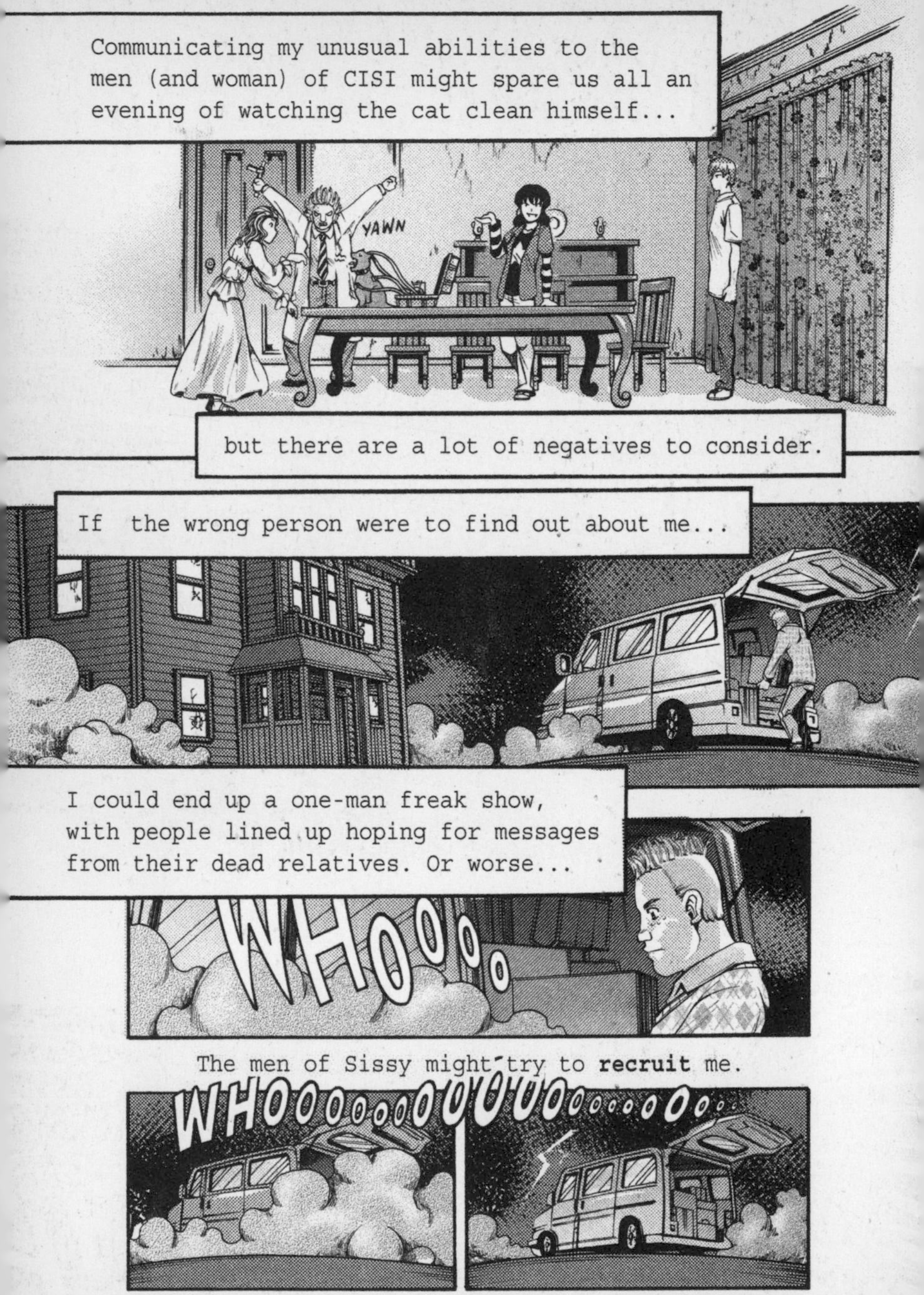

Communicating my unusual abilities to the men (and woman) of CISI might spare us all an evening of watching the cat clean himself...
YAWN
but there are a lot of negatives to consider.
If the wrong person were to find out about me...
I could end up a one-man freak show, with people lined up hoping for messages from their dead relatives. Or worse...
WHOooo
The men of Sissy might try to **recruit** me.
WHOOooooOOOOOoooooOoo

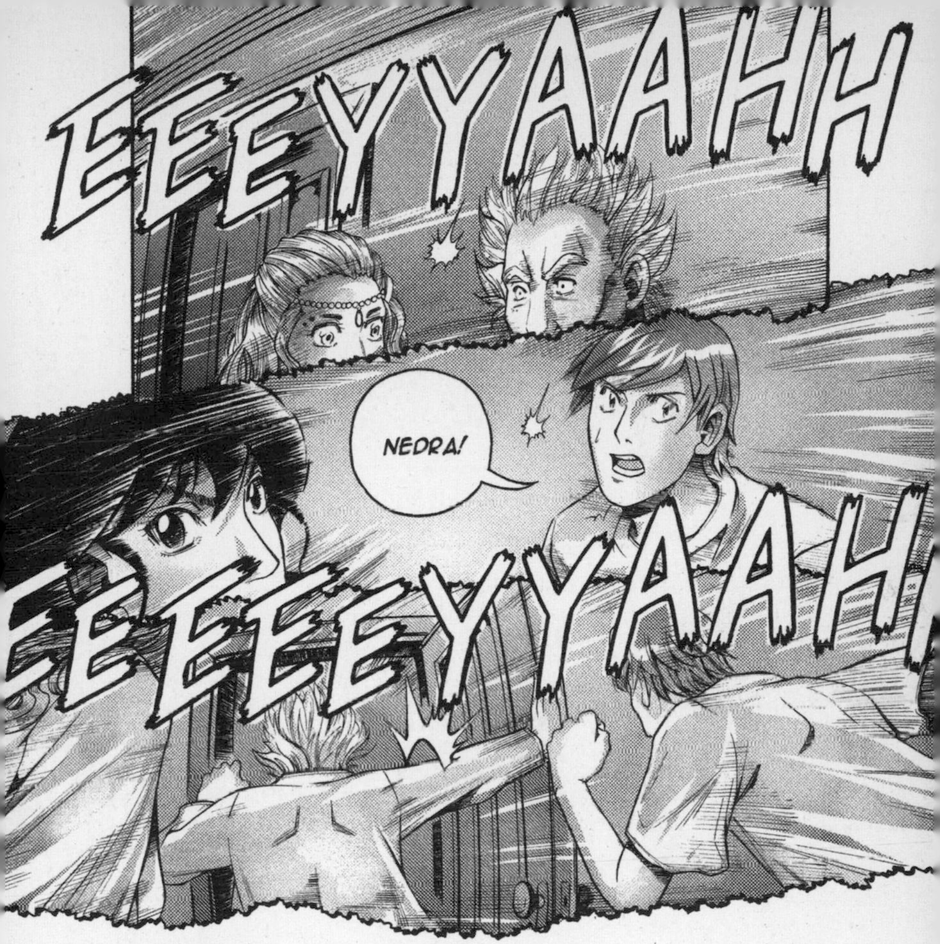
EEEYYAAHH
NEDRA!
EEEEEYYAAH

All my experiences indicate that ghosts cannot injure the living.

Except in one case...

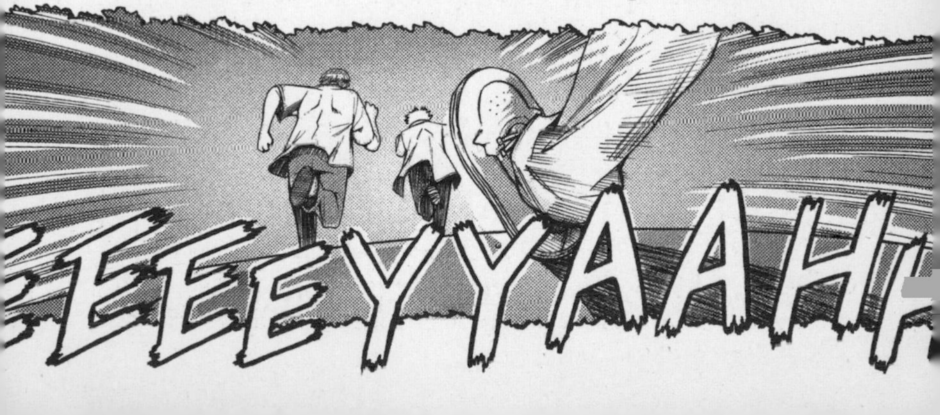
EEEEYYAAH

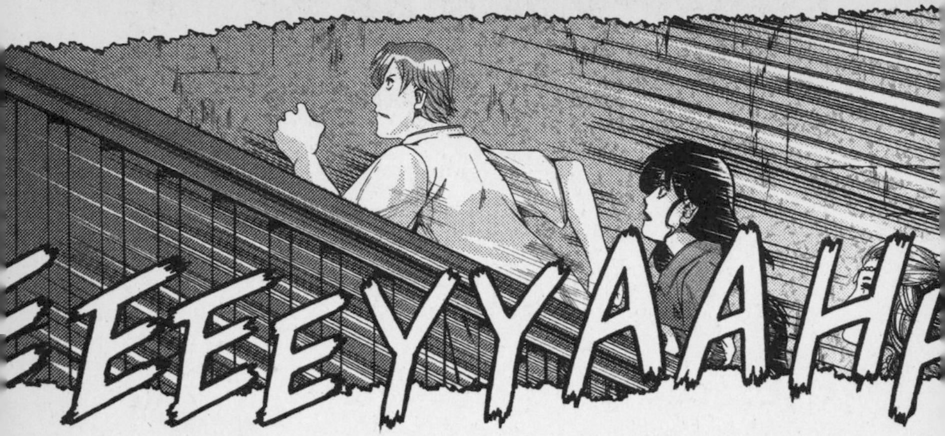
EEEYYAAH

When a spirit reaches a sufficiently volatile emotional state, it can "go poltergeist."

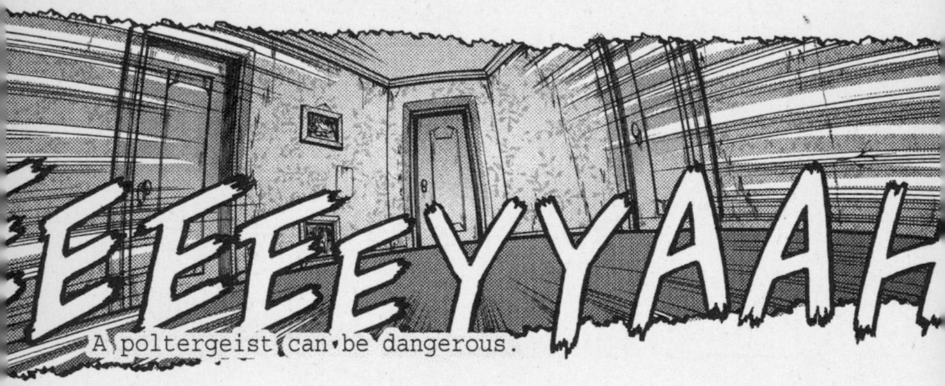
EEEEYYAAH
A poltergeist can be dangerous.

A poltergeist once destroyed my brand-new music system.

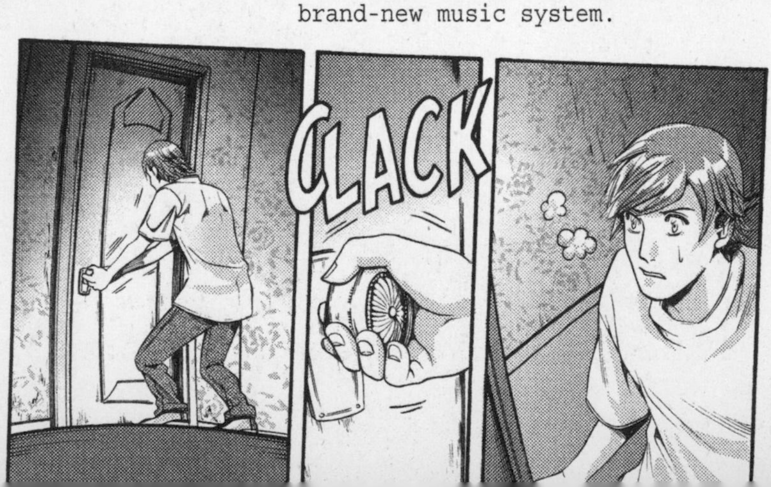
CLACK

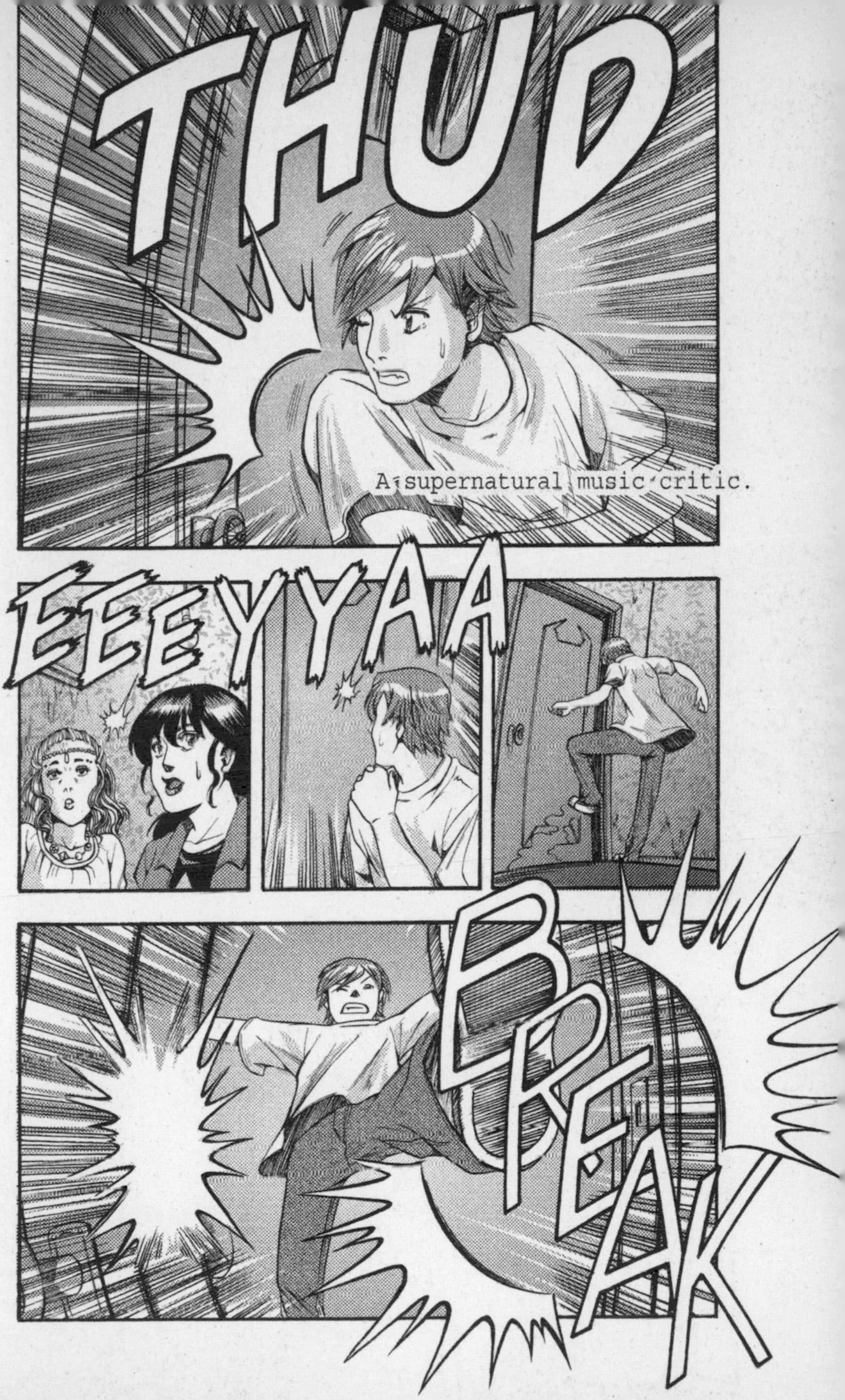
THUD
A supernatural music critic.
EEEYYAA
BREAK

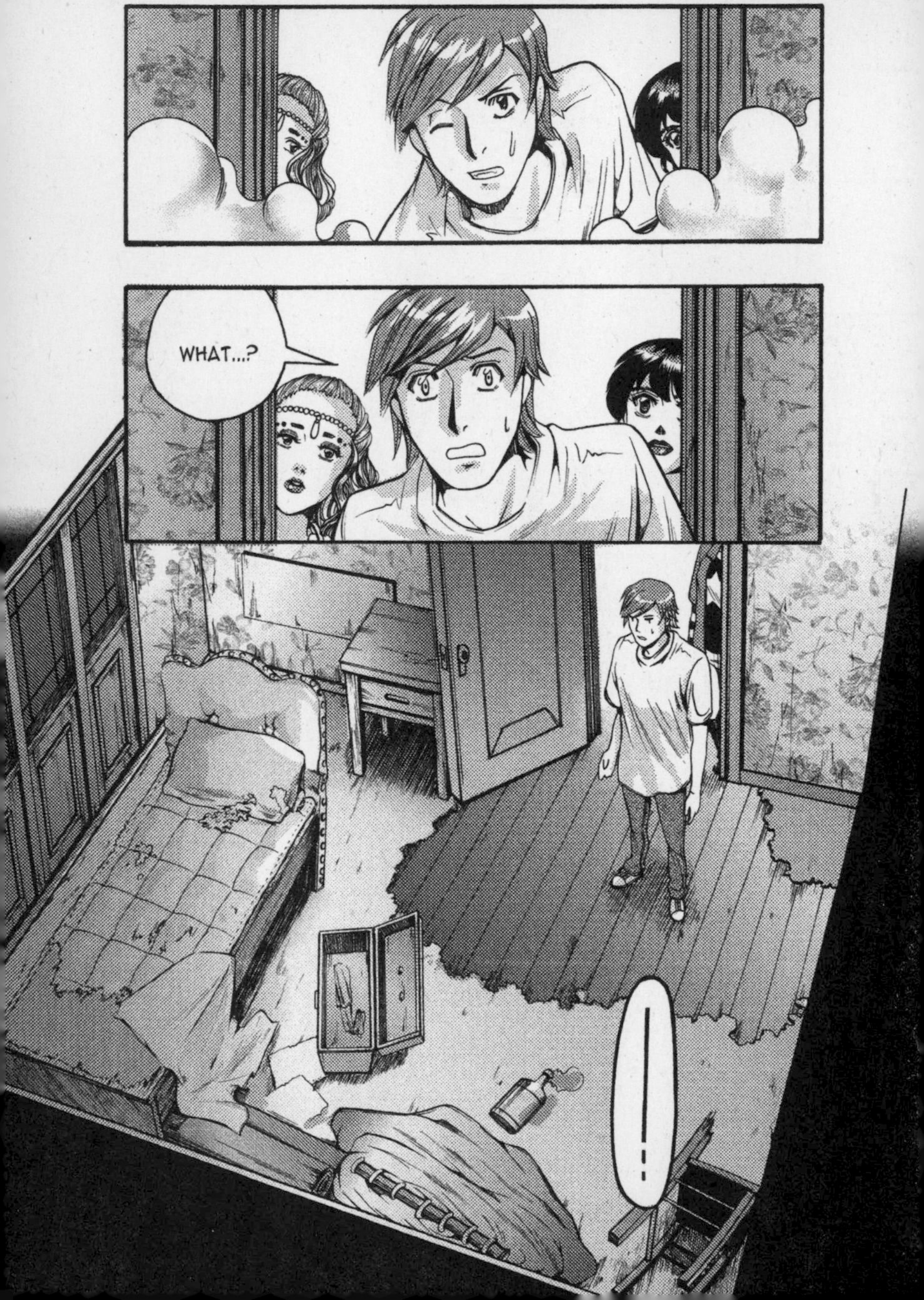
WHAT...?
!

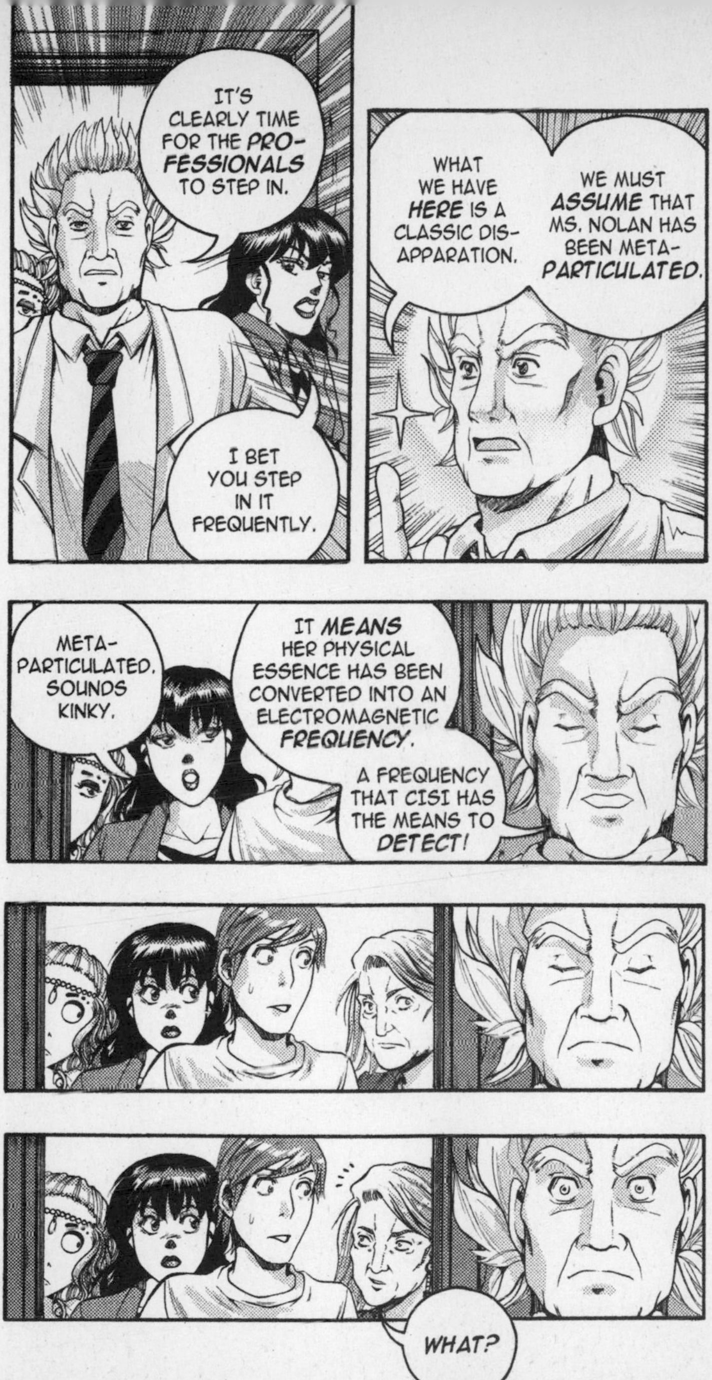
IT'S CLEARLY TIME FOR THE PRO-FESSIONALS TO STEP IN.
I BET YOU STEP IN IT FREQUENTLY.
WHAT WE HAVE HERE IS A CLASSIC DIS-APPARATION.
WE MUST ASSUME THAT MS. NOLAN HAS BEEN META-PARTICULATED.
META-PARTICULATED. SOUNDS KINKY.
IT MEANS HER PHYSICAL ESSENCE HAS BEEN CONVERTED INTO AN ELECTROMAGNETIC FREQUENCY.
A FREQUENCY THAT CISI HAS THE MEANS TO DETECT!
WHAT?

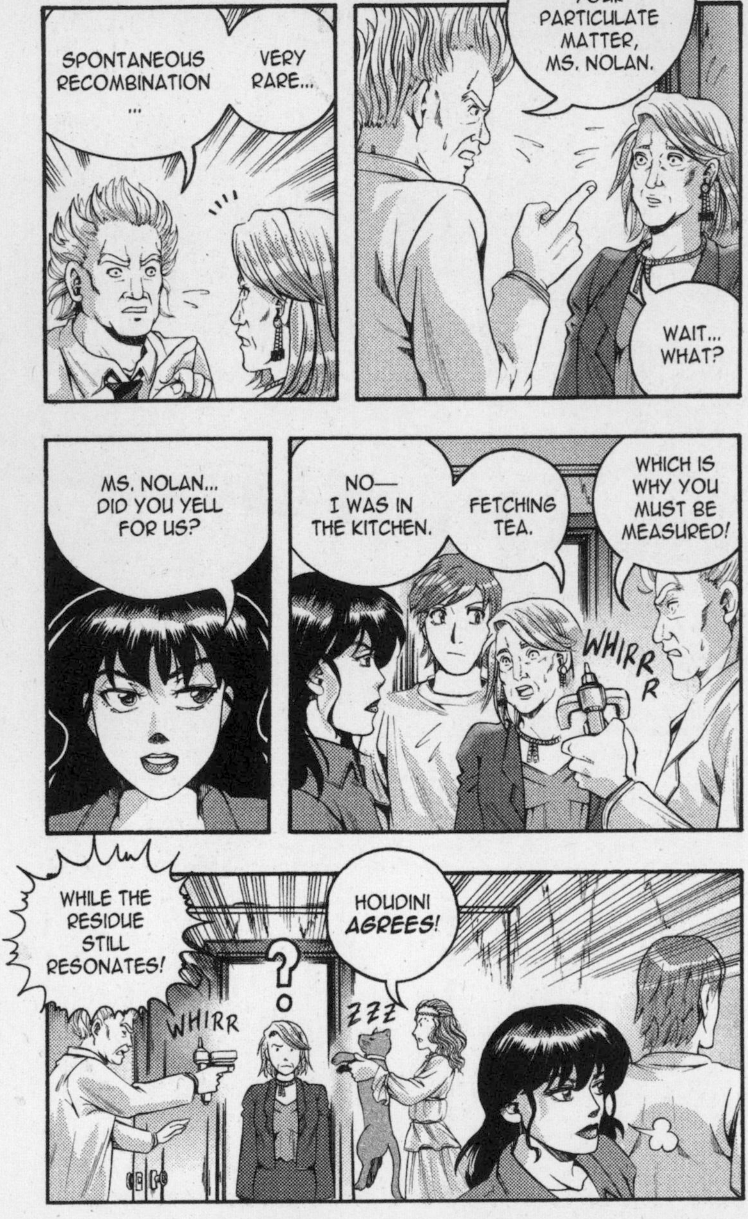
SPONTANEOUS RECOMBINATION ...
VERY RARE...
WE MUST MEASURE YOUR PARTICULATE MATTER, MS. NOLAN.
WAIT... WHAT?
MS. NOLAN... DID YOU YELL FOR US?
NO— I WAS IN THE KITCHEN.
FETCHING TEA.
WHICH IS WHY YOU MUST BE MEASURED!
WHIRRR
WHILE THE RESIDUE STILL RESONATES!
HOUDINI AGREES!
?
WHIRR
ZZZ

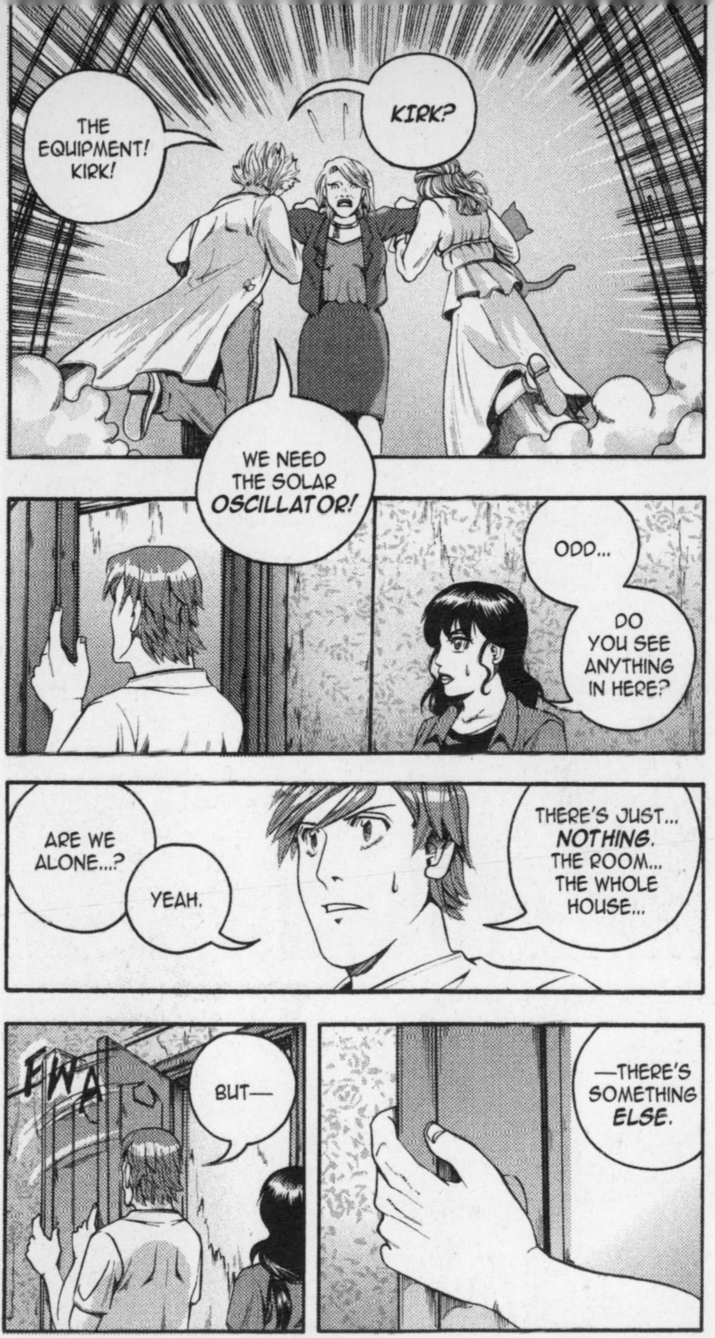
KIRK?
THE EQUIPMENT! KIRK!
WE NEED THE SOLAR OSCILLATOR!
ODD...
DO YOU SEE ANYTHING IN HERE?
THERE'S JUST... NOTHING. THE ROOM... THE WHOLE HOUSE...
ARE WE ALONE...?
YEAH.
FWA
BUT—
—THERE'S SOMETHING ELSE.

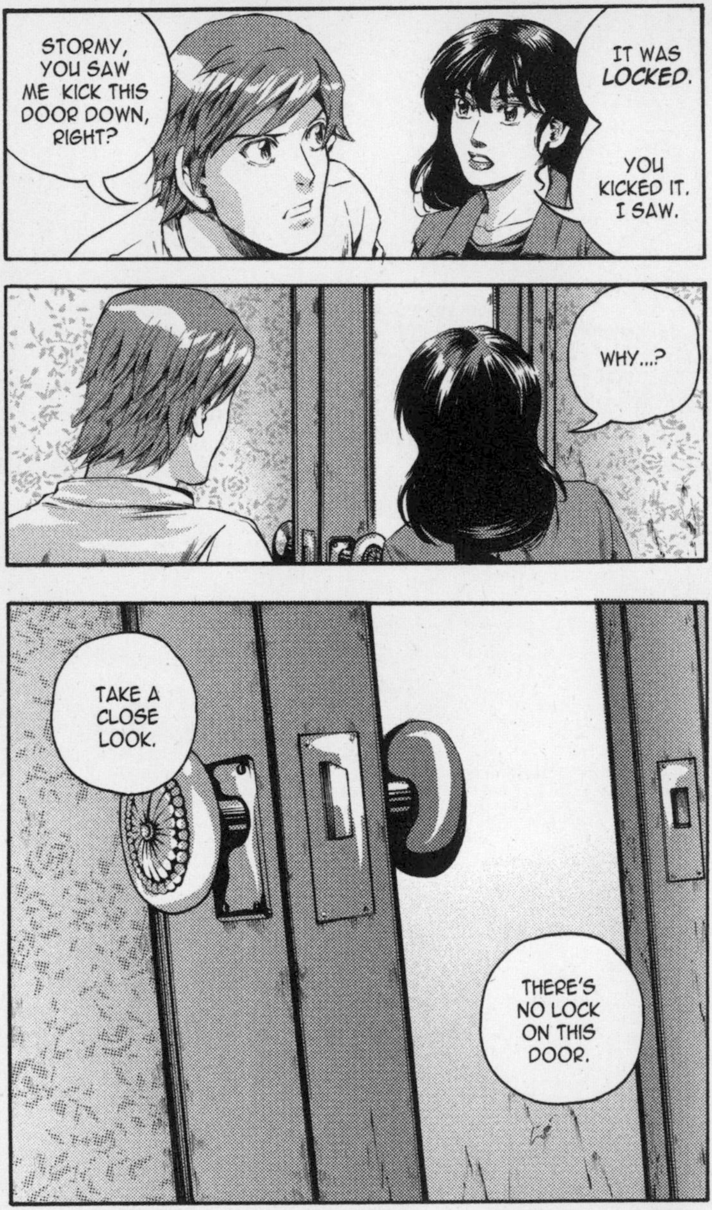
STORMY, YOU SAW ME KICK THIS DOOR DOWN, RIGHT?
IT WAS LOCKED.
YOU KICKED IT. I SAW.
WHY...?
TAKE A CLOSE LOOK.
THERE'S NO LOCK ON THIS DOOR.

Chapter 5

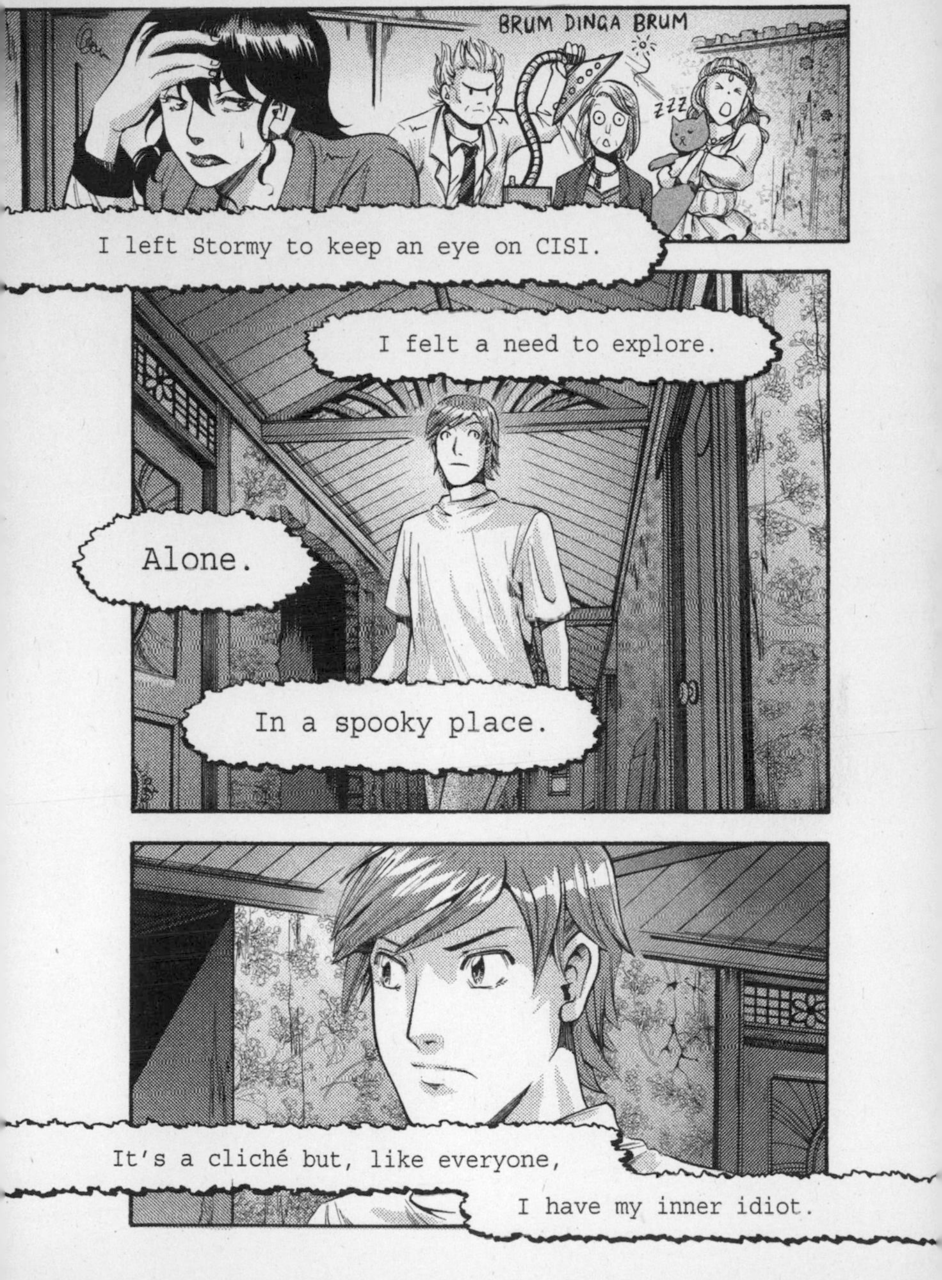
BRUM DINGA BRUM
ZZZ
I left Stormy to keep an eye on CISI.
I felt a need to explore.
Alone.
In a spooky place.
It's a cliché but, like everyone,
I have my inner idiot.

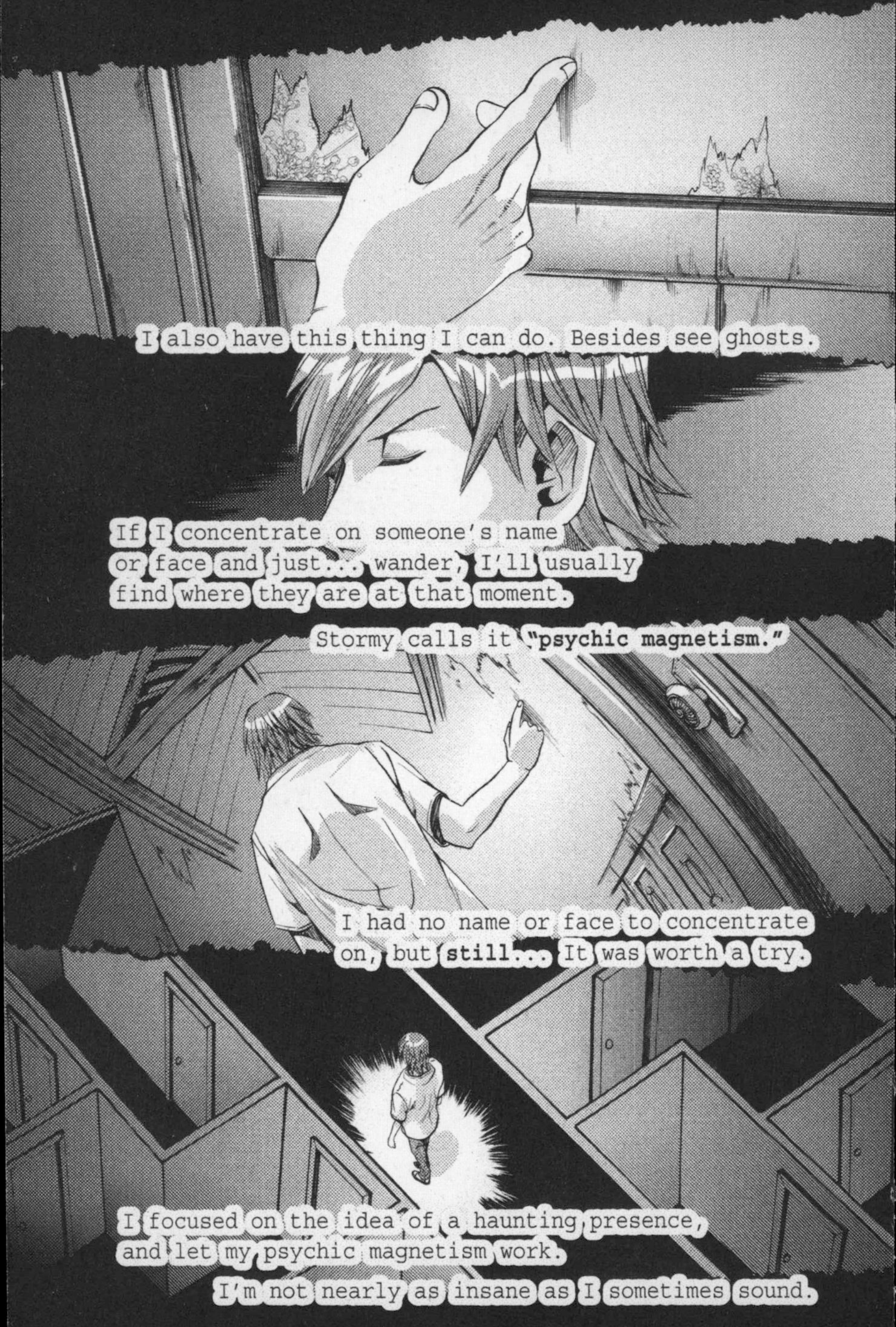
I also have this thing I can do. Besides see ghosts.
If I concentrate on someone's name or face and just... wander, I'll usually find where they are at that moment.
Stormy calls it **"psychic magnetism."**
I had no name or face to concentrate on, but **still...** It was worth a try.
I focused on the idea of a haunting presence, and let my psychic magnetism work.
I'm not nearly as insane as I sometimes sound.

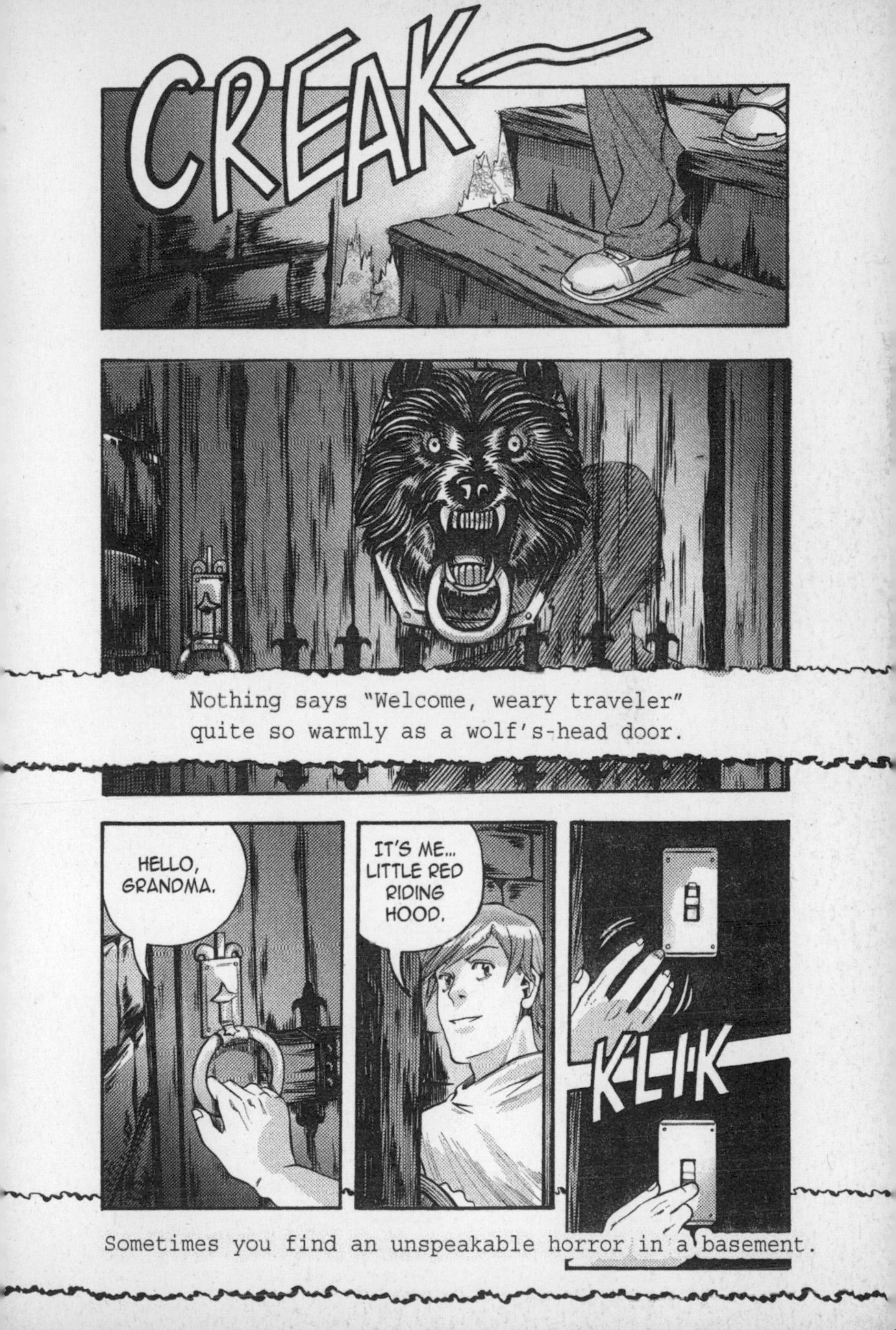
CREAK
Nothing says "Welcome, weary traveler" quite so warmly as a wolf's-head door.
HELLO, GRANDMA.
IT'S ME... LITTLE RED RIDING HOOD.
K-L-I-K
Sometimes you find an unspeakable horror in a basement.

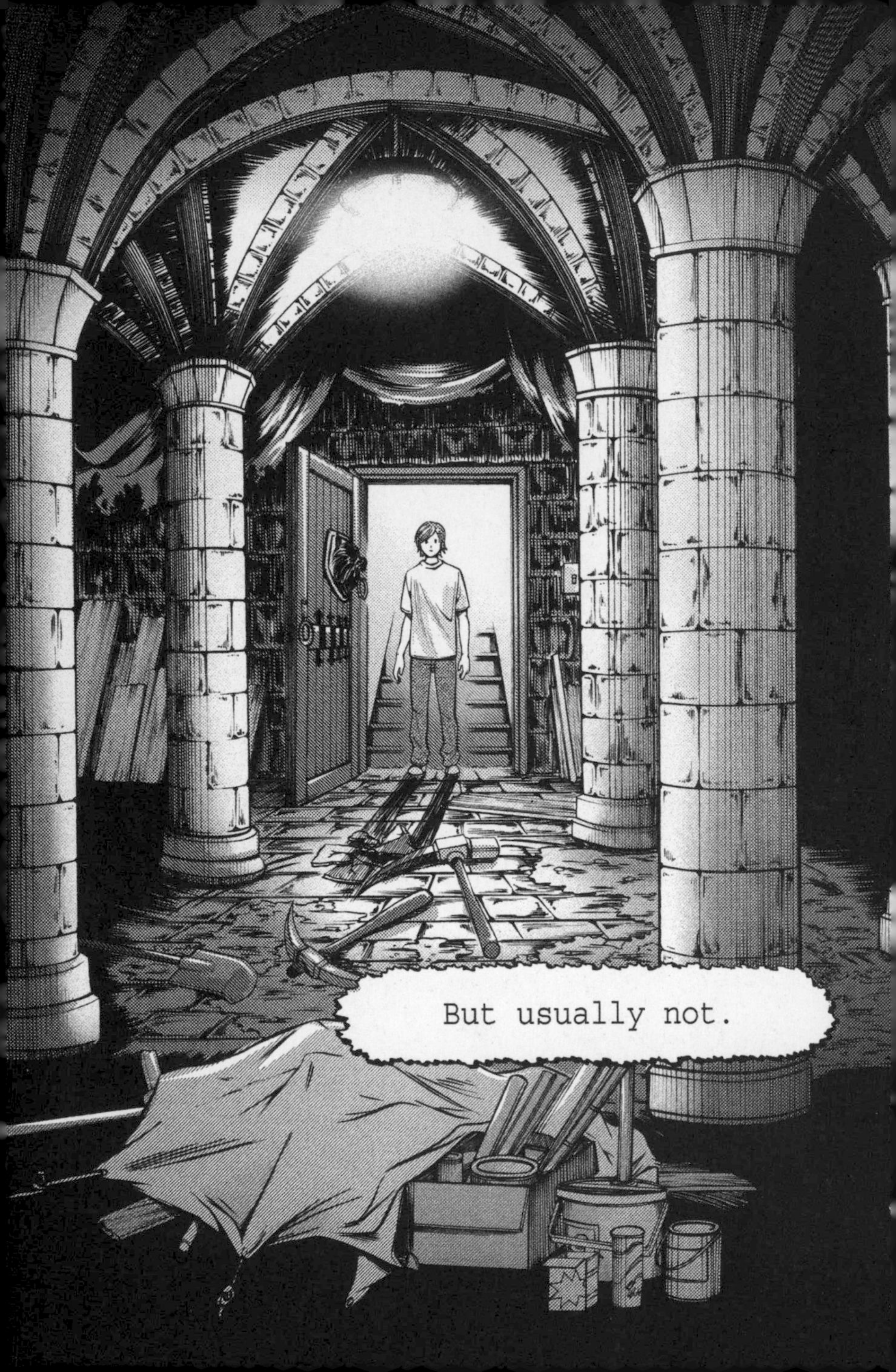
But usually not.

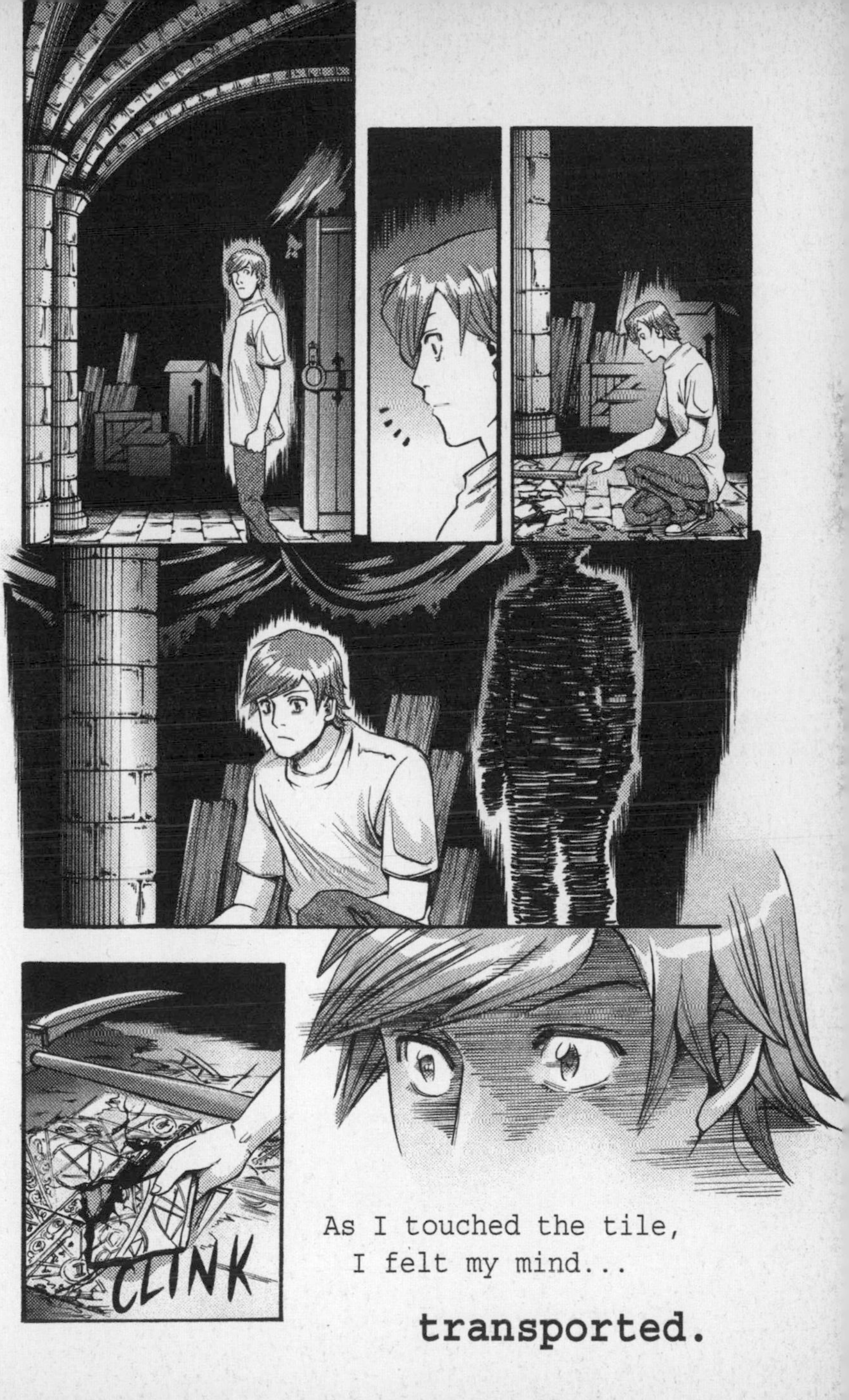
CLINK
As I touched the tile,
I felt my mind...
transported.

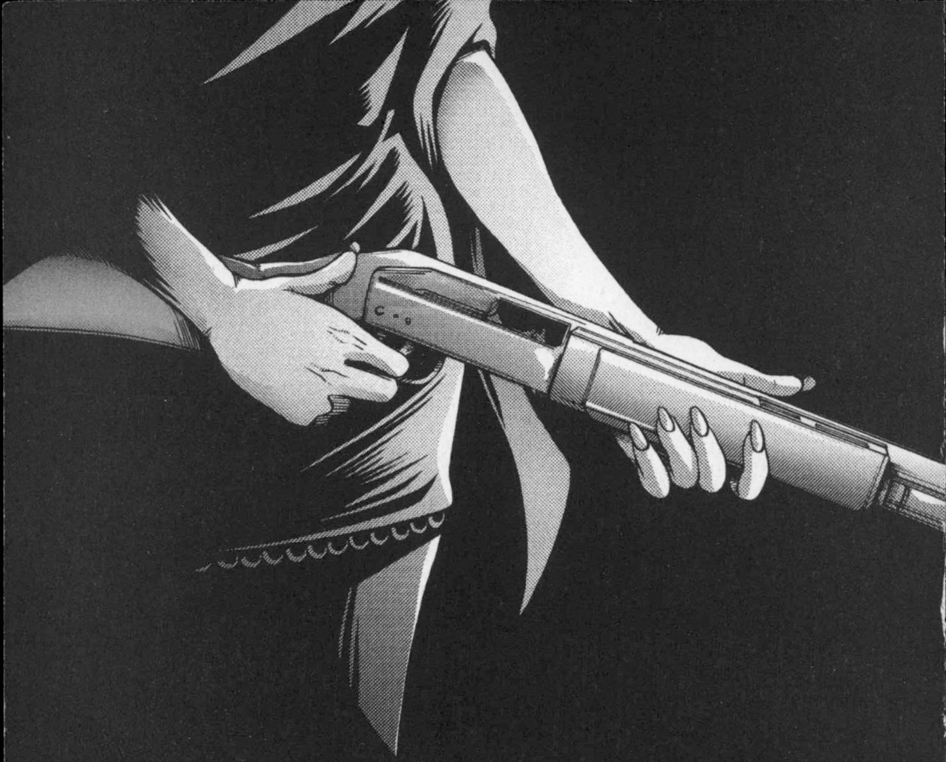

I had been cast back into the past.

Back to my

childhood...

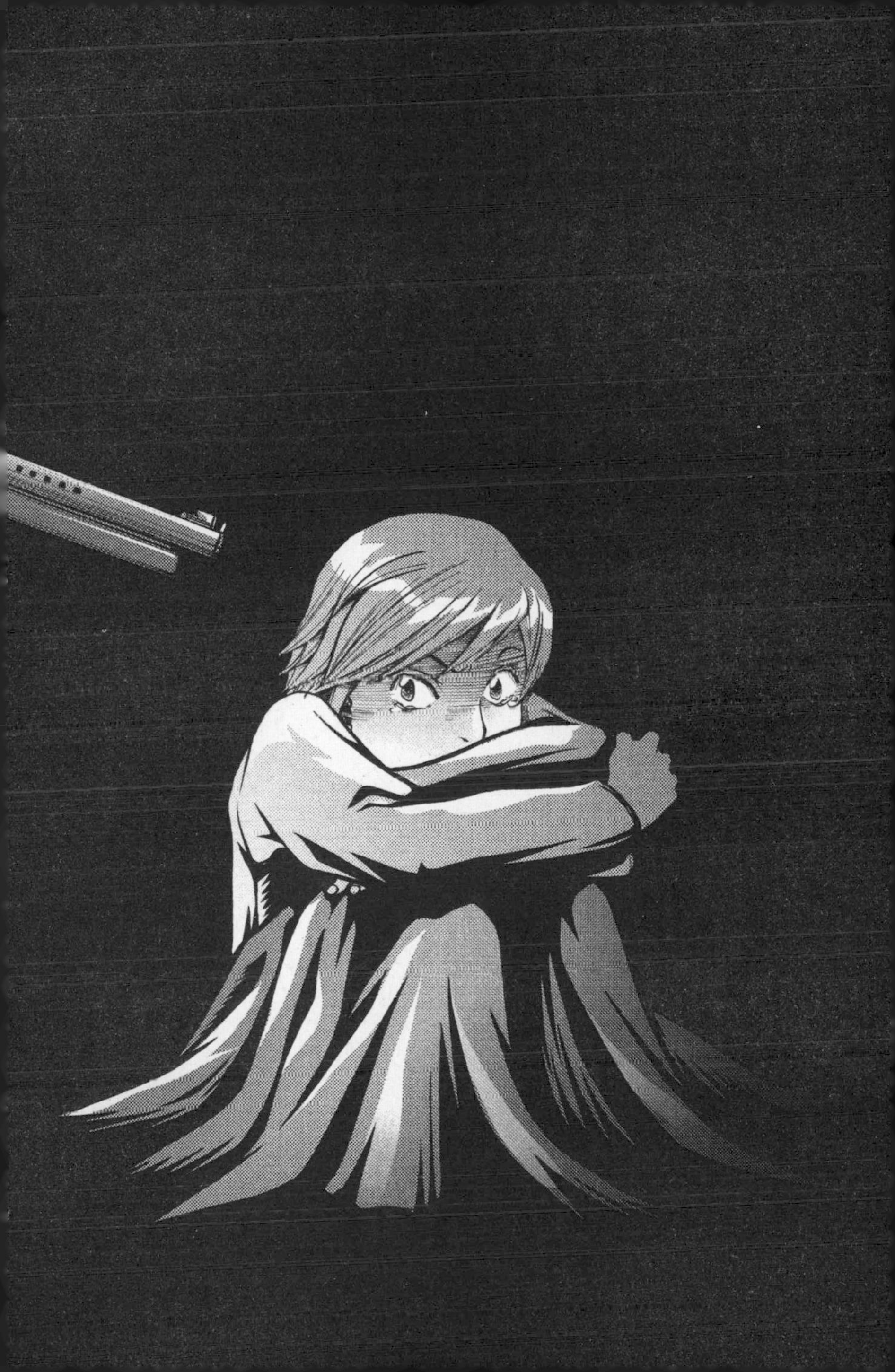

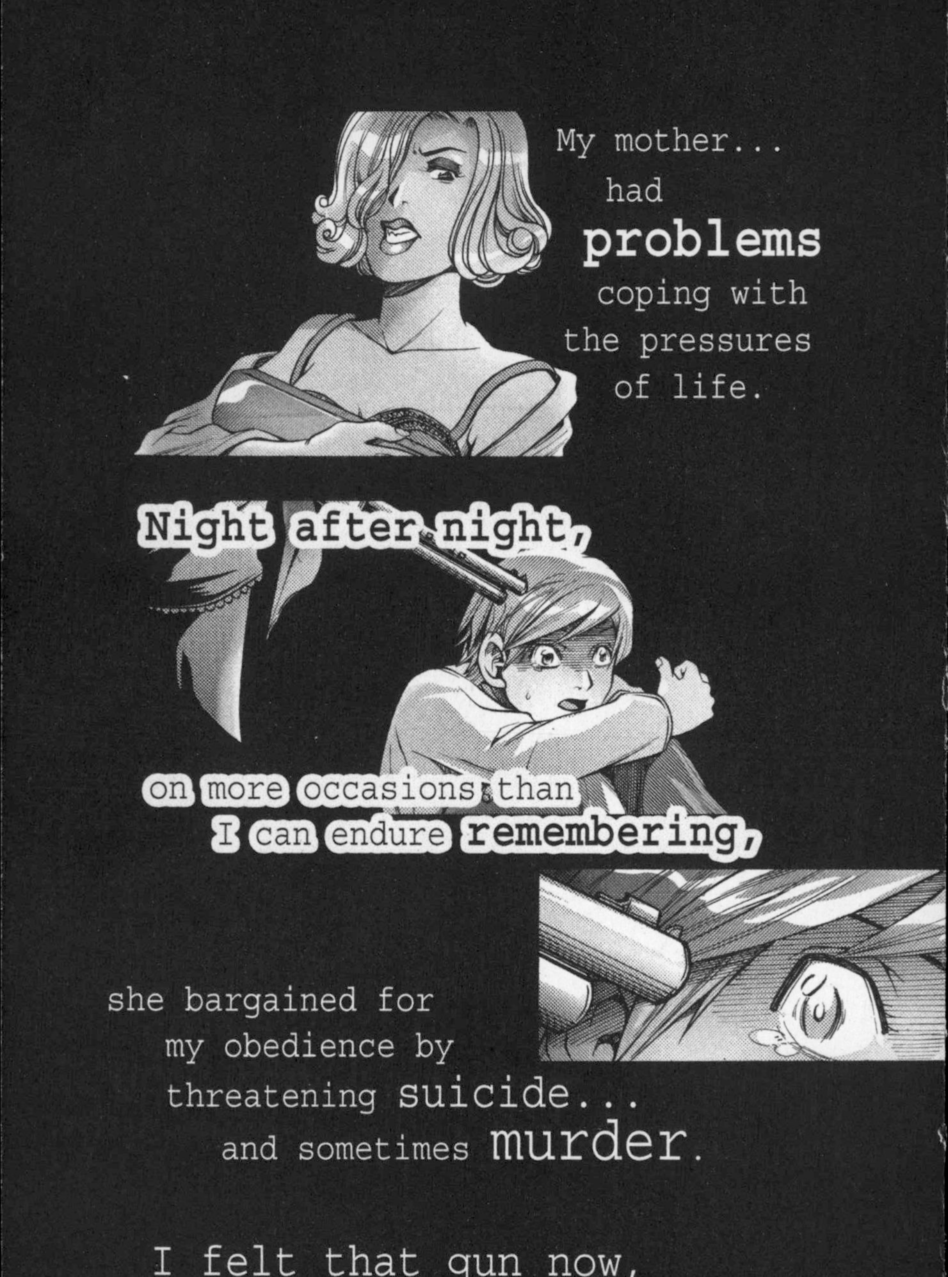
My mother... had **problems** coping with the pressures of life.
Night after night,
on more occasions than I can endure remembering,
she bargained for my obedience by threatening suicide... and sometimes murder.
I felt that gun now,

I was a **child** again,

experiencing **fear**

beyond my ability
to **process**...

The sensation lasted less than a second, though it felt like an eternity.

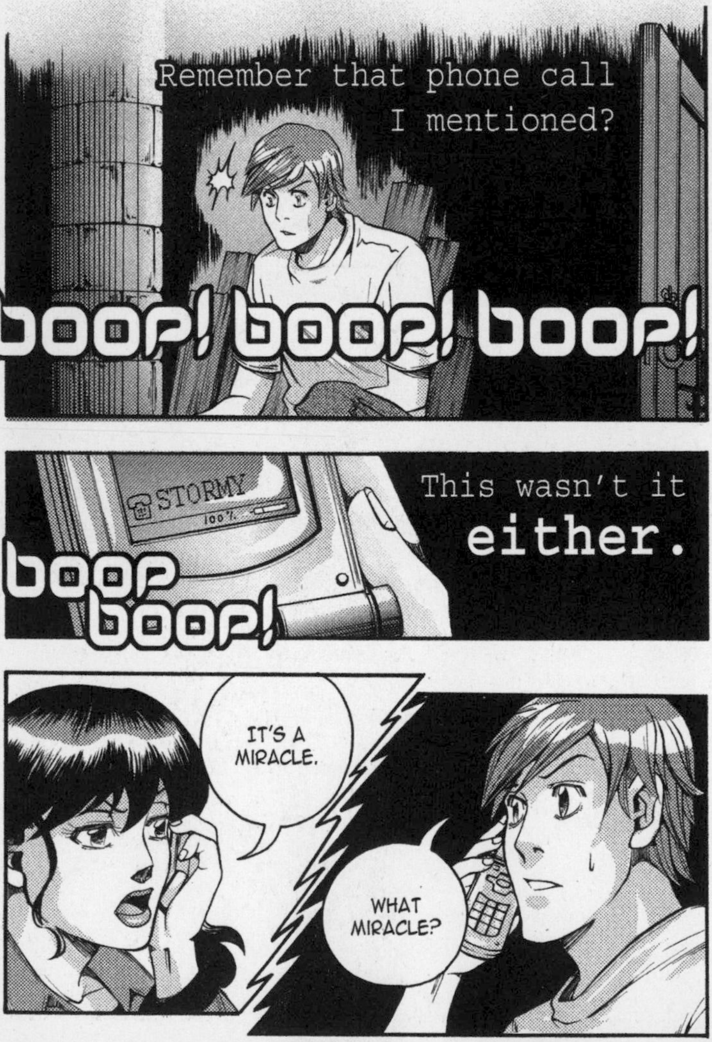

Remember that phone call I mentioned?
boop! boop! boop!
STORMY
100%
This wasn't it either.
boop boop!
IT'S A MIRACLE.
WHAT MIRACLE?

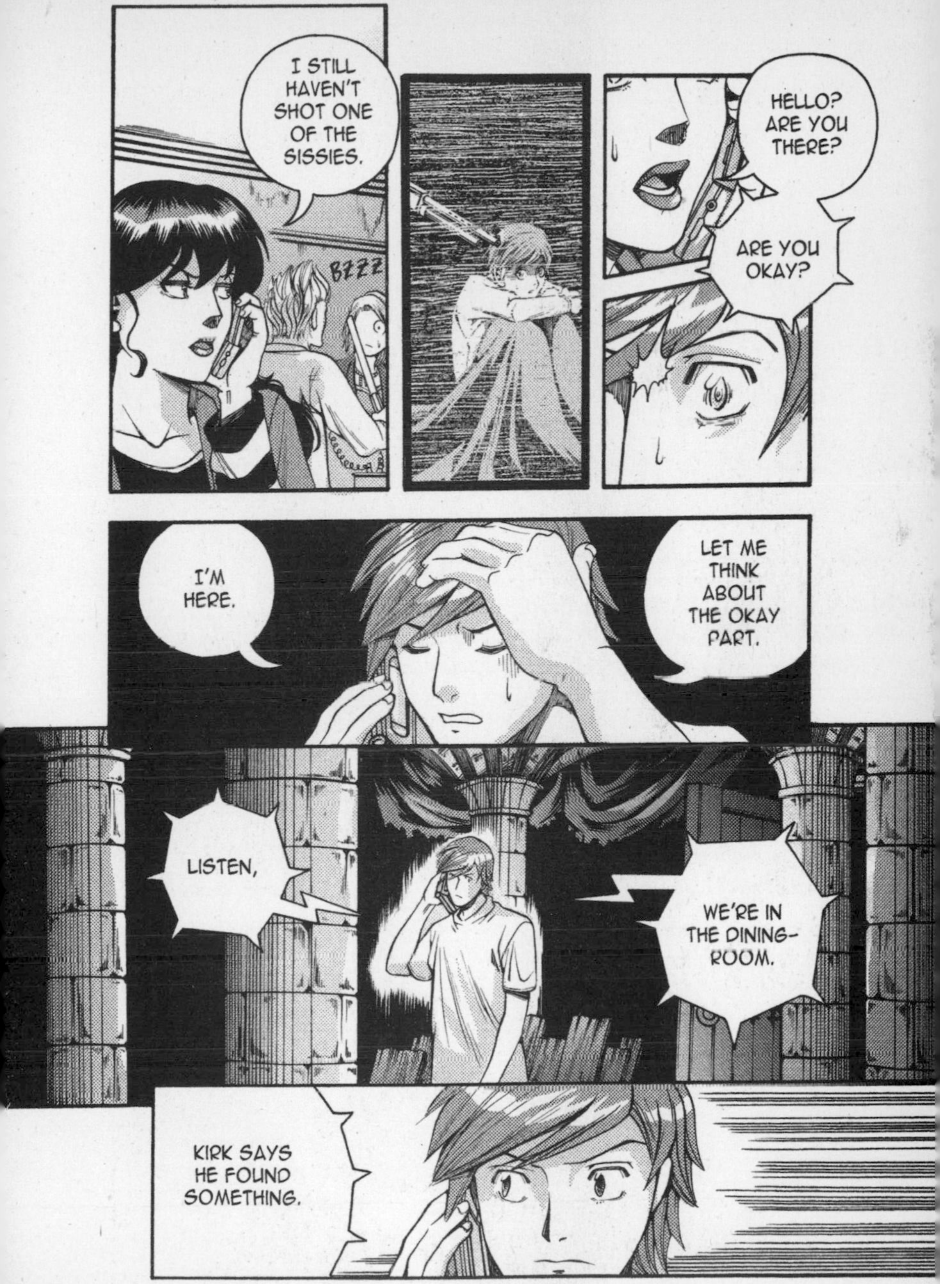
I STILL HAVEN'T SHOT ONE OF THE SISSIES.
BZZZ
HELLO? ARE YOU THERE?
ARE YOU OKAY?
I'M HERE.
LET ME THINK ABOUT THE OKAY PART.
LISTEN,
WE'RE IN THE DINING-ROOM.
KIRK SAYS HE FOUND SOMETHING.

Chapter 6

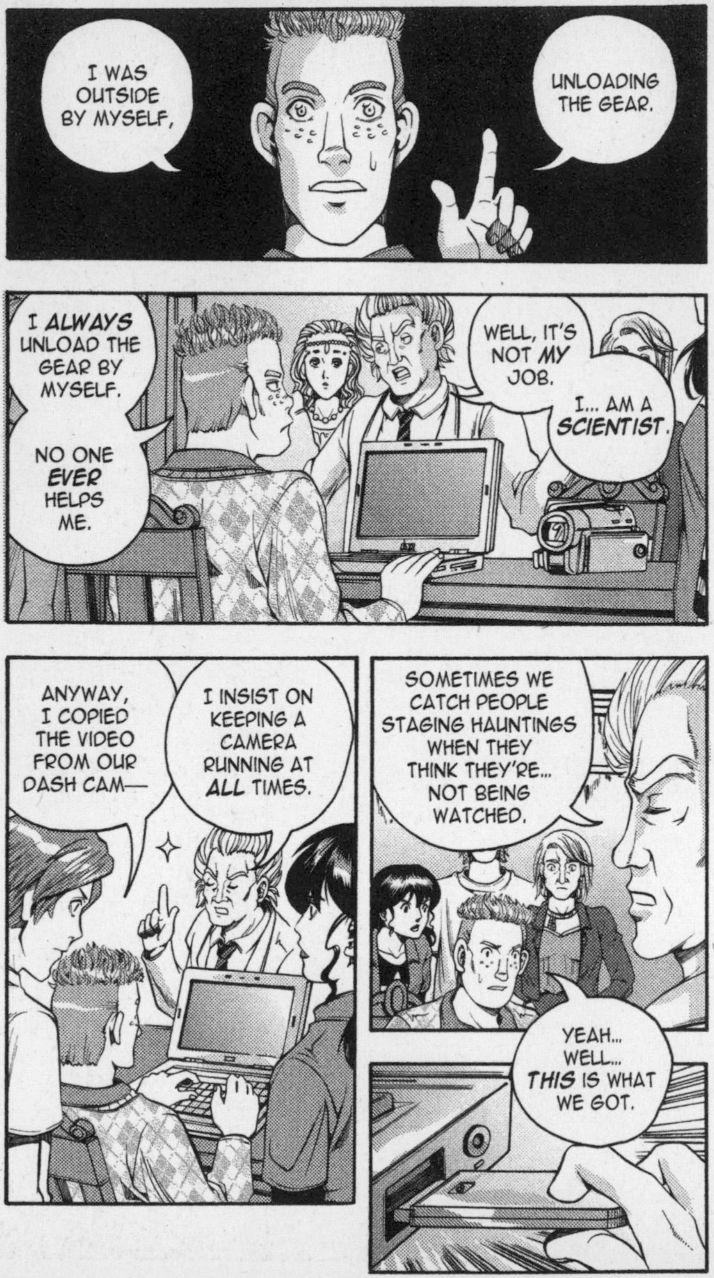
I WAS OUTSIDE BY MYSELF,
UNLOADING THE GEAR.
I *ALWAYS* UNLOAD THE GEAR BY MYSELF.
NO ONE *EVER* HELPS ME.
WELL, IT'S NOT *MY* JOB.
I... AM A *SCIENTIST*.
ANYWAY, I COPIED THE VIDEO FROM OUR DASH CAM—
I INSIST ON KEEPING A CAMERA RUNNING AT *ALL* TIMES.
SOMETIMES WE CATCH PEOPLE STAGING HAUNTINGS WHEN THEY THINK THEY'RE... NOT BEING WATCHED.
YEAH... WELL... *THIS* IS WHAT WE GOT.

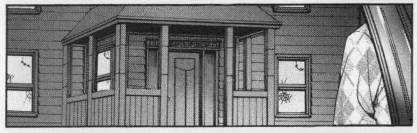

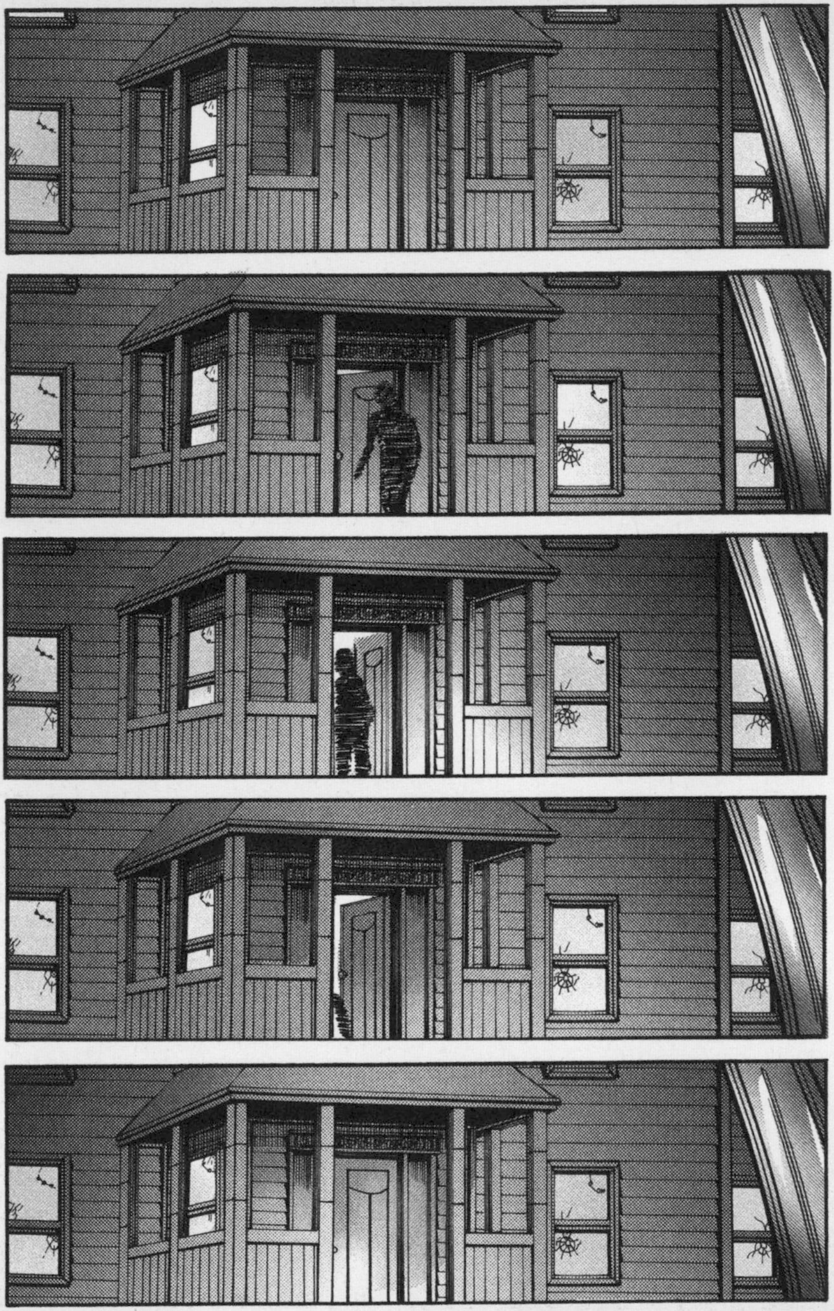

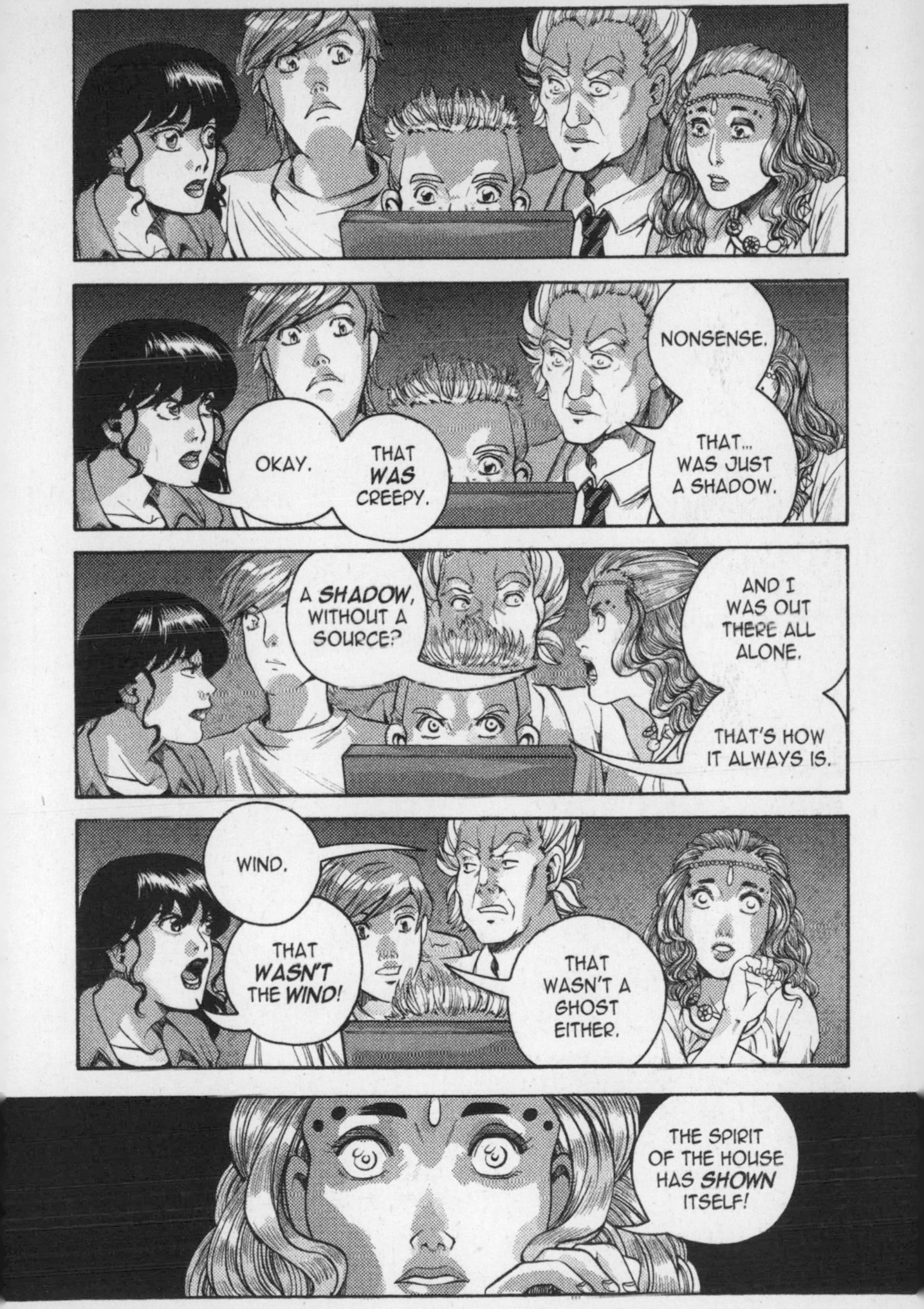
NONSENSE.
THAT... WAS JUST A SHADOW.
OKAY.
THAT *WAS* CREEPY.
A *SHADOW*, WITHOUT A SOURCE?
AND I WAS OUT THERE ALL ALONE.
THAT'S HOW IT ALWAYS IS.
WIND.
THAT *WASN'T* THE *WIND*!
THAT WASN'T A GHOST EITHER.
THE SPIRIT OF THE HOUSE HAS *SHOWN* ITSELF!

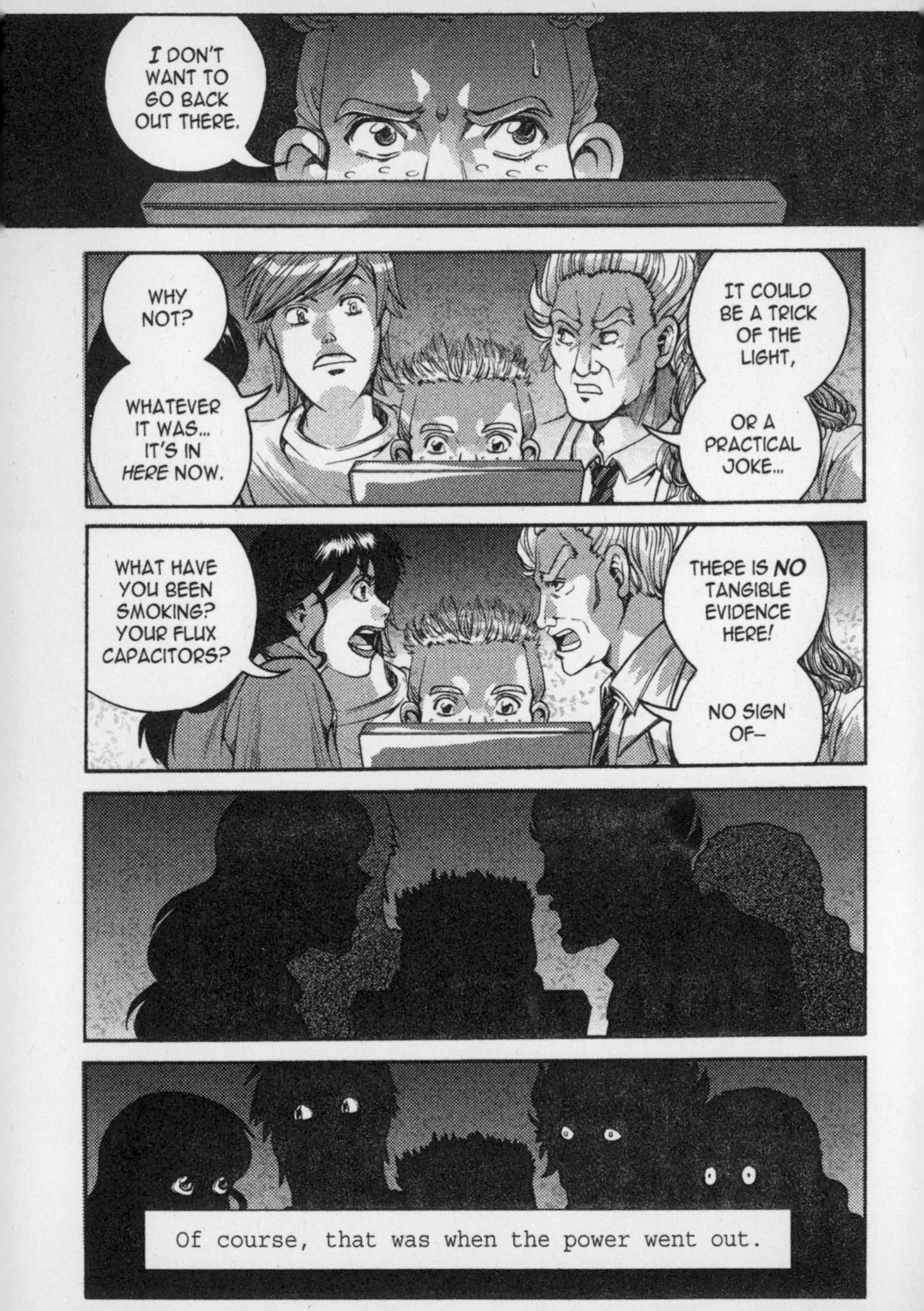
I DON'T WANT TO GO BACK OUT THERE.
WHY NOT?
WHATEVER IT WAS... IT'S IN HERE NOW.
IT COULD BE A TRICK OF THE LIGHT,
OR A PRACTICAL JOKE...
WHAT HAVE YOU BEEN SMOKING? YOUR FLUX CAPACITORS?
THERE IS NO TANGIBLE EVIDENCE HERE!
NO SIGN OF–
Of course, that was when the power went out.

Chapter 7

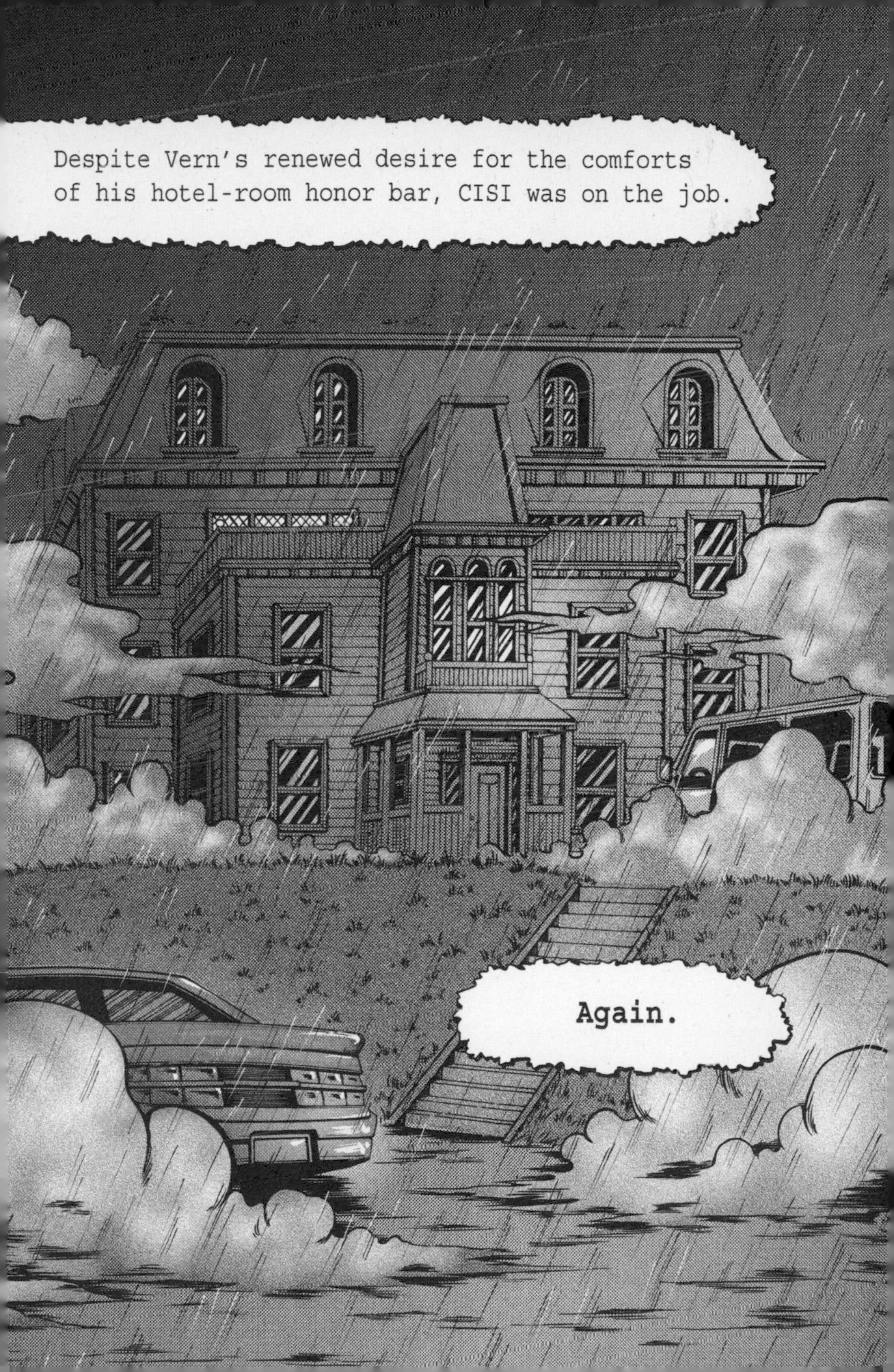
Despite Vern's renewed desire for the comforts of his hotel-room honor bar, CISI was on the job.
Again.

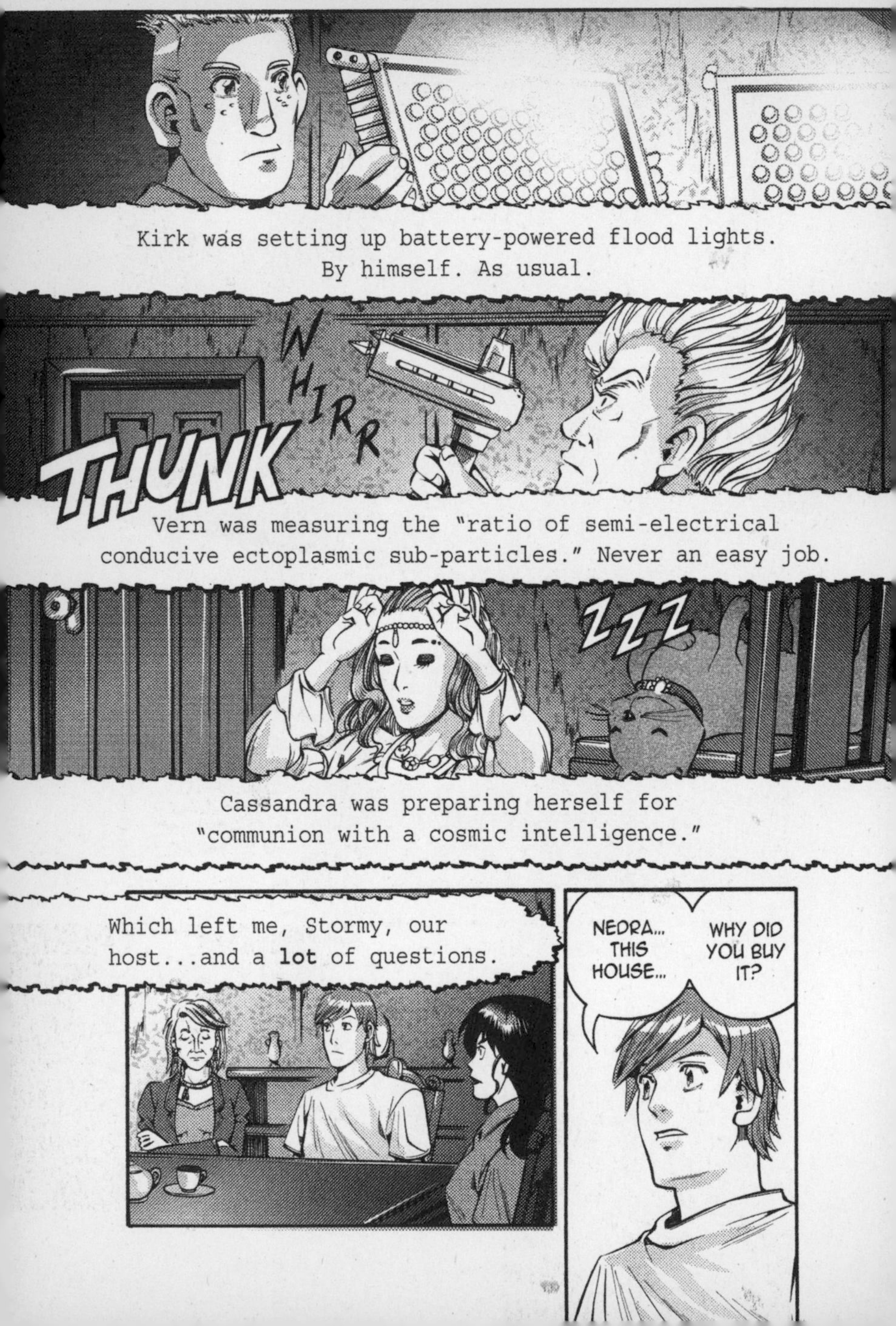
Kirk was setting up battery-powered flood lights.
By himself. As usual.
WHIRR
THUNK
Vern was measuring the "ratio of semi-electrical conducive ectoplasmic sub-particles." Never an easy job.
ZZZ
Cassandra was preparing herself for "communion with a cosmic intelligence."
Which left me, Stormy, our host...and a **lot** of questions.
NEDRA... THIS HOUSE...
WHY DID YOU BUY IT?

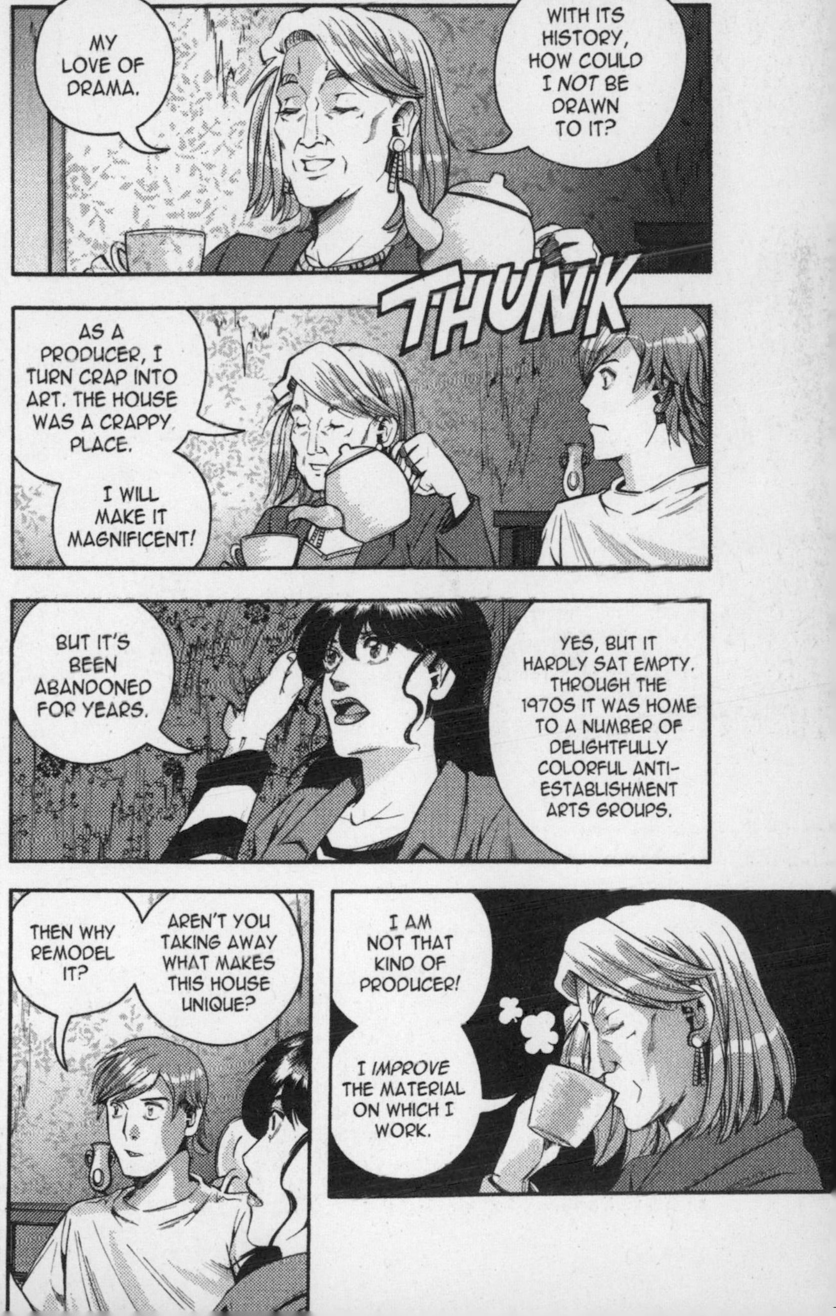
MY LOVE OF DRAMA.
WITH ITS HISTORY, HOW COULD I *NOT* BE DRAWN TO IT?
THUNK
AS A PRODUCER, I TURN CRAP INTO ART. THE HOUSE WAS A CRAPPY PLACE.
I WILL MAKE IT MAGNIFICENT!
BUT IT'S BEEN ABANDONED FOR YEARS.
YES, BUT IT HARDLY SAT EMPTY. THROUGH THE 1970S IT WAS HOME TO A NUMBER OF DELIGHTFULLY COLORFUL ANTI-ESTABLISHMENT ARTS GROUPS.
THEN WHY REMODEL IT?
AREN'T YOU TAKING AWAY WHAT MAKES THIS HOUSE UNIQUE?
I AM NOT THAT KIND OF PRODUCER!
I *IMPROVE* THE MATERIAL ON WHICH I WORK.

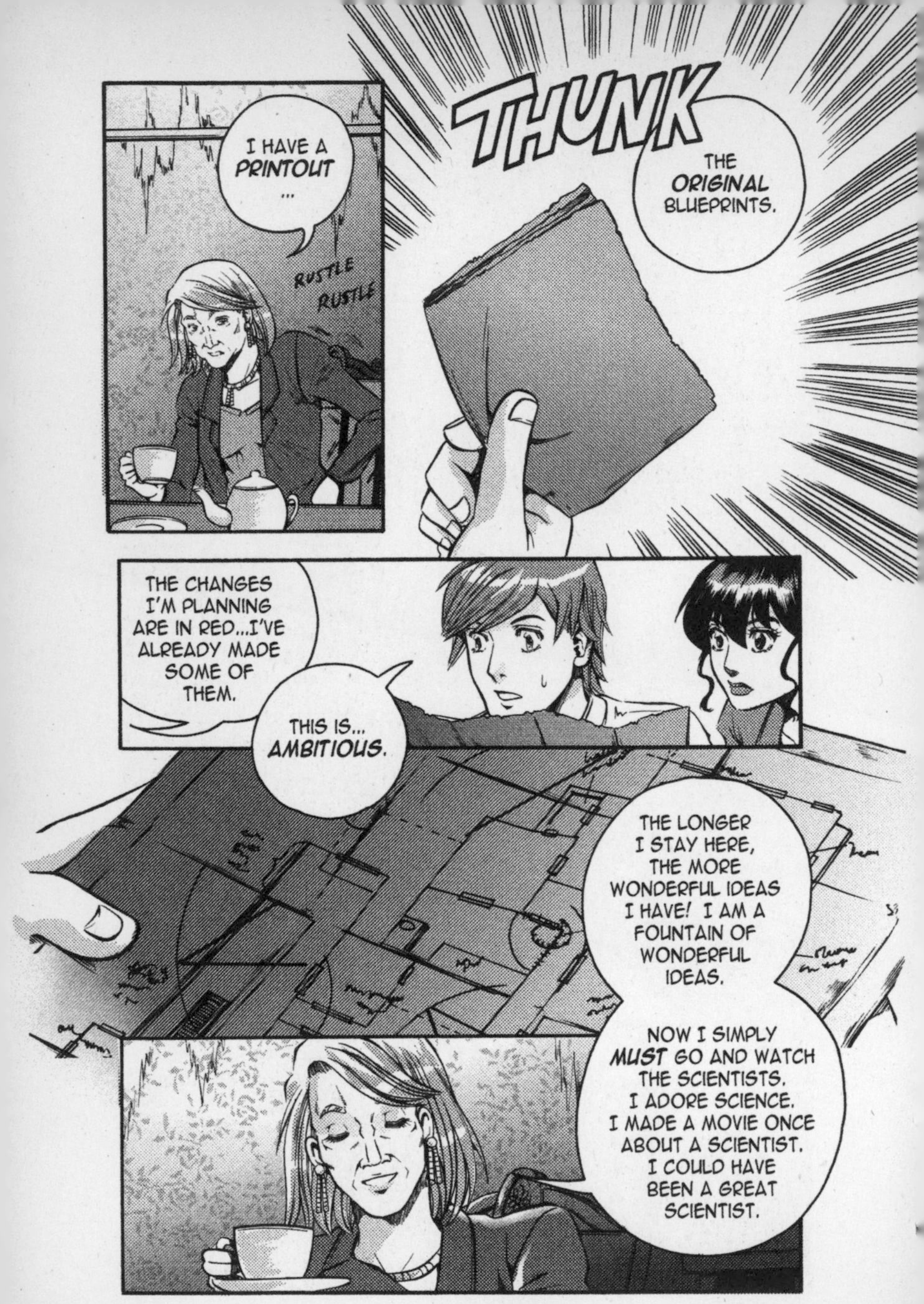
I HAVE A PRINTOUT ...
RUSTLE RUSTLE
THUNK
THE ORIGINAL BLUEPRINTS.
THE CHANGES I'M PLANNING ARE IN RED...I'VE ALREADY MADE SOME OF THEM.
THIS IS... AMBITIOUS.
THE LONGER I STAY HERE, THE MORE WONDERFUL IDEAS I HAVE! I AM A FOUNTAIN OF WONDERFUL IDEAS.
NOW I SIMPLY MUST GO AND WATCH THE SCIENTISTS. I ADORE SCIENCE. I MADE A MOVIE ONCE ABOUT A SCIENTIST. I COULD HAVE BEEN A GREAT SCIENTIST.

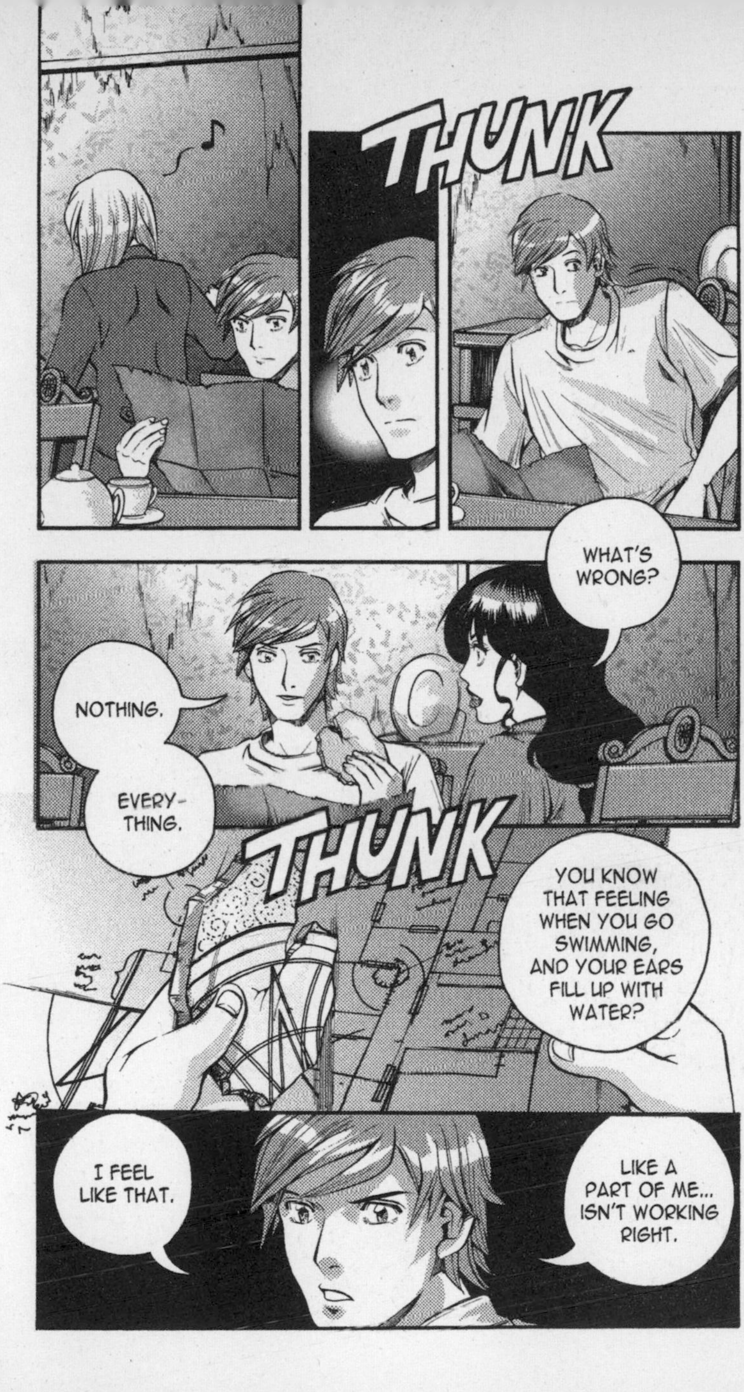
THUNK
WHAT'S WRONG?
NOTHING.
EVERY-THING.
THUNK
YOU KNOW THAT FEELING WHEN YOU GO SWIMMING, AND YOUR EARS FILL UP WITH WATER?
I FEEL LIKE THAT.
LIKE A PART OF ME... ISN'T WORKING RIGHT.

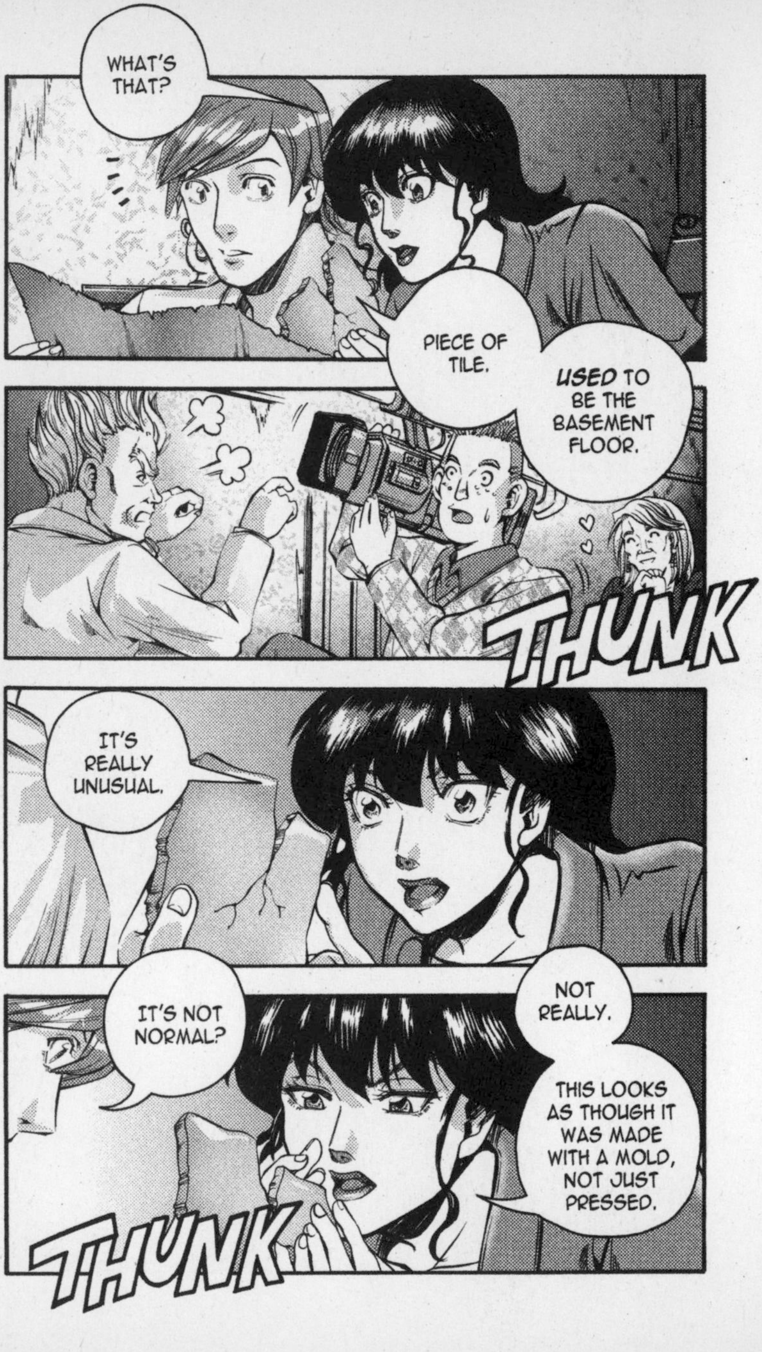
WHAT'S THAT?
PIECE OF TILE.
USED TO BE THE BASEMENT FLOOR.
THUNK
IT'S REALLY UNUSUAL.
IT'S NOT NORMAL?
NOT REALLY.
THIS LOOKS AS THOUGH IT WAS MADE WITH A MOLD, NOT JUST PRESSED.
THUNK

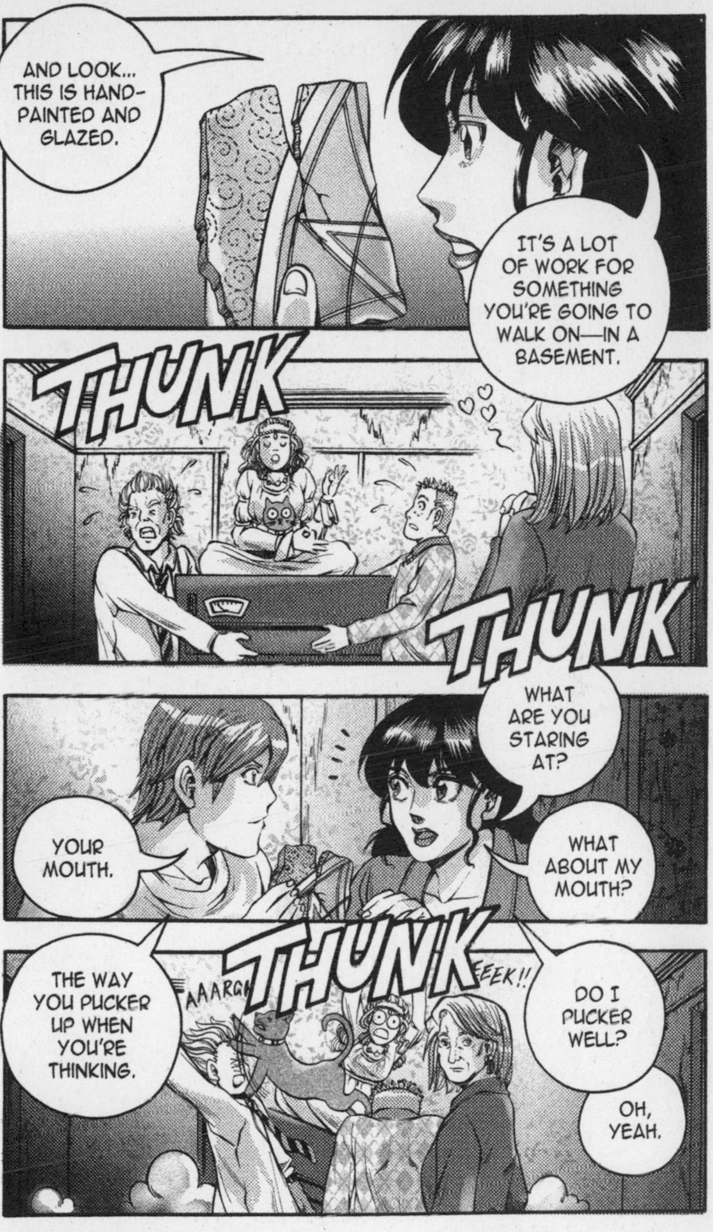
AND LOOK... THIS IS HAND-PAINTED AND GLAZED.
IT'S A LOT OF WORK FOR SOMETHING YOU'RE GOING TO WALK ON—IN A BASEMENT.
THUNK
THUNK
WHAT ARE YOU STARING AT?
YOUR MOUTH.
WHAT ABOUT MY MOUTH?
THE WAY YOU PUCKER UP WHEN YOU'RE THINKING.
AAARGH
THUNK
EEEK!!
DO I PUCKER WELL?
OH, YEAH.

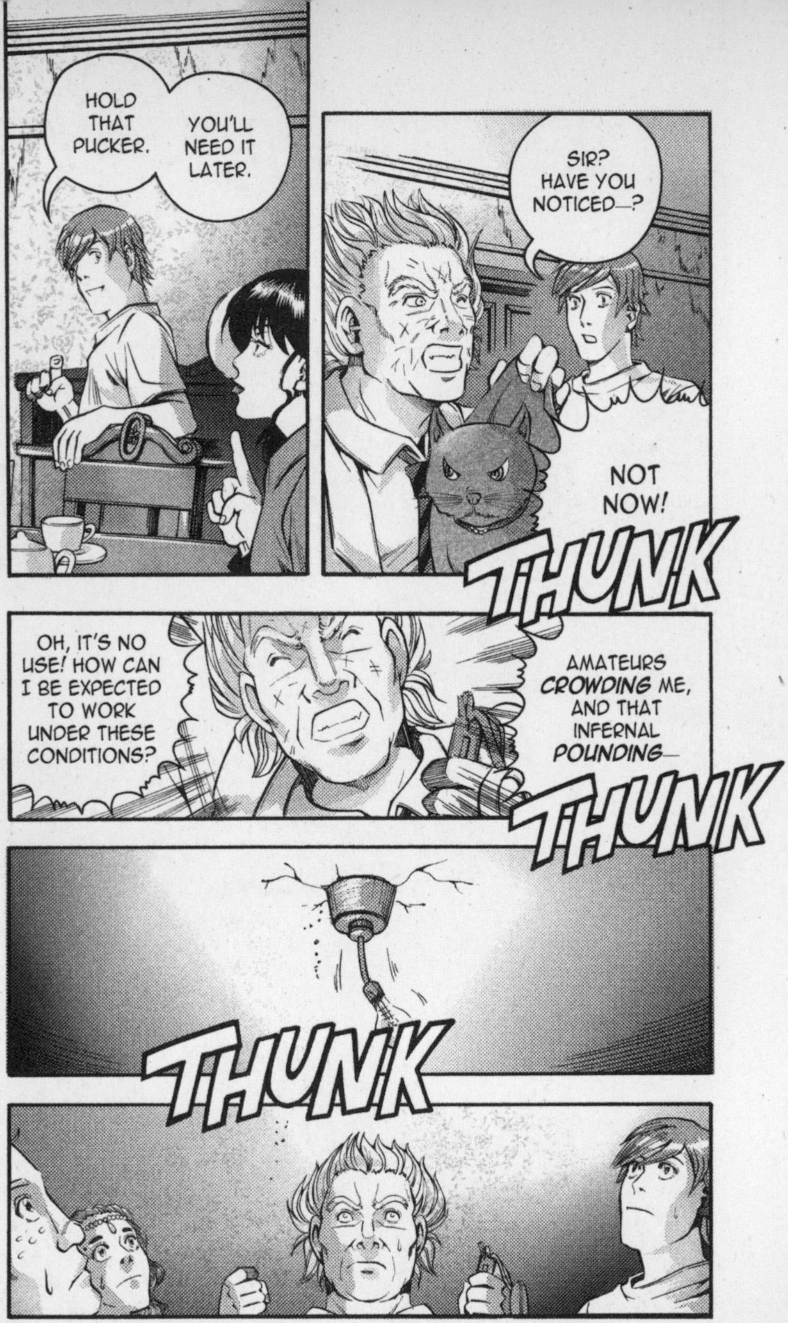
HOLD THAT PUCKER.
YOU'LL NEED IT LATER.
SIR? HAVE YOU NOTICED—?
NOT NOW!
THUNK
OH, IT'S NO USE! HOW CAN I BE EXPECTED TO WORK UNDER THESE CONDITIONS?
AMATEURS CROWDING ME, AND THAT INFERNAL POUNDING—
THUNK
THUNK

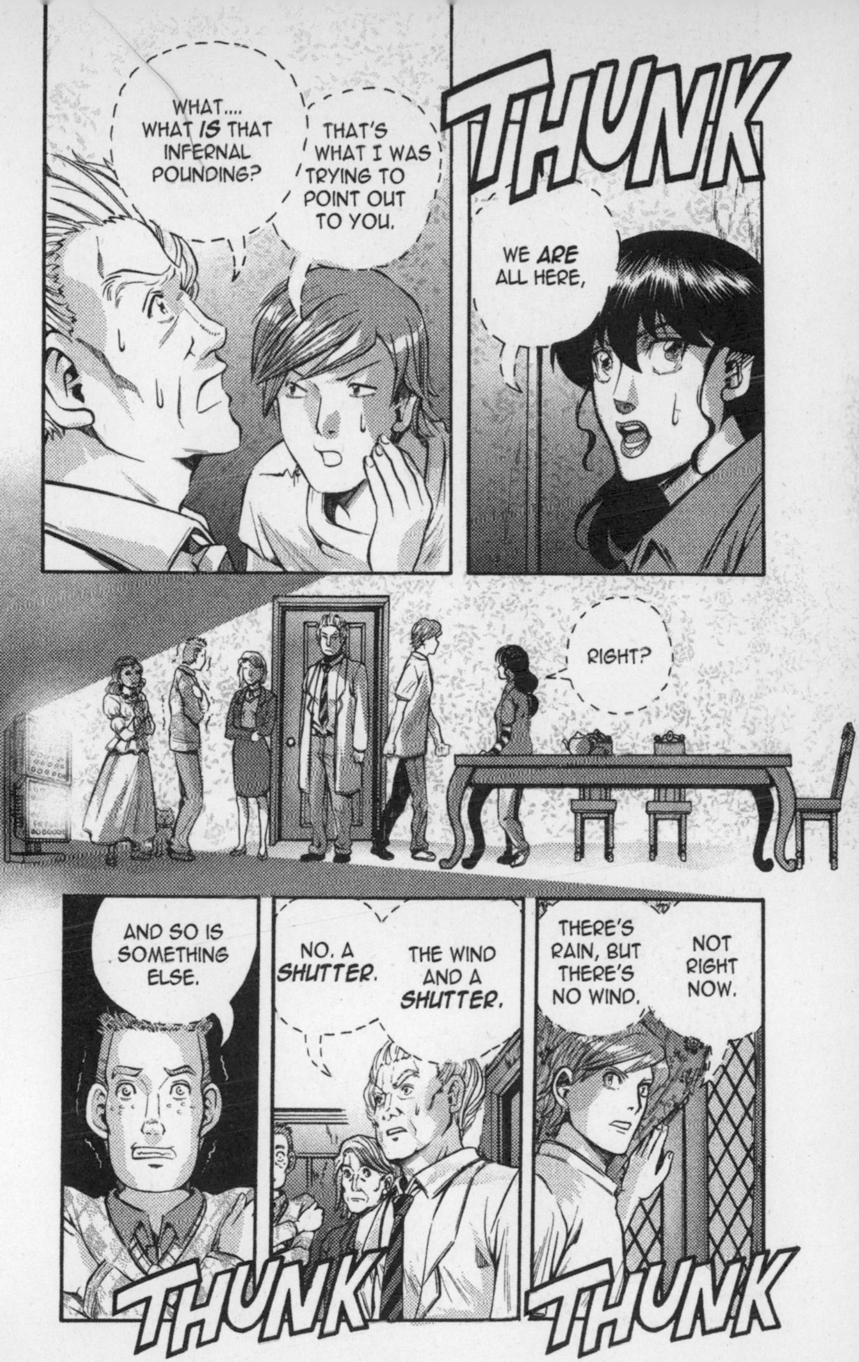
WHAT.... WHAT IS THAT INFERNAL POUNDING?
THAT'S WHAT I WAS TRYING TO POINT OUT TO YOU.
THUNK
WE ARE ALL HERE,
RIGHT?
AND SO IS SOMETHING ELSE.
THE WIND AND A SHUTTER.
NO. A SHUTTER.
NOT RIGHT NOW.
THERE'S RAIN, BUT THERE'S NO WIND.
THUNK
THUNK

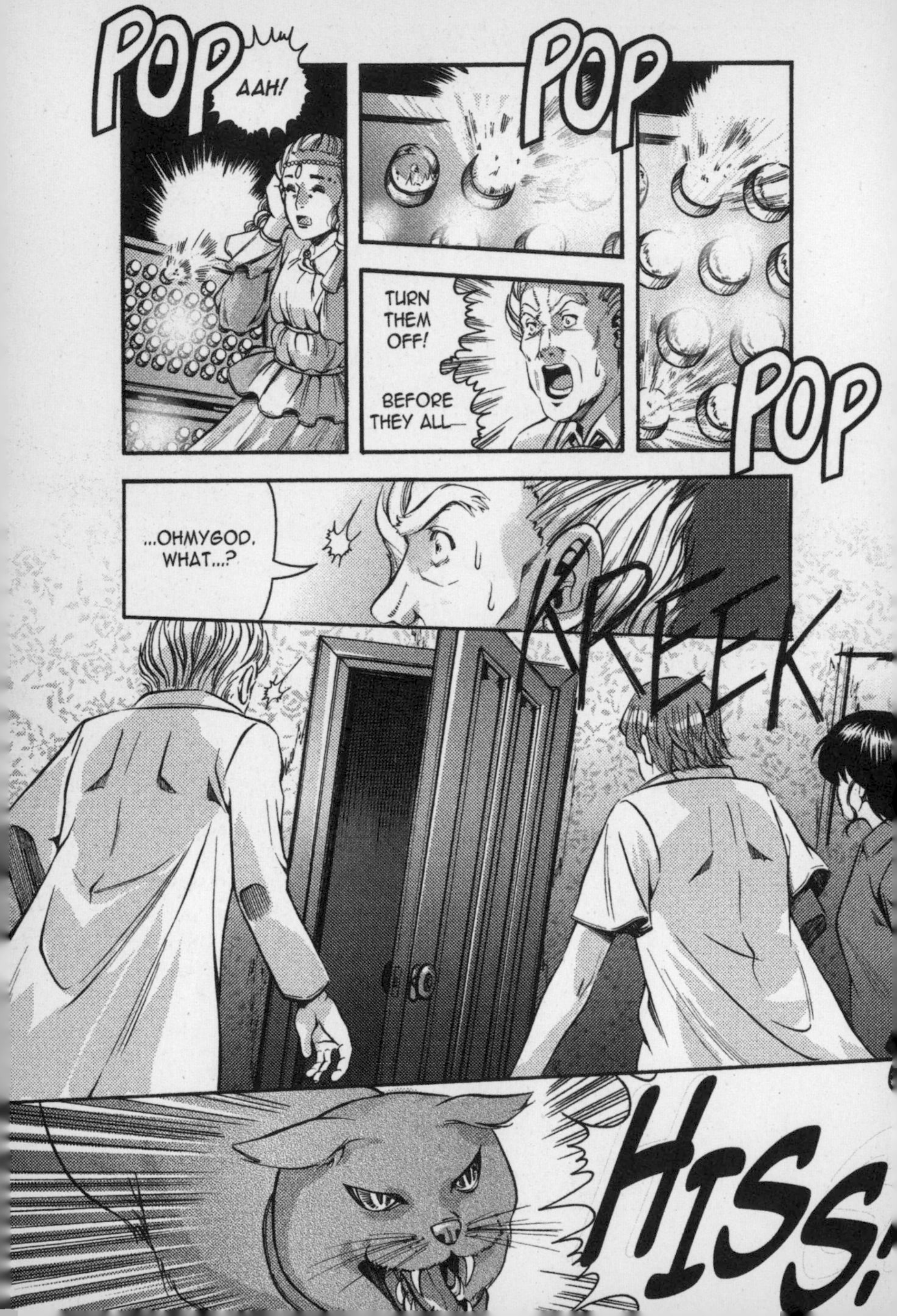
POP
AAH!
POP
TURN THEM OFF!
BEFORE THEY ALL—
POP
...OHMYGOD. WHAT...?
KREEK
HISS!

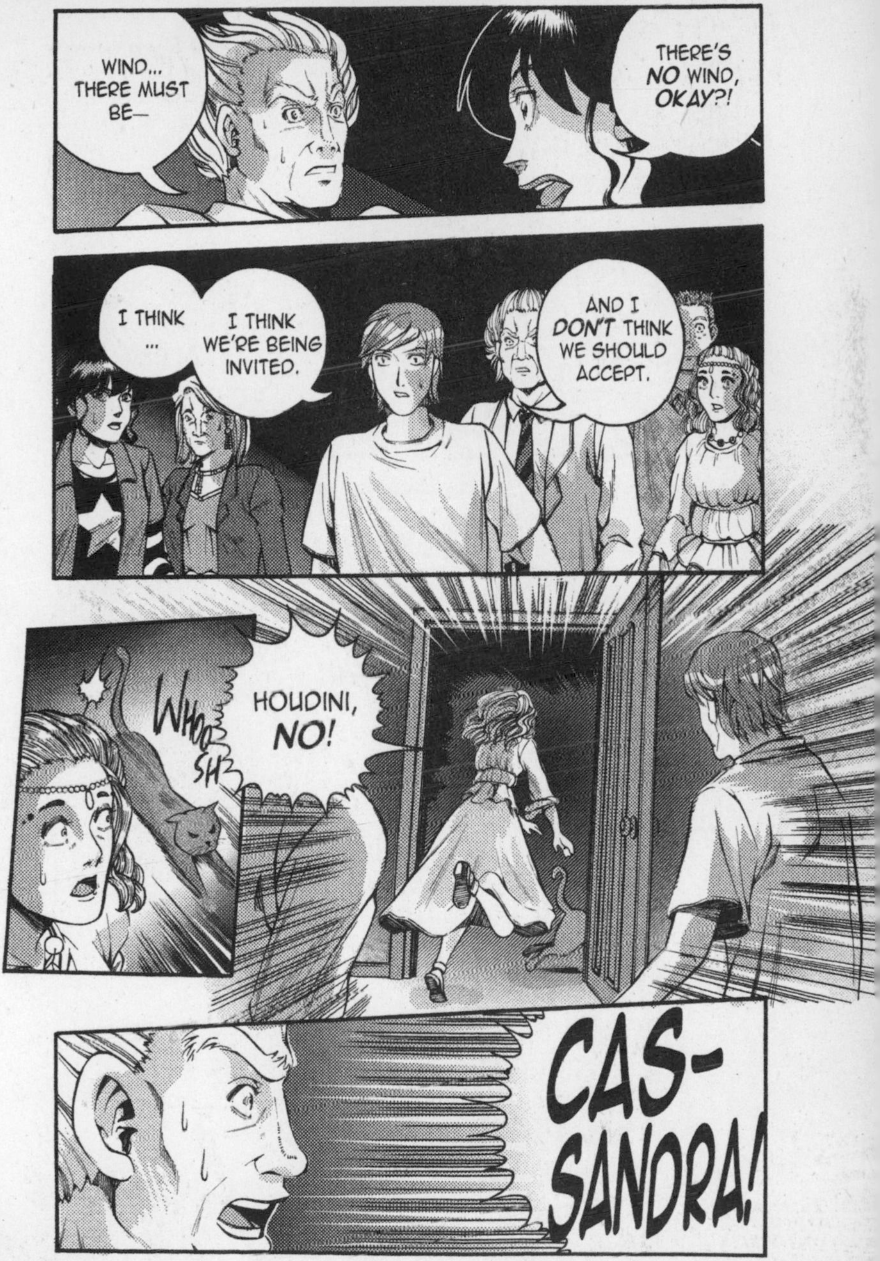
WIND... THERE MUST BE—
THERE'S NO WIND, OKAY?!
I THINK ...
I THINK WE'RE BEING INVITED.
AND I DON'T THINK WE SHOULD ACCEPT.
WHOOSH
HOUDINI, NO!
CAS-SANDRA!

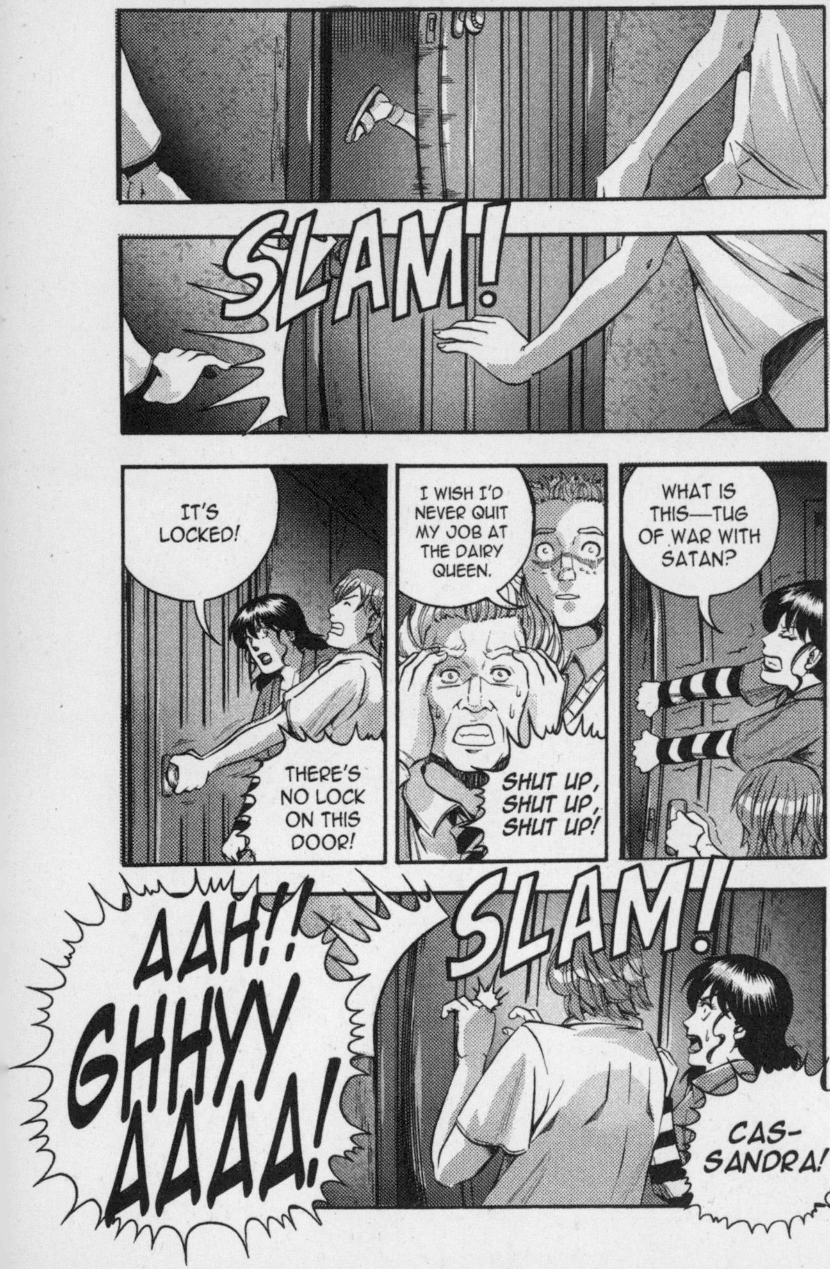
SLAM!
IT'S LOCKED!
THERE'S NO LOCK ON THIS DOOR!
I WISH I'D NEVER QUIT MY JOB AT THE DAIRY QUEEN.
SHUT UP, SHUT UP, SHUT UP!
WHAT IS THIS—TUG OF WAR WITH SATAN?
SLAM!
AAH!! GHHYY AAAA!
CAS-SANDRA!

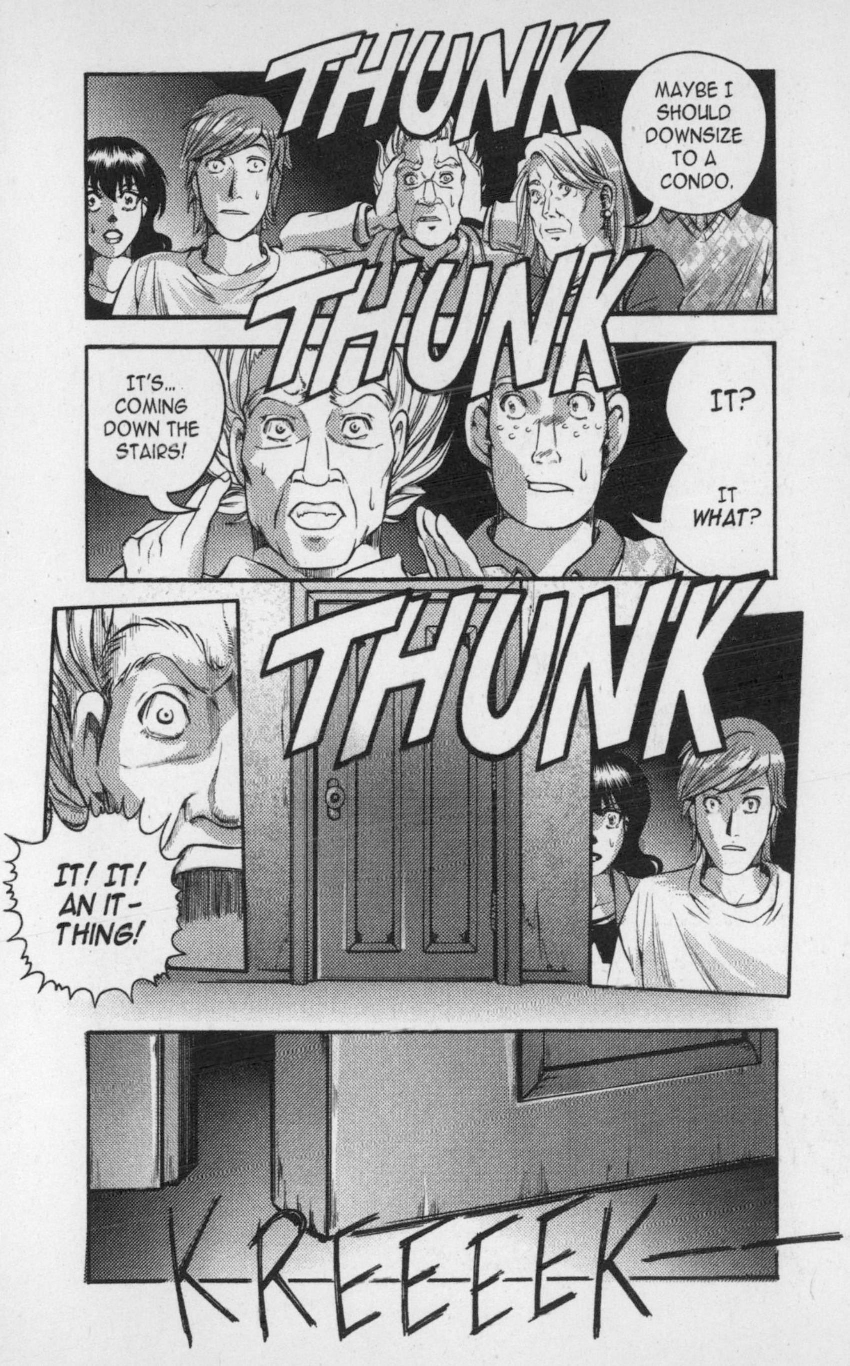
THUNK
MAYBE I SHOULD DOWNSIZE TO A CONDO.
THUNK
IT'S... COMING DOWN THE STAIRS!
IT?
IT WHAT?
THUNK
IT! IT! AN IT-THING!
KREEEEK

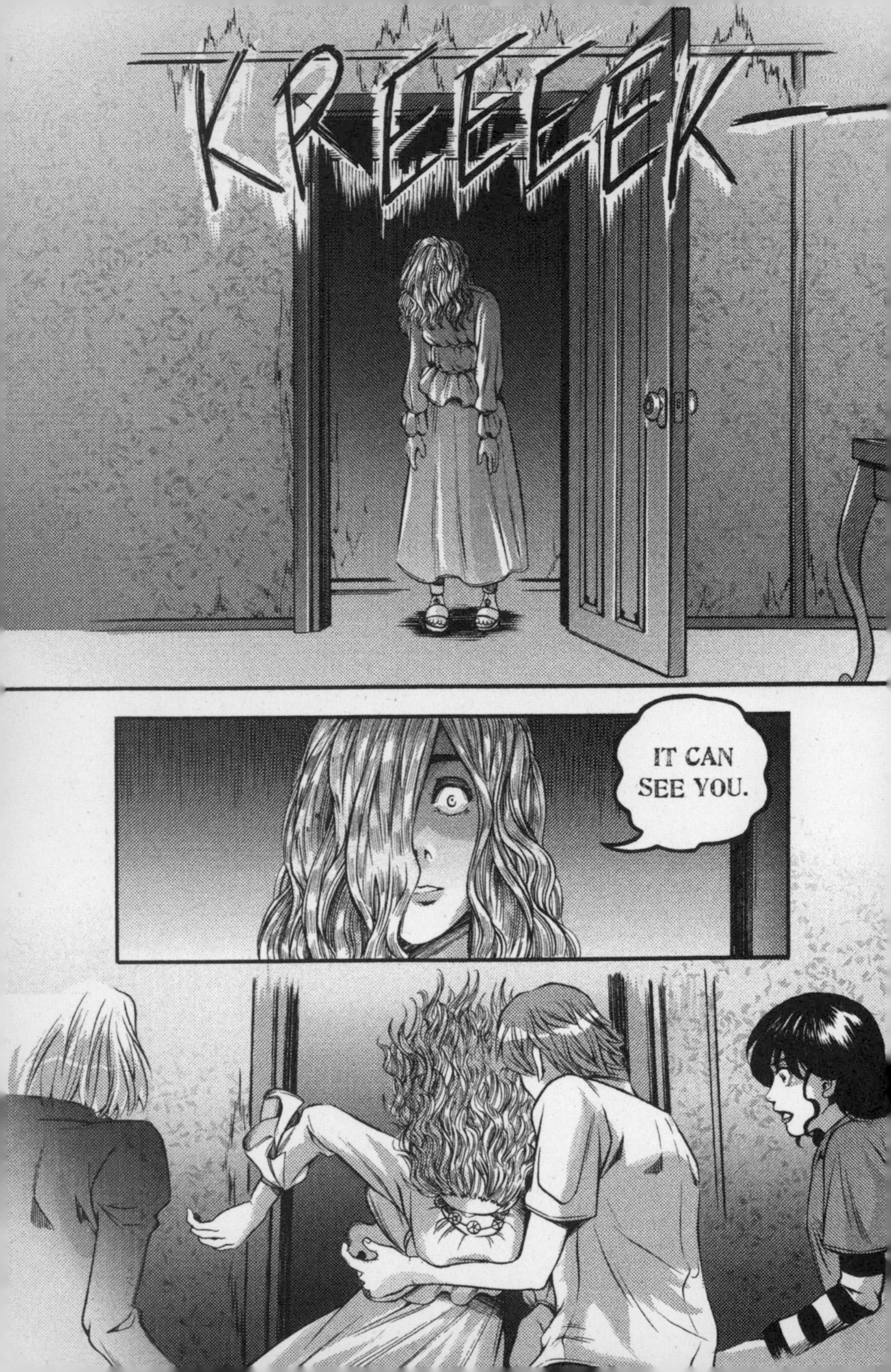
KREEEEK
IT CAN SEE YOU.

Chapter 8

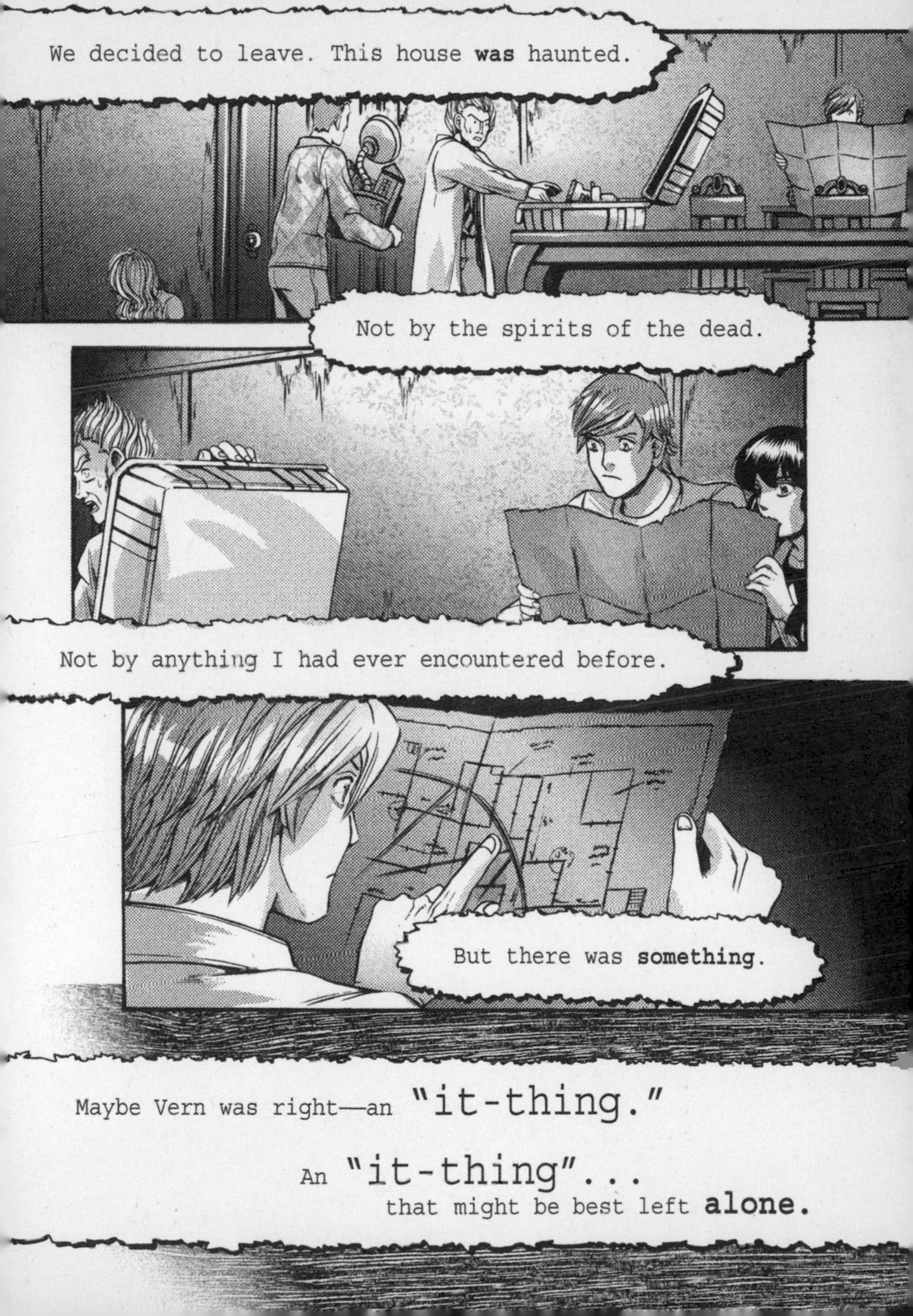
We decided to leave. This house **was** haunted.
Not by the spirits of the dead.
Not by anything I had ever encountered before.
But there was **something**.
Maybe Vern was right—an "it-thing."
An "it-thing"...
that might be best left **alone**.

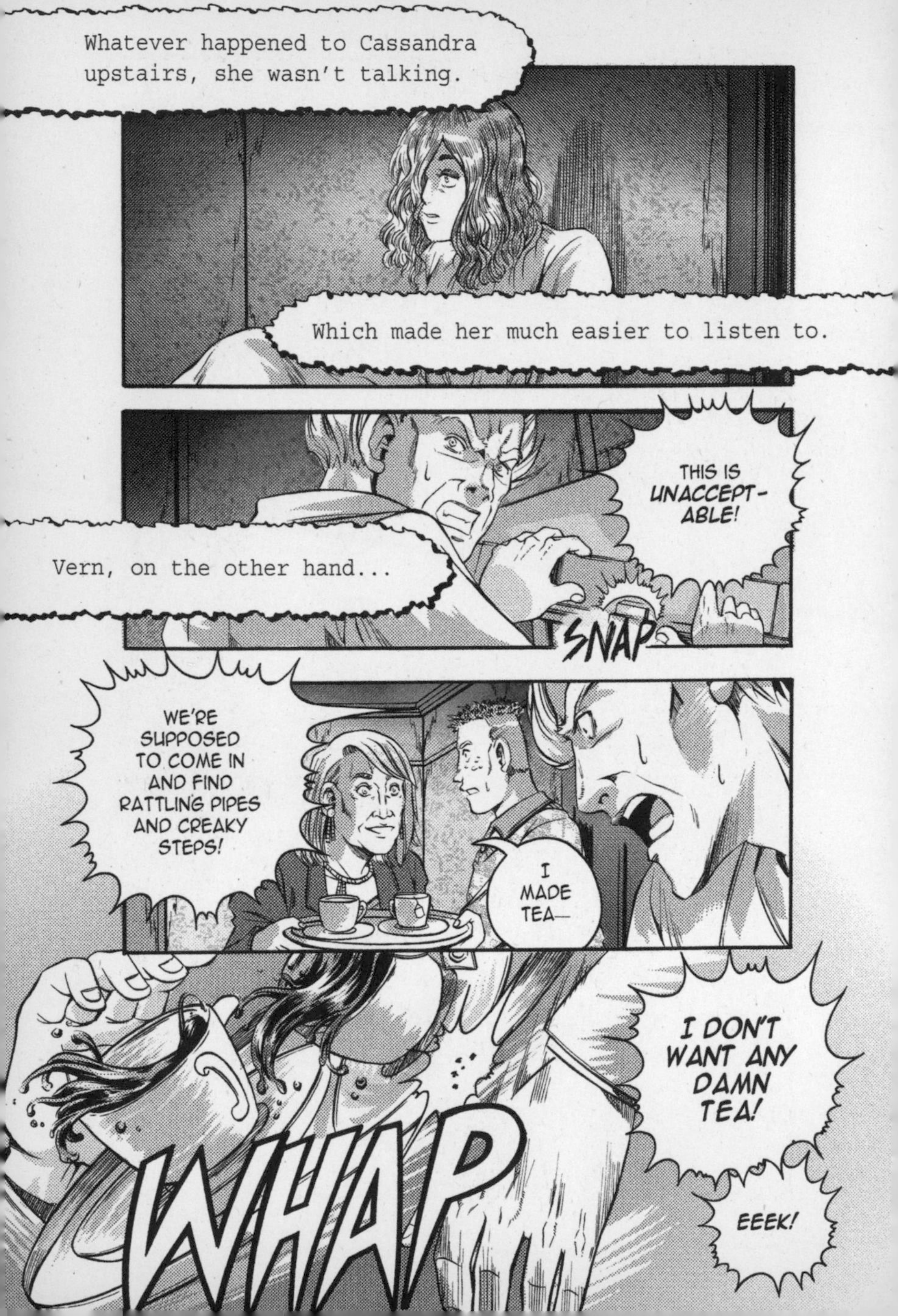
Whatever happened to Cassandra upstairs, she wasn't talking.
Which made her much easier to listen to.
Vern, on the other hand...
THIS IS UNACCEPT-ABLE!
SNAP
WE'RE SUPPOSED TO COME IN AND FIND RATTLING PIPES AND CREAKY STEPS!
I MADE TEA—
I DON'T WANT ANY DAMN TEA!
WHAP
EEEK!

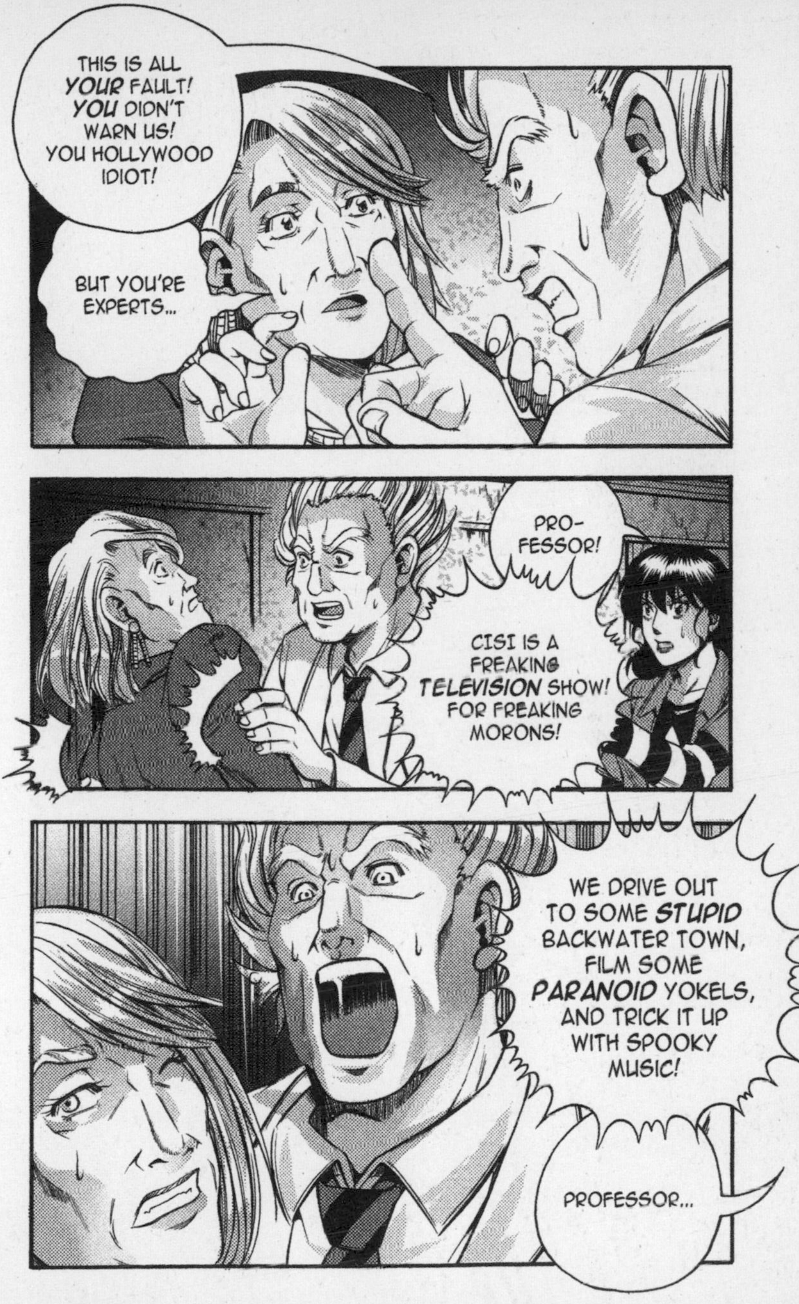
THIS IS ALL YOUR FAULT! YOU DIDN'T WARN US! YOU HOLLYWOOD IDIOT!
BUT YOU'RE EXPERTS...
PRO-FESSOR!
CISI IS A FREAKING TELEVISION SHOW! FOR FREAKING MORONS!
WE DRIVE OUT TO SOME STUPID BACKWATER TOWN, FILM SOME PARANOID YOKELS, AND TRICK IT UP WITH SPOOKY MUSIC!
PROFESSOR...

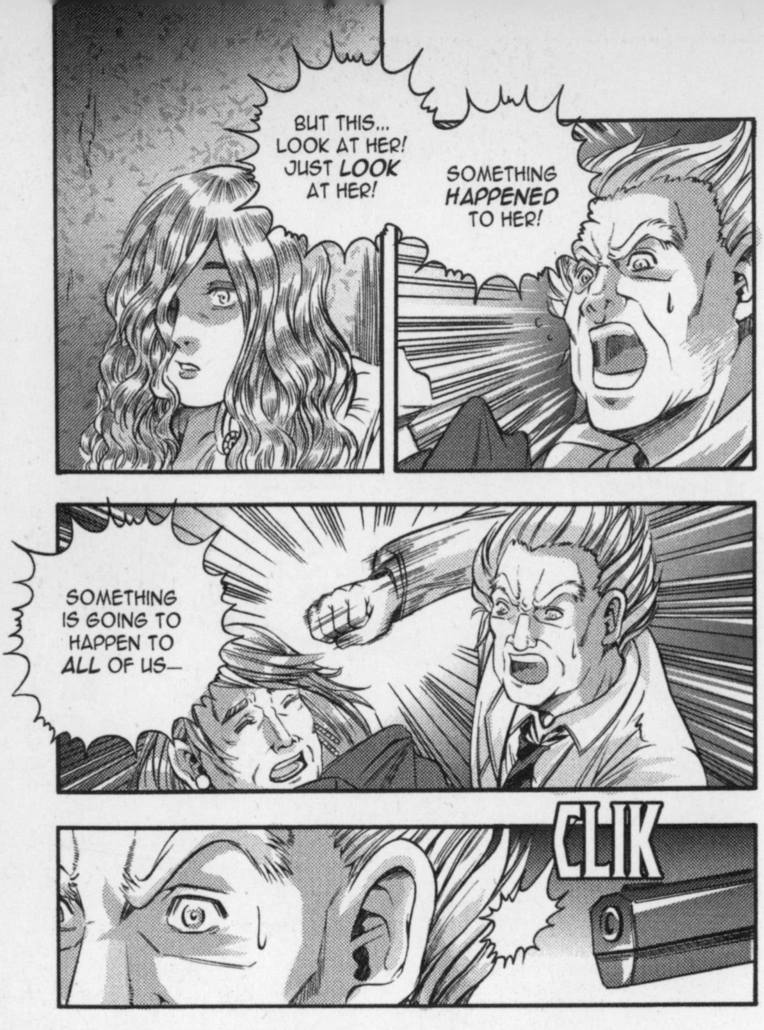
BUT THIS... LOOK AT HER! JUST LOOK AT HER!
SOMETHING HAPPENED TO HER!
SOMETHING IS GOING TO HAPPEN TO ALL OF US—
CLIK

Because of the experiences
with my mother I mentioned previously,
I won't carry a gun.

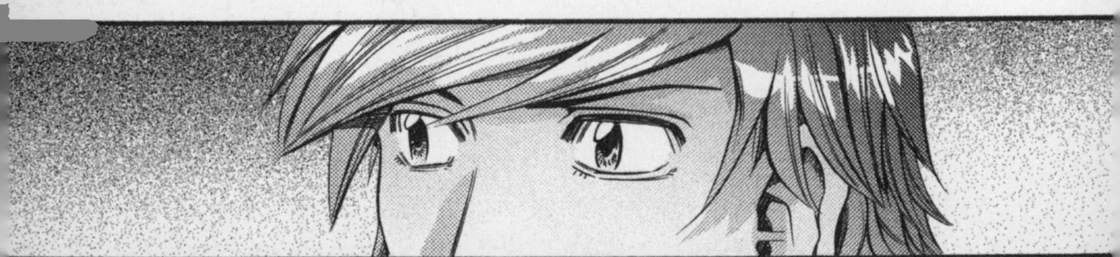

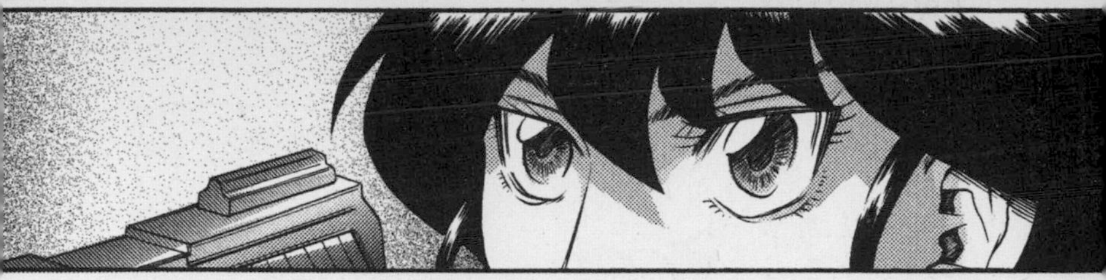

My position is not one founded on a sense of moral superiority. I don't believe that avoiding the use of guns makes me better than those who choose to arm themselves. It's simply a matter of personal discomfort.

Fortunately, Stormy has no such issues.

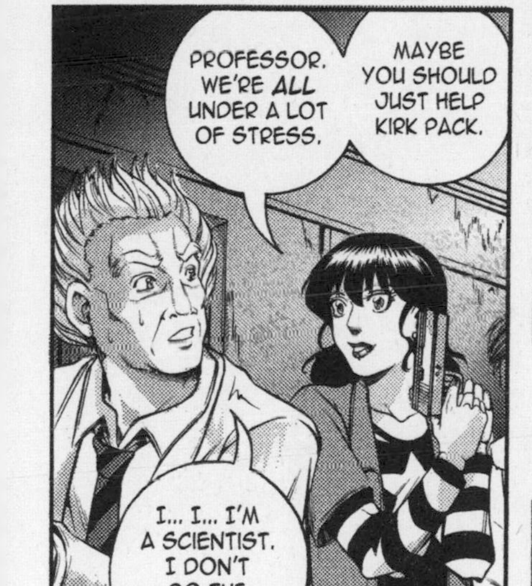
PROFESSOR. WE'RE ALL UNDER A LOT OF STRESS.
MAYBE YOU SHOULD JUST HELP KIRK PACK.
I... I... I'M A SCIENTIST. I DON'T DO THE PACKING.

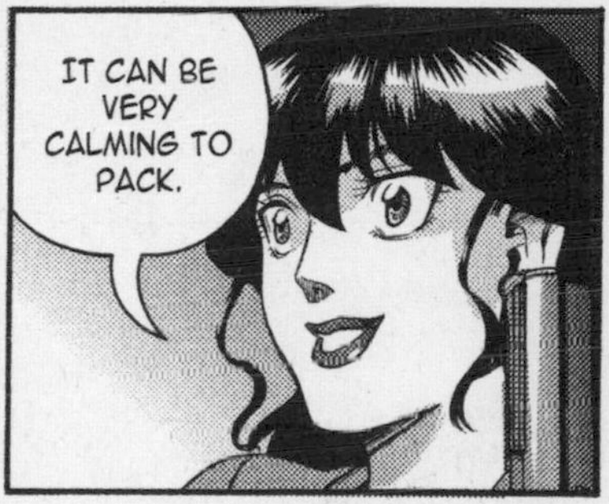
IT CAN BE VERY CALMING TO PACK.

It's one of the many ways in which we complement one another.

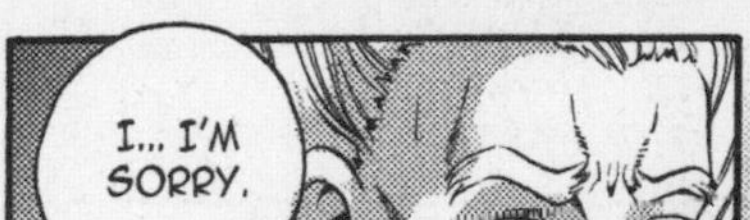
I... I'M SORRY.

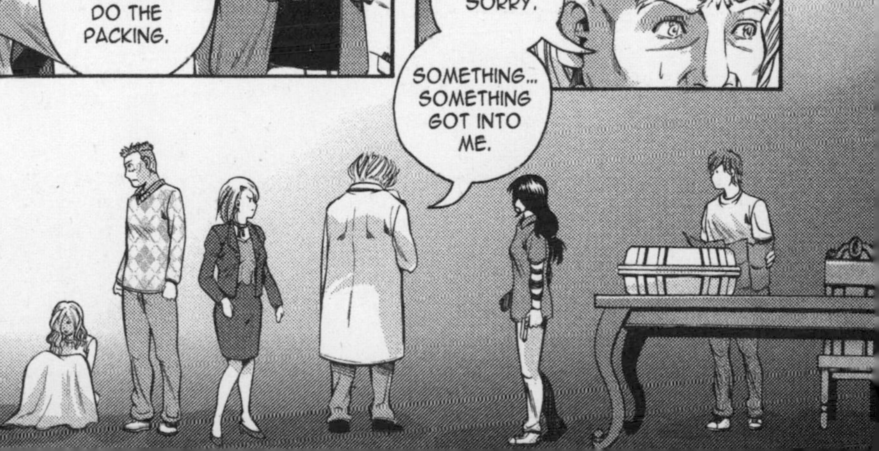
SOMETHING... SOMETHING GOT INTO ME.

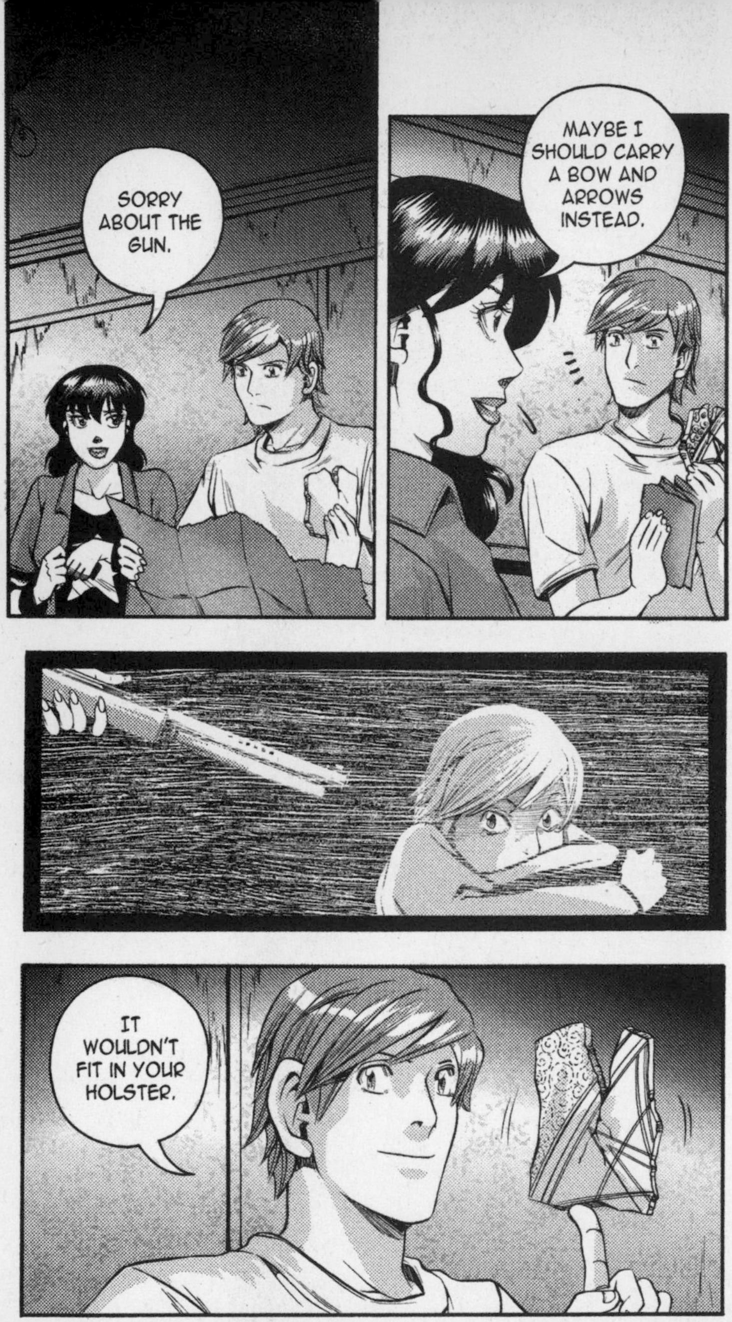
SORRY ABOUT THE GUN.
MAYBE I SHOULD CARRY A BOW AND ARROWS INSTEAD.
IT WOULDN'T FIT IN YOUR HOLSTER.

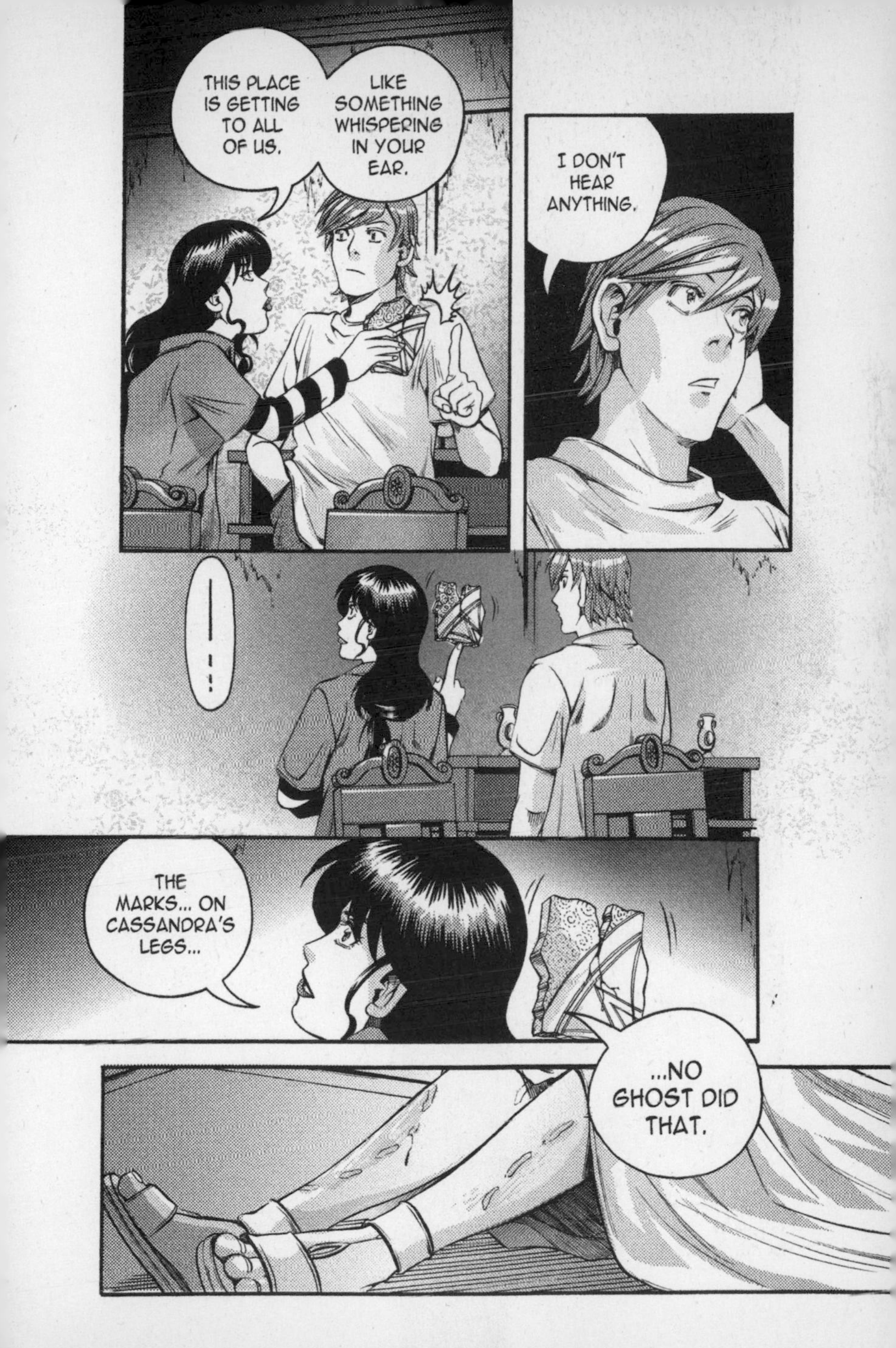

THIS PLACE IS GETTING TO ALL OF US.
LIKE SOMETHING WHISPERING IN YOUR EAR.
I DON'T HEAR ANYTHING.
—!
THE MARKS... ON CASSANDRA'S LEGS...
...NO GHOST DID THAT.

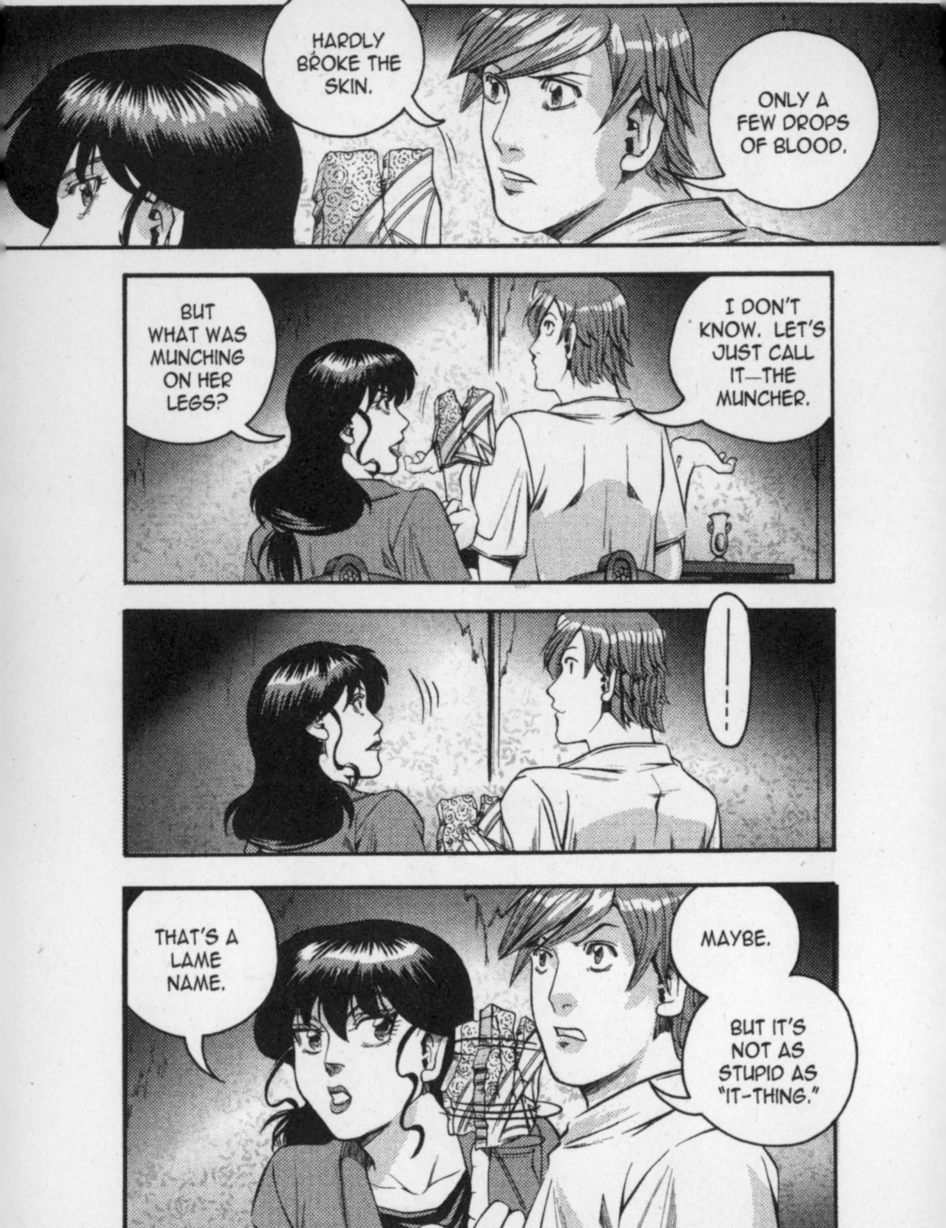
HARDLY BROKE THE SKIN.
ONLY A FEW DROPS OF BLOOD.
BUT WHAT WAS MUNCHING ON HER LEGS?
I DON'T KNOW. LET'S JUST CALL IT—THE MUNCHER.
!
THAT'S A LAME NAME.
MAYBE.
BUT IT'S NOT AS STUPID AS "IT-THING."

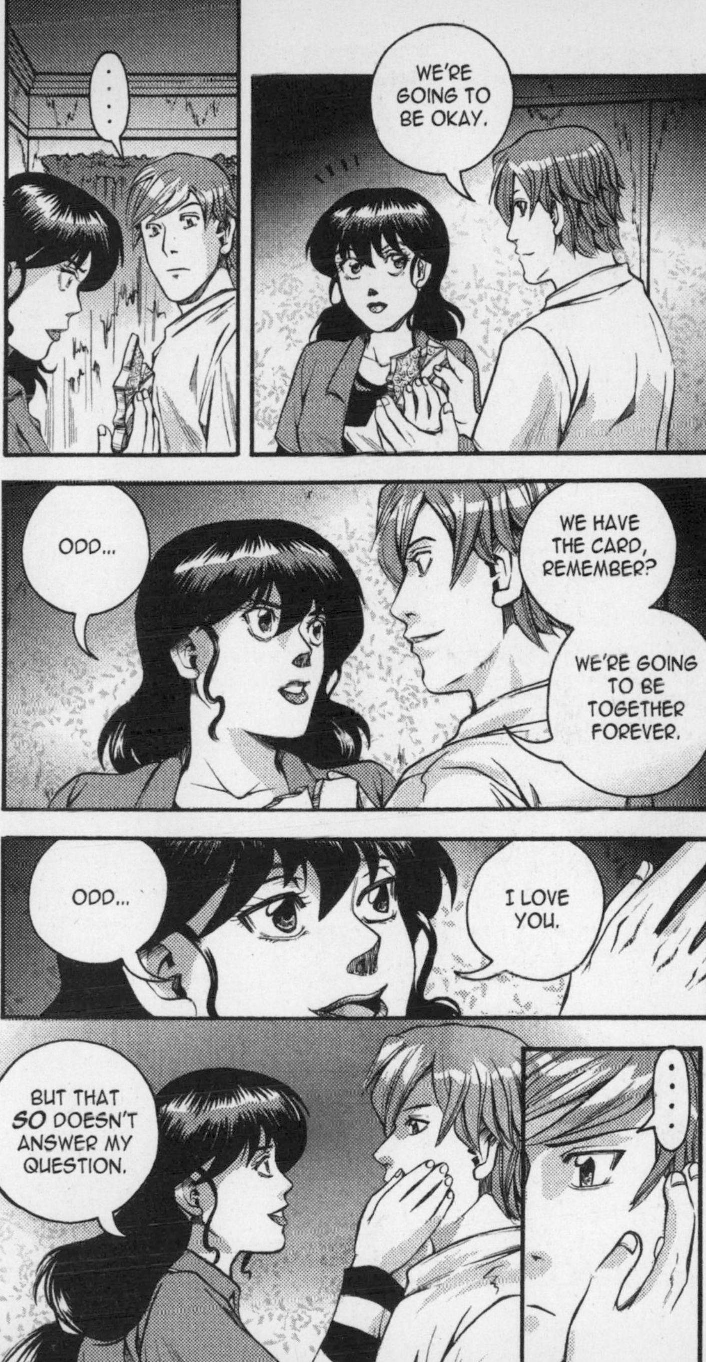
. . . .
WE'RE GOING TO BE OKAY.
ODD...
WE HAVE THE CARD, REMEMBER?
WE'RE GOING TO BE TOGETHER FOREVER.
ODD...
I LOVE YOU.
BUT THAT SO DOESN'T ANSWER MY QUESTION.
. . . .

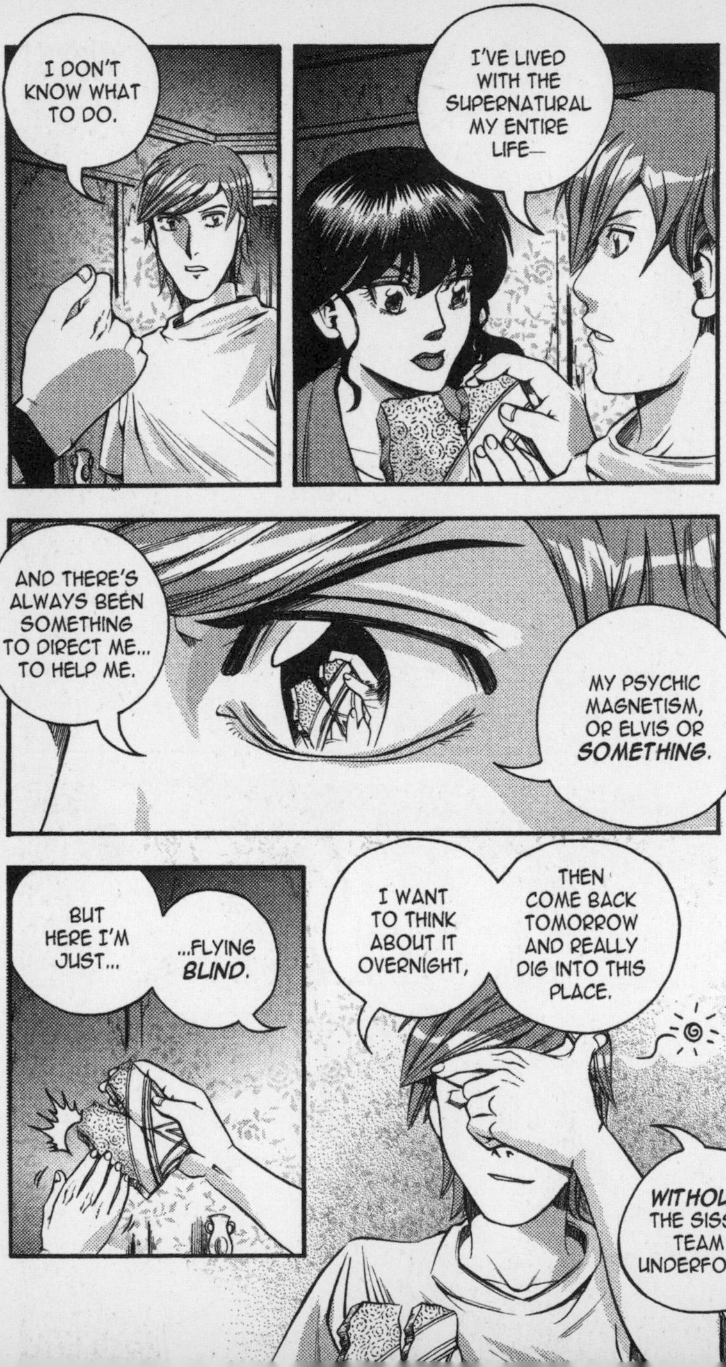
I DON'T KNOW WHAT TO DO.
I'VE LIVED WITH THE SUPERNATURAL MY ENTIRE LIFE—
AND THERE'S ALWAYS BEEN SOMETHING TO DIRECT ME... TO HELP ME.
MY PSYCHIC MAGNETISM, OR ELVIS OR *SOMETHING*.
BUT HERE I'M JUST...
...FLYING *BLIND*.
I WANT TO THINK ABOUT IT OVERNIGHT,
THEN COME BACK TOMORROW AND REALLY DIG INTO THIS PLACE.
WITHOUT THE SISSY TEAM UNDERFOOT.

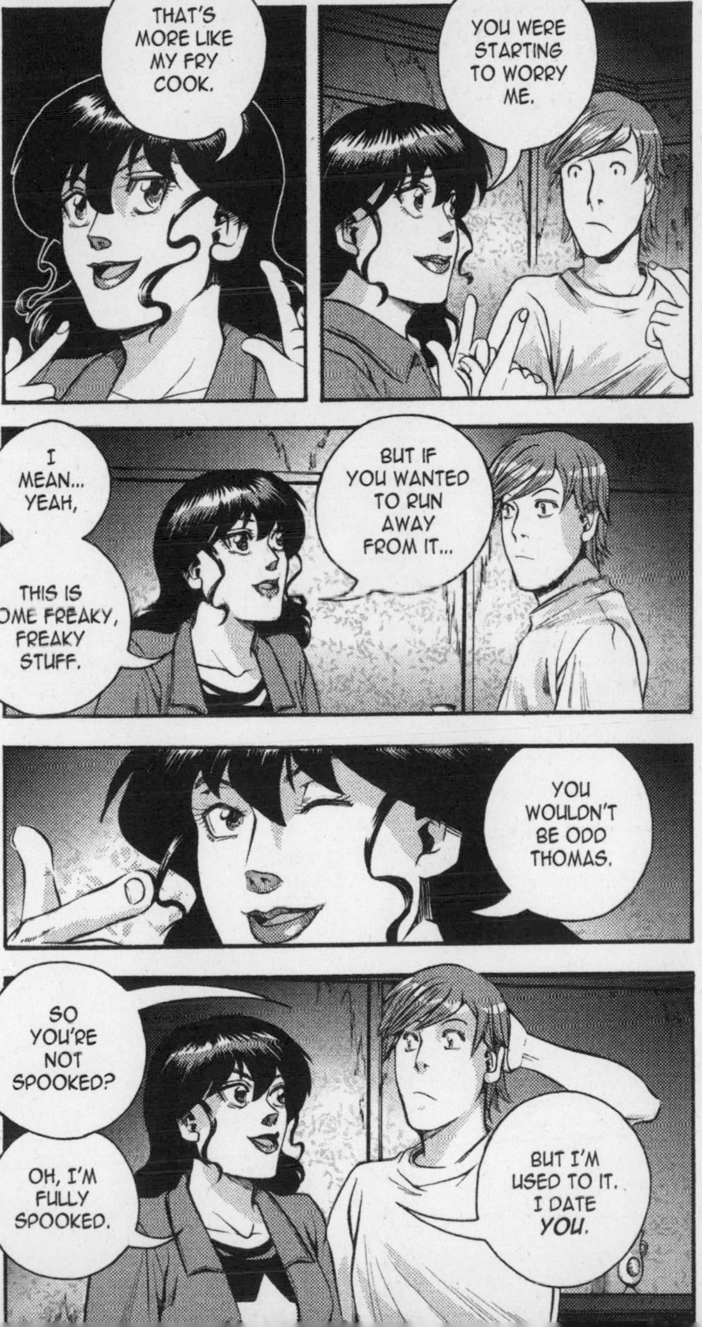
THAT'S MORE LIKE MY FRY COOK.
YOU WERE STARTING TO WORRY ME.
I MEAN... YEAH,
THIS IS SOME FREAKY, FREAKY STUFF.
BUT IF YOU WANTED TO RUN AWAY FROM IT...
YOU WOULDN'T BE ODD THOMAS.
SO YOU'RE NOT SPOOKED?
OH, I'M FULLY SPOOKED.
BUT I'M USED TO IT. I DATE YOU.

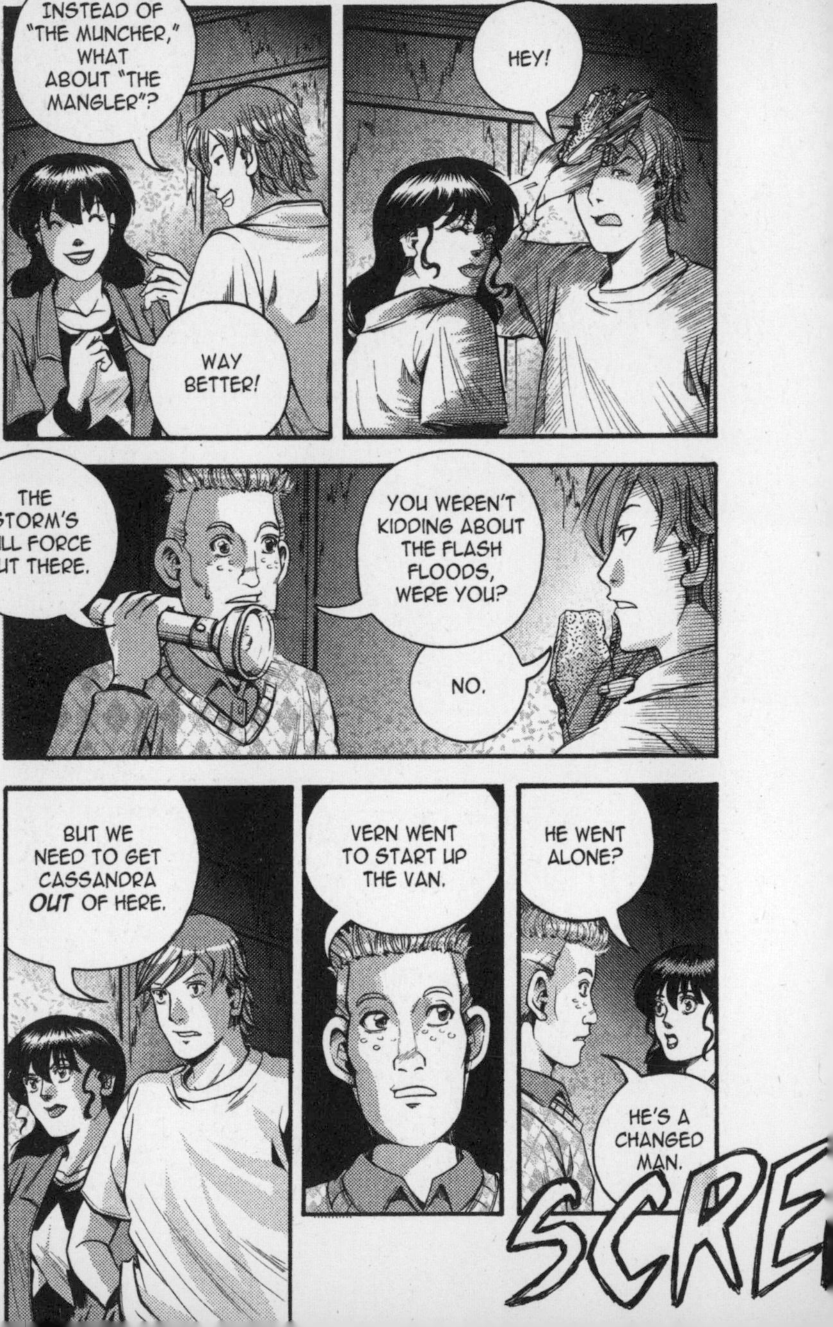
INSTEAD OF "THE MUNCHER," WHAT ABOUT "THE MANGLER"?
WAY BETTER!
HEY!
THE STORM'S FULL FORCE OUT THERE.
YOU WEREN'T KIDDING ABOUT THE FLASH FLOODS, WERE YOU?
NO.
BUT WE NEED TO GET CASSANDRA *OUT* OF HERE.
VERN WENT TO START UP THE VAN.
HE WENT ALONE?
HE'S A CHANGED MAN.
SCRE

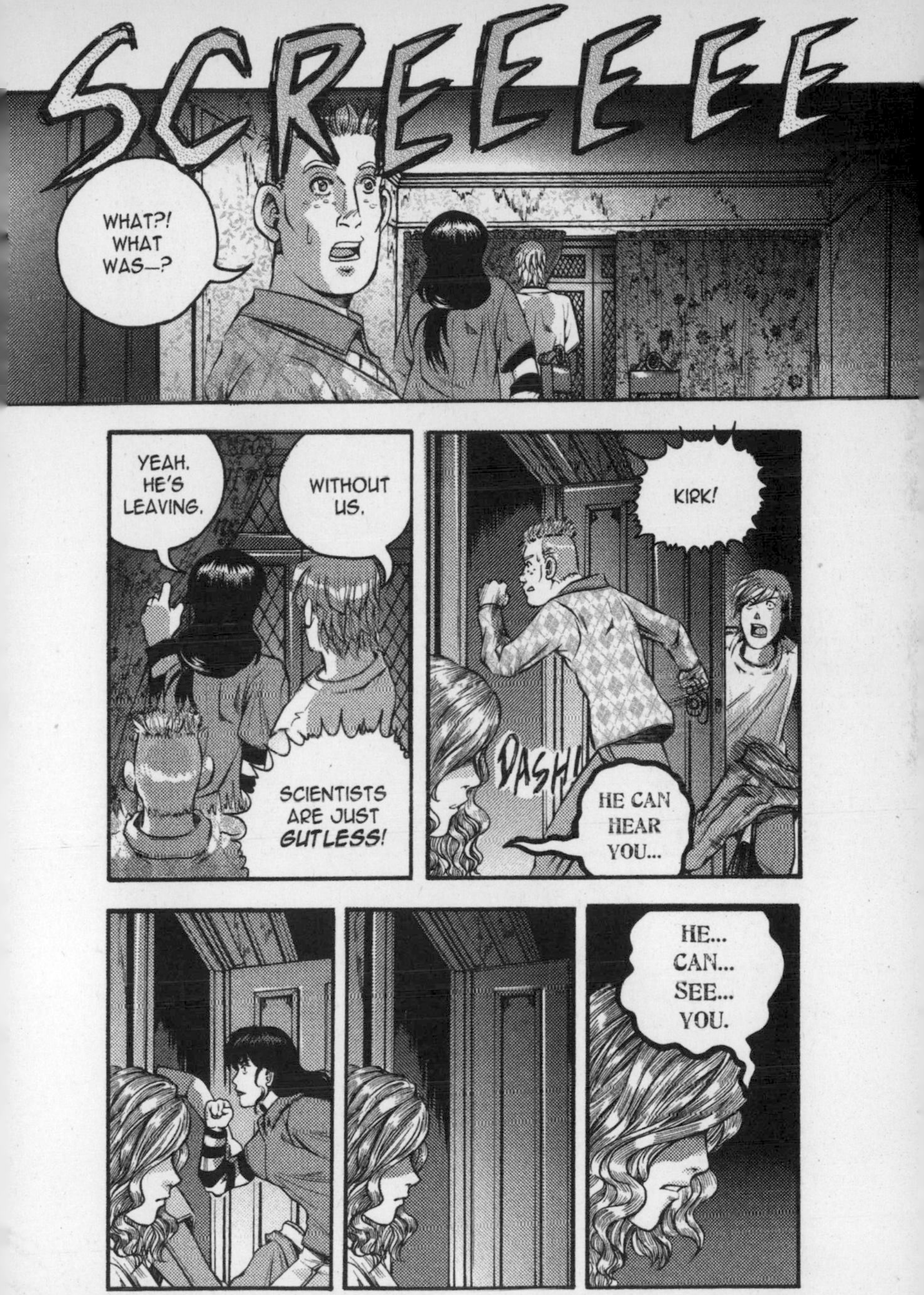
SCREEEEEE
WHAT?! WHAT WAS—?
YEAH. HE'S LEAVING.
WITHOUT US.
SCIENTISTS ARE JUST GUTLESS!
KIRK!
DASH
HE CAN HEAR YOU...
HE... CAN... SEE... YOU.

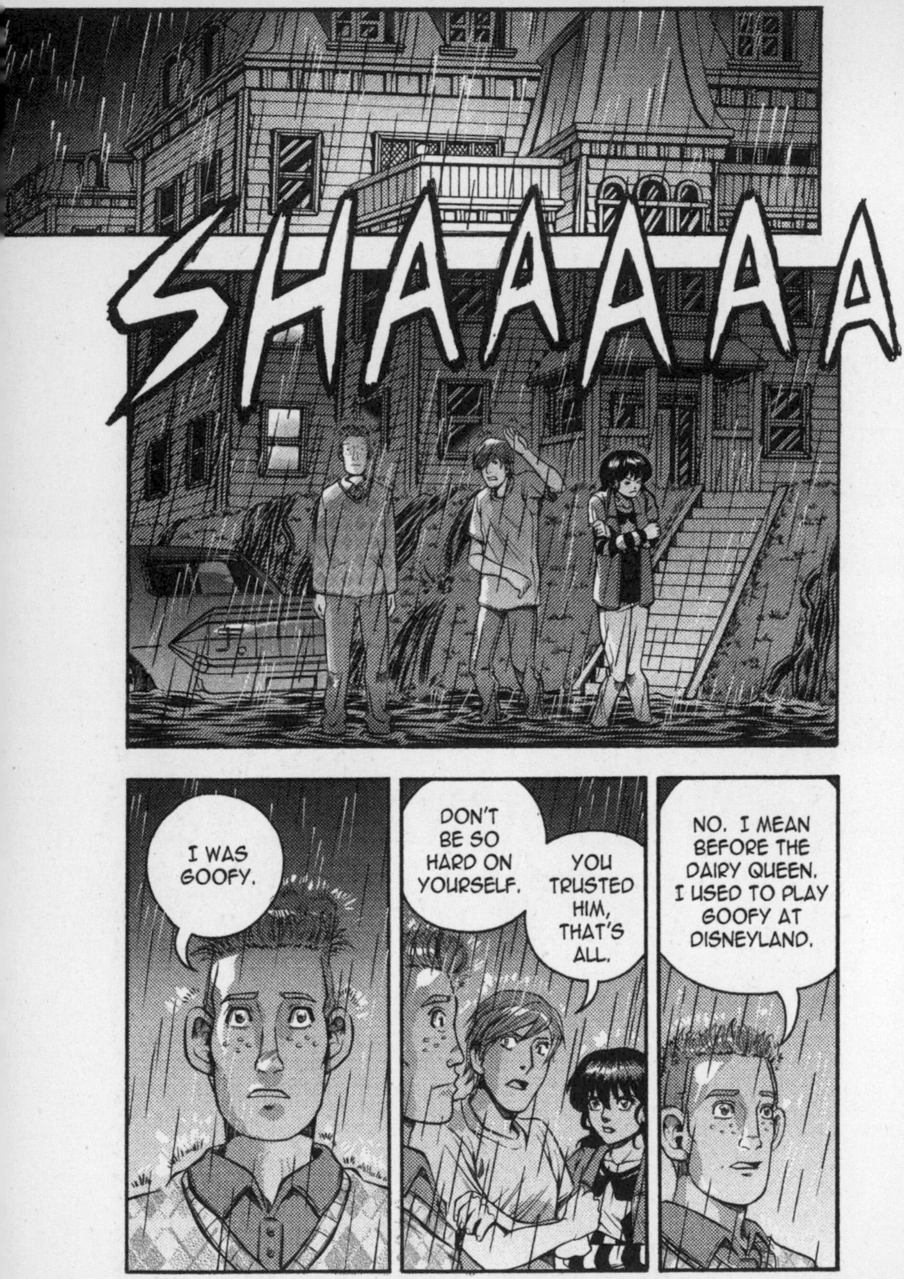
SHAAAAA
I WAS GOOFY.
DON'T BE SO HARD ON YOURSELF.
YOU TRUSTED HIM, THAT'S ALL.
NO. I MEAN BEFORE THE DAIRY QUEEN. I USED TO PLAY GOOFY AT DISNEYLAND.

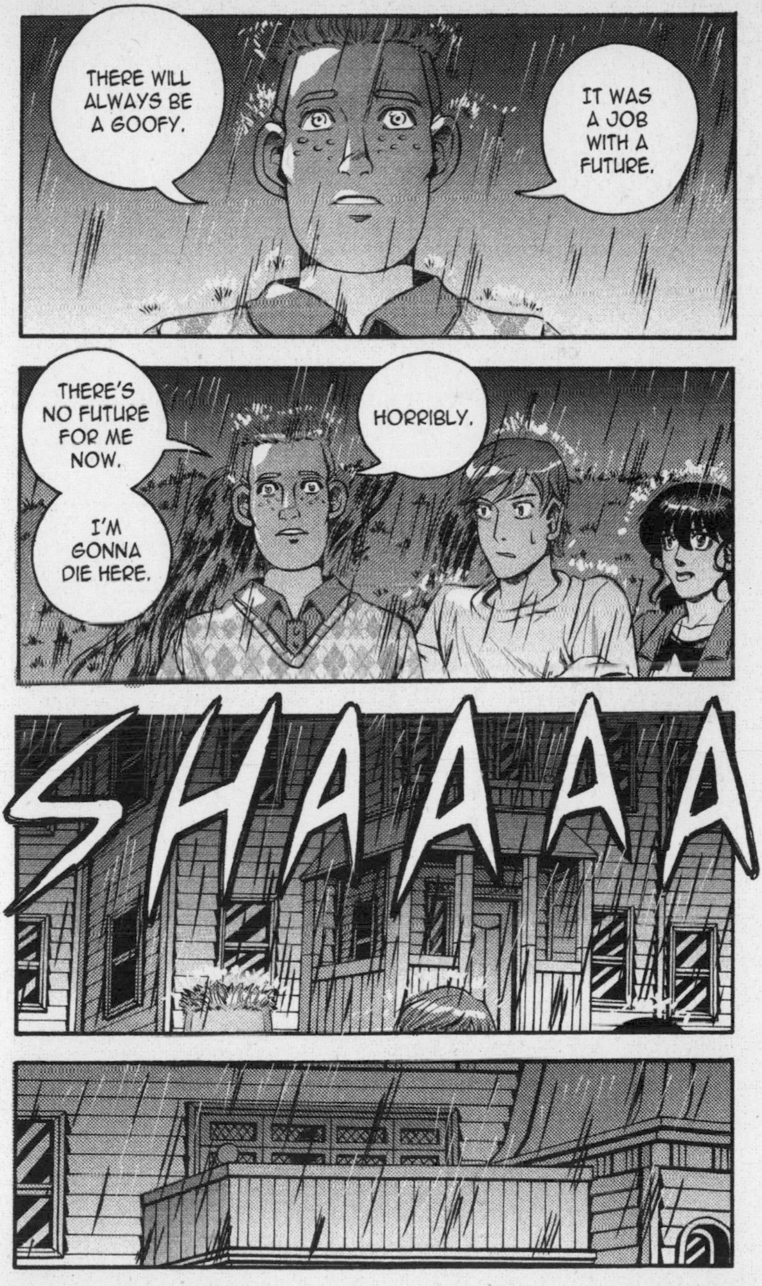
THERE WILL ALWAYS BE A GOOFY.
IT WAS A JOB WITH A FUTURE.
THERE'S NO FUTURE FOR ME NOW.
I'M GONNA DIE HERE.
HORRIBLY.
SHAAAAA

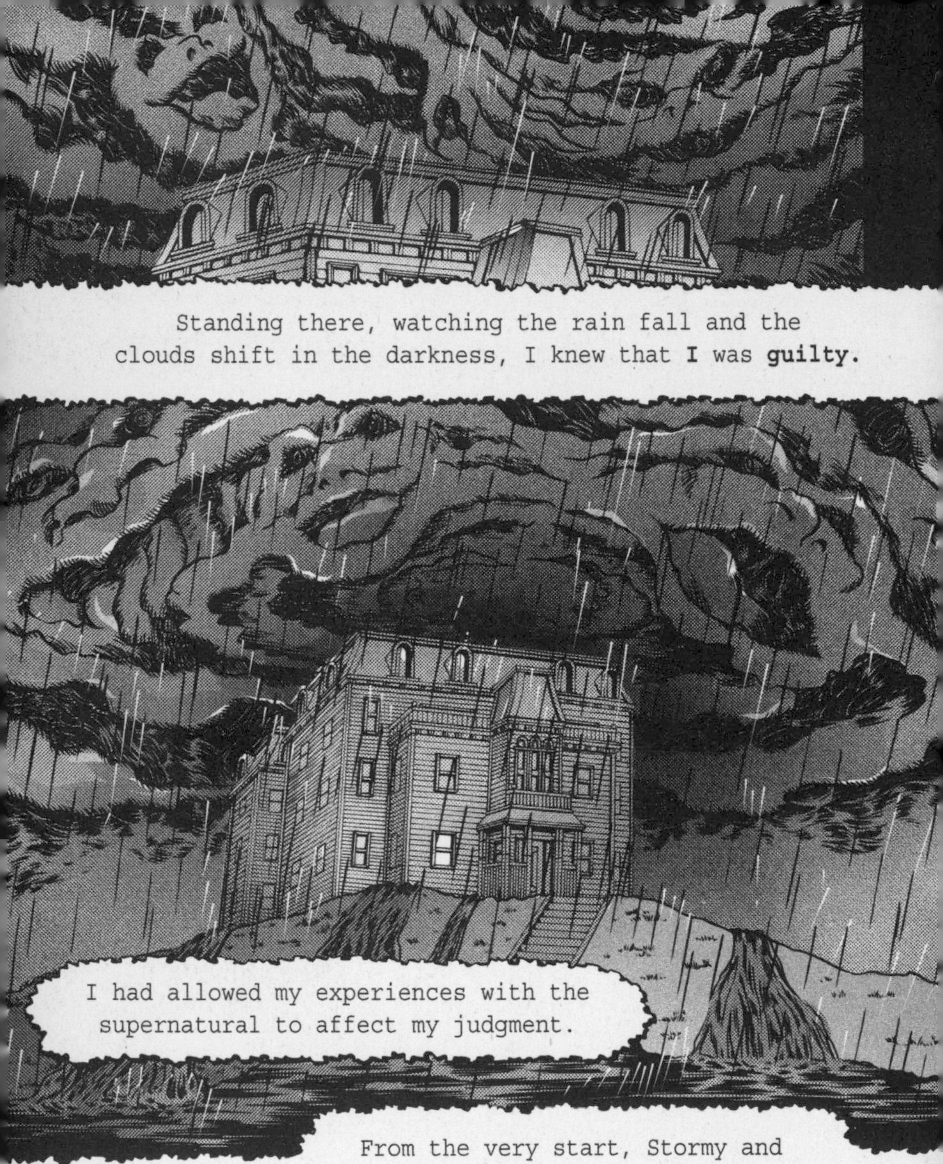
Standing there, watching the rain fall and the clouds shift in the darkness, I knew that **I** was **guilty.**
I had allowed my experiences with the supernatural to affect my judgment.
From the very start, Stormy and I had assumed CISI was a joke.

To a degree, we had been correct.
Vern was a fraud. Kirk was...Kirk.

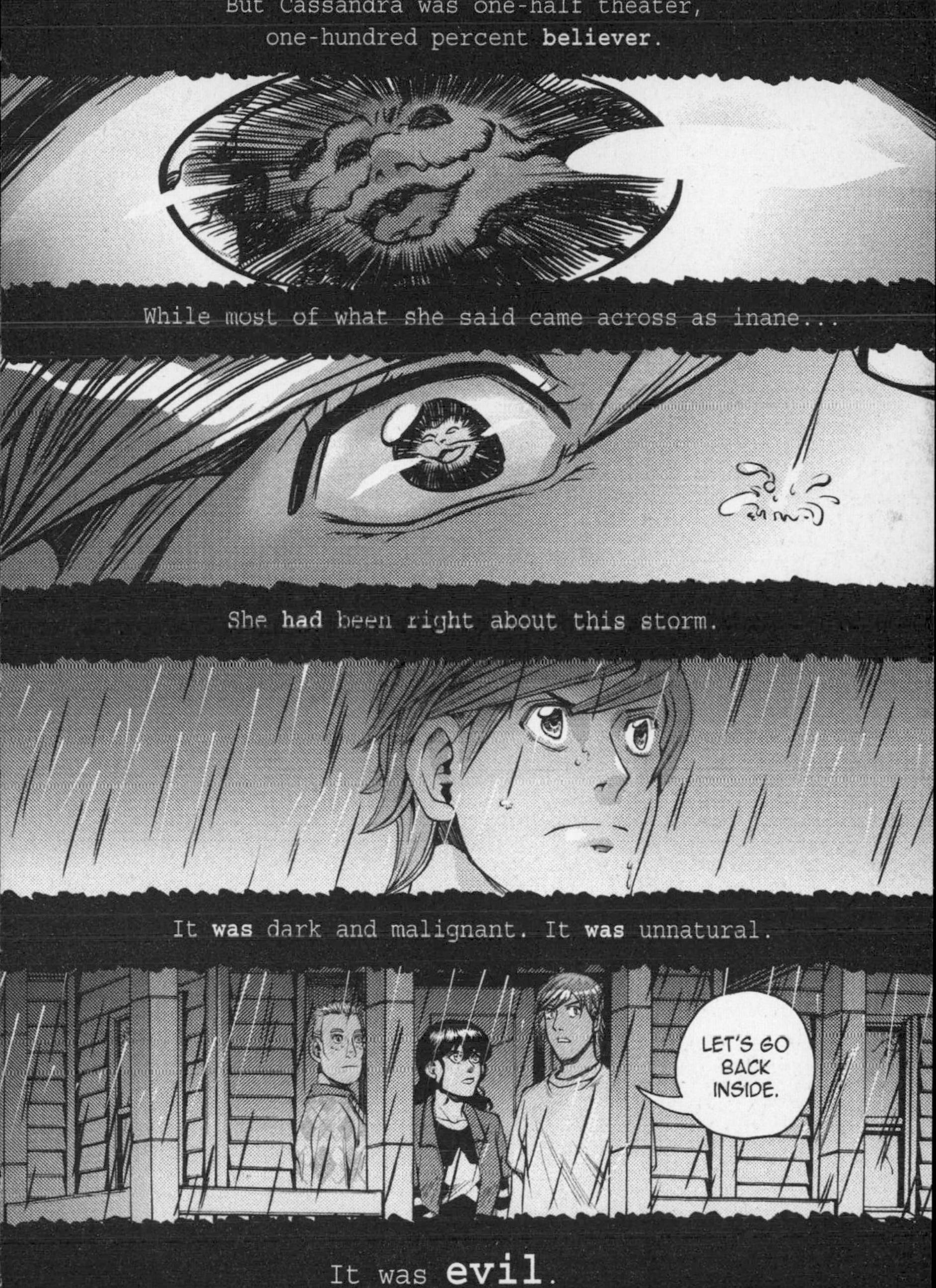
But Cassandra was one-half theater,
one-hundred percent **believer**.
While most of what she said came across as inane...
She **had** been right about this storm.
It **was** dark and malignant. It **was** unnatural.
LET'S GO BACK INSIDE.
It was **evil**.

Chapter 9

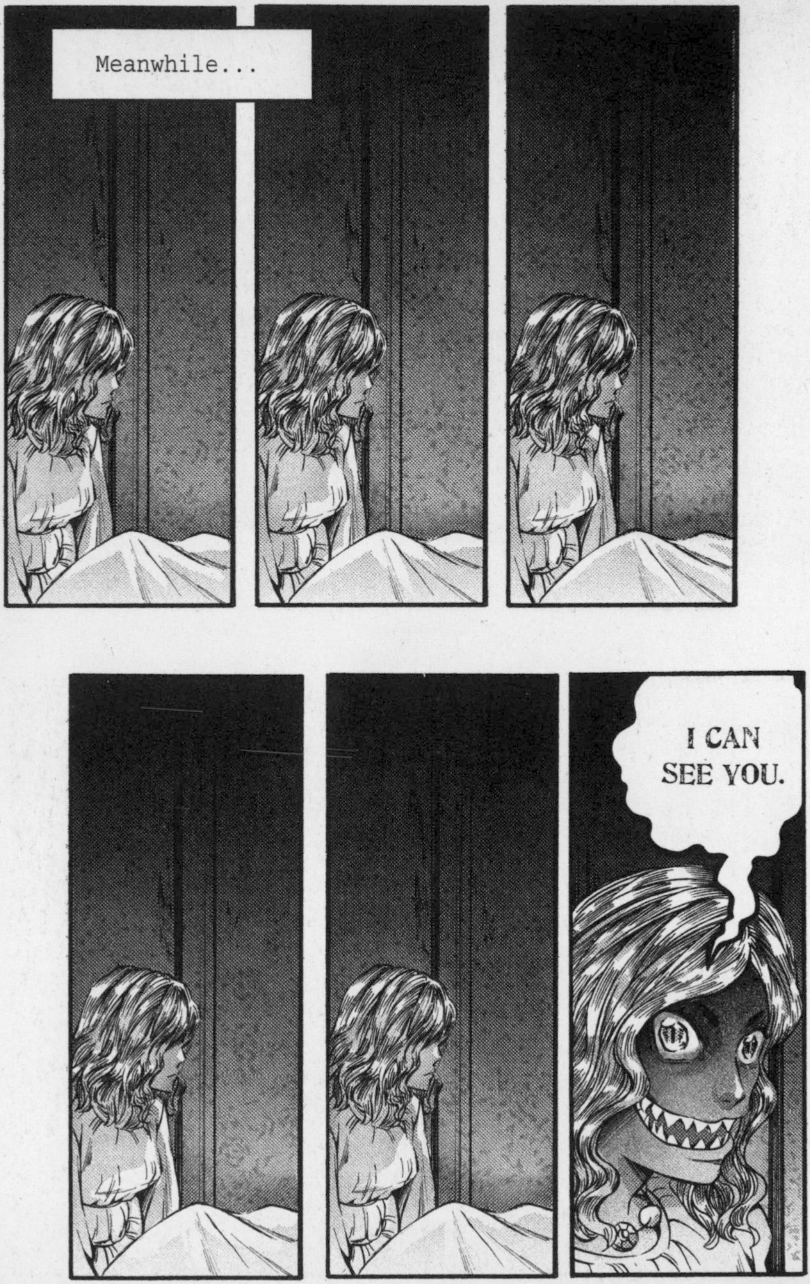
Meanwhile...
I CAN SEE YOU.

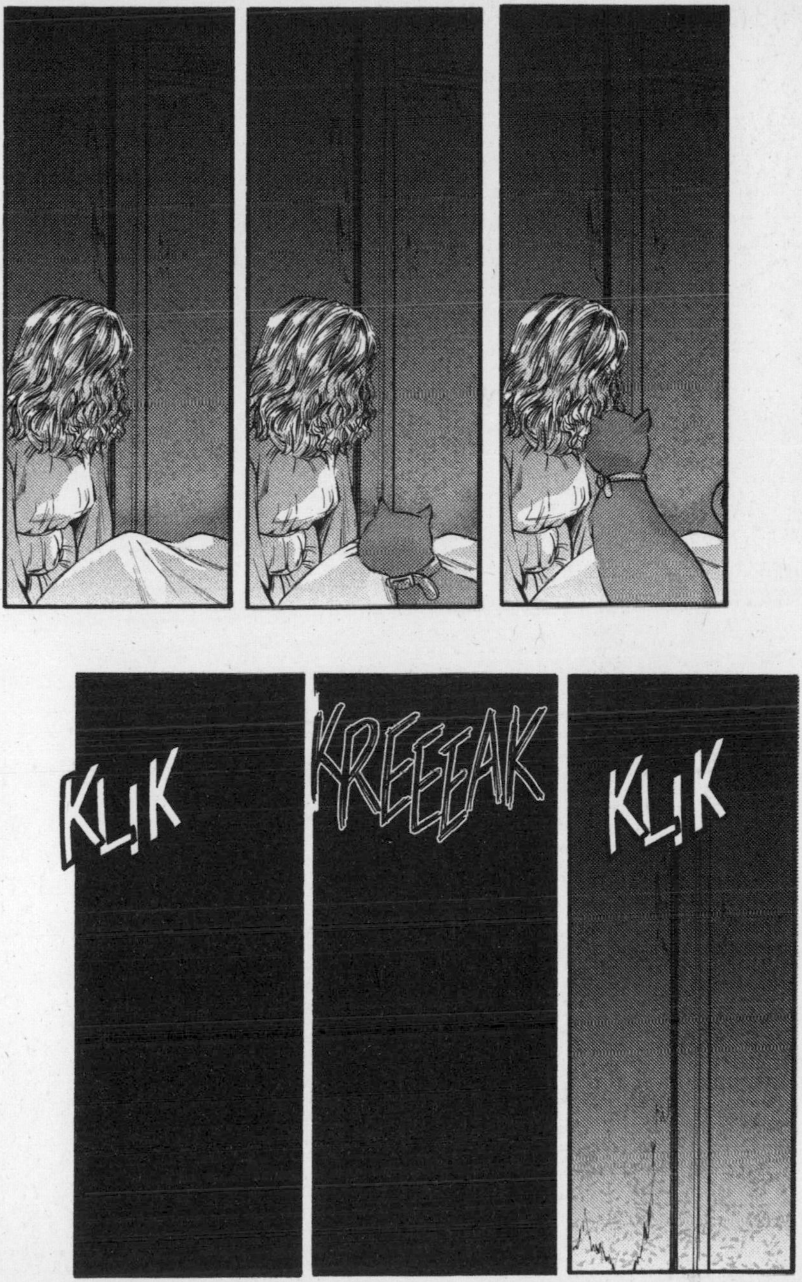
KLIK
KREEEAK
KLIK

Chapter 10

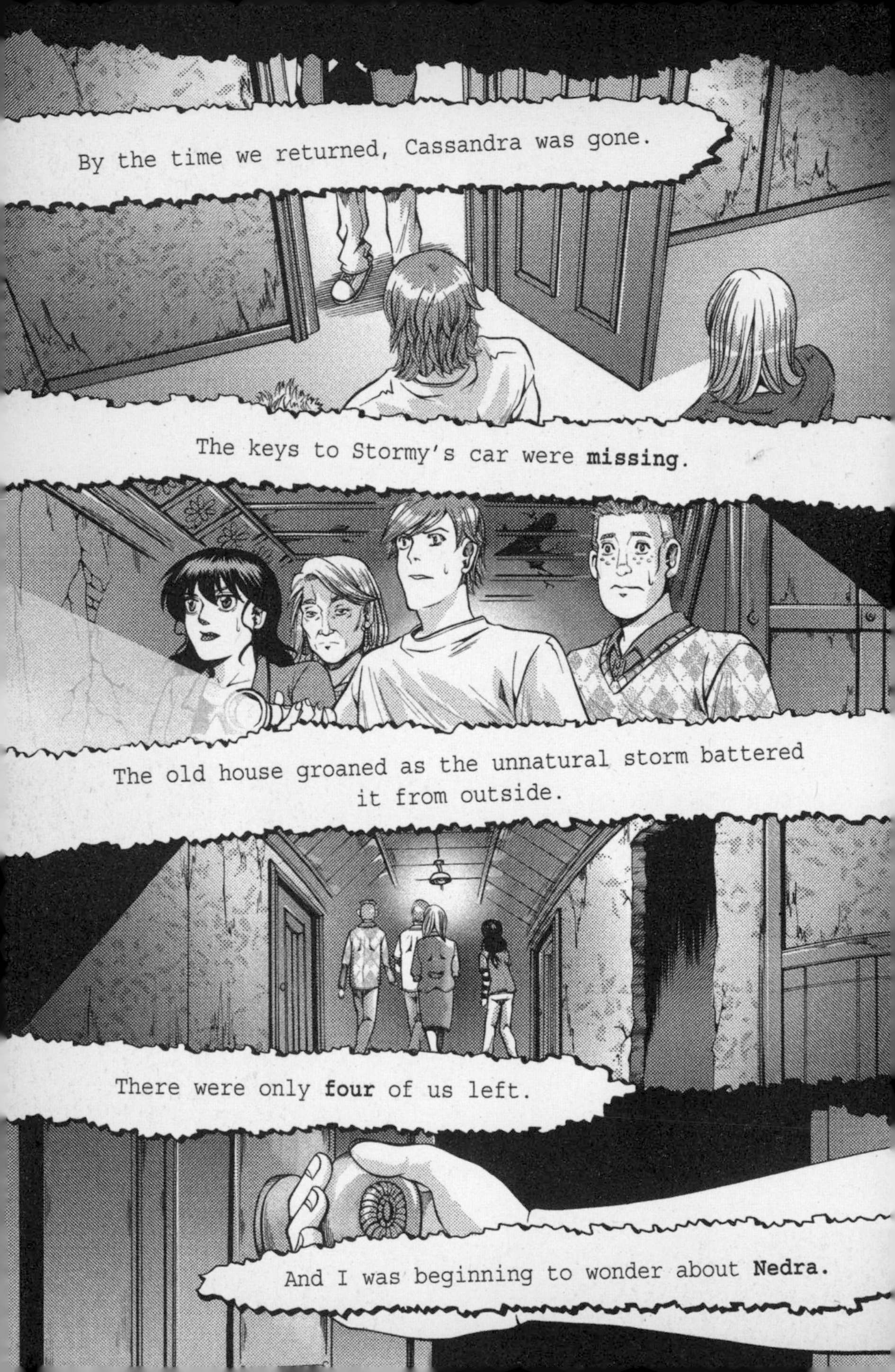
By the time we returned, Cassandra was gone.
The keys to Stormy's car were **missing**.
The old house groaned as the unnatural storm battered it from outside.
There were only **four** of us left.
And I was beginning to wonder about **Nedra**.

For an hour we had been searching this nightmare mansion for Cassandra. The place had become impossibly vast.

We were all frightened. On edge.

Yet every once in a while...

When she thought no one was looking...

Nedra would smile.

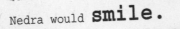

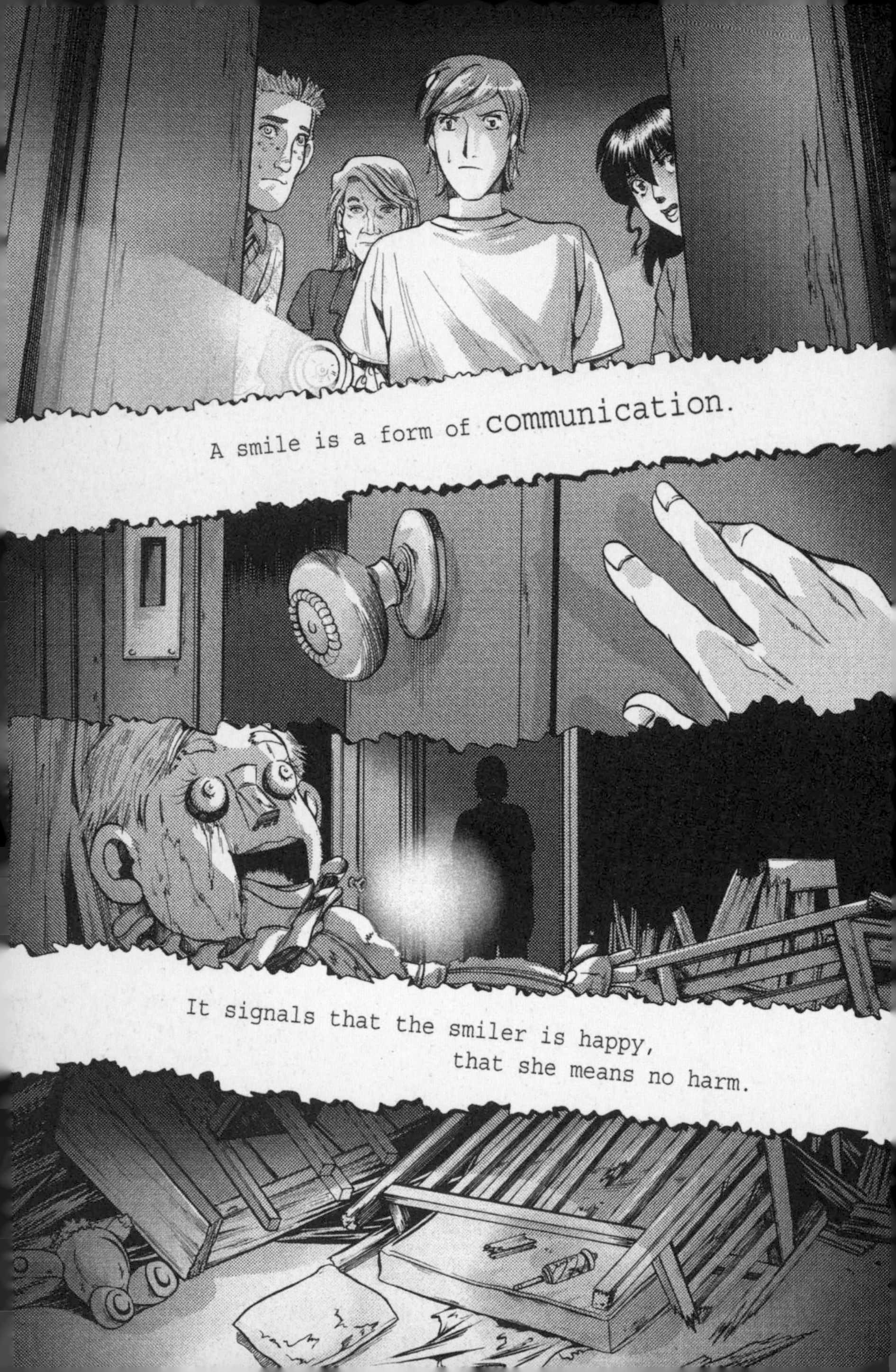
A smile is a form of communication.
It signals that the smiler is happy,
that she means no harm.

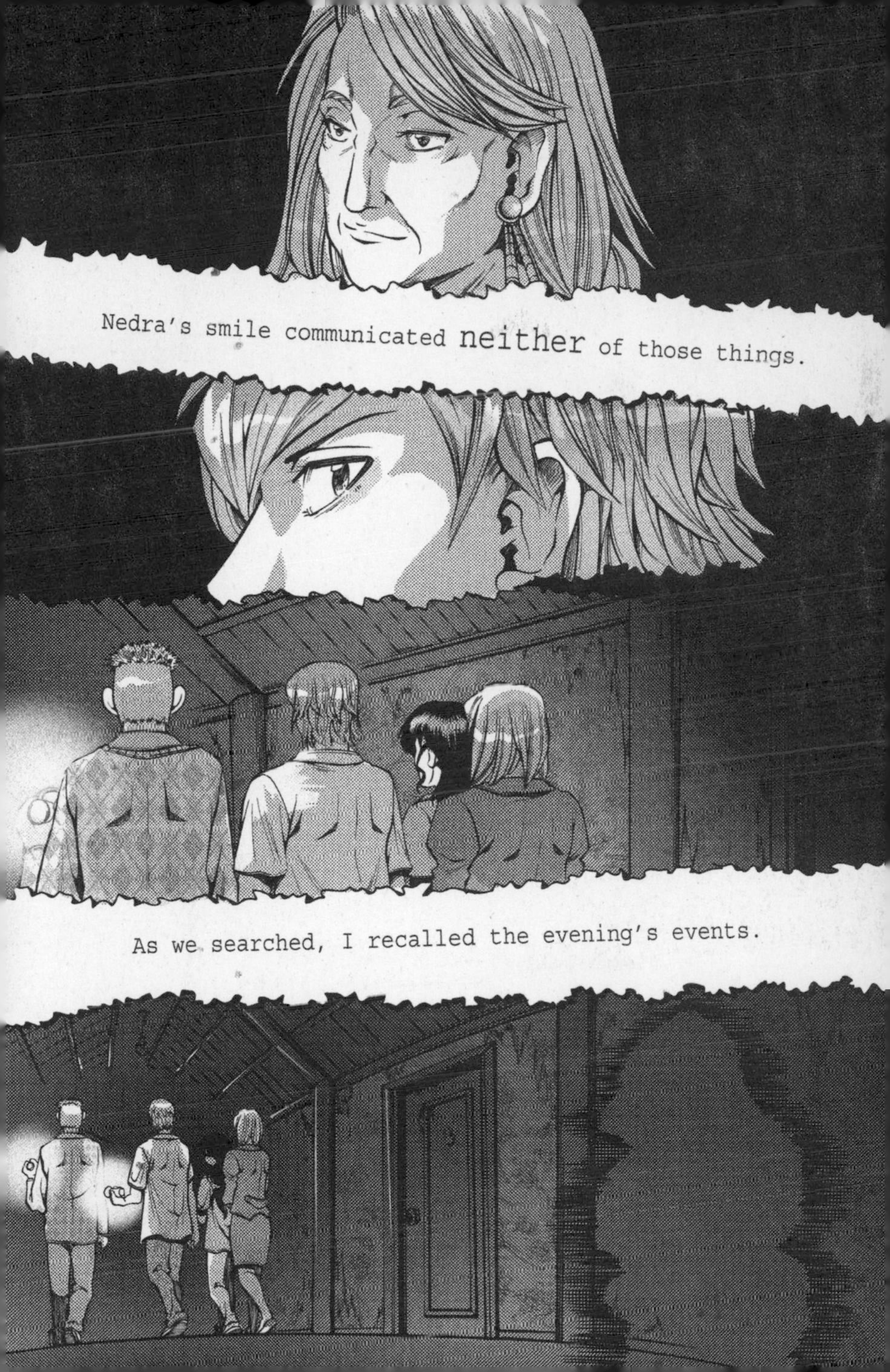
Nedra's smile communicated neither of those things.
As we searched, I recalled the evening's events.

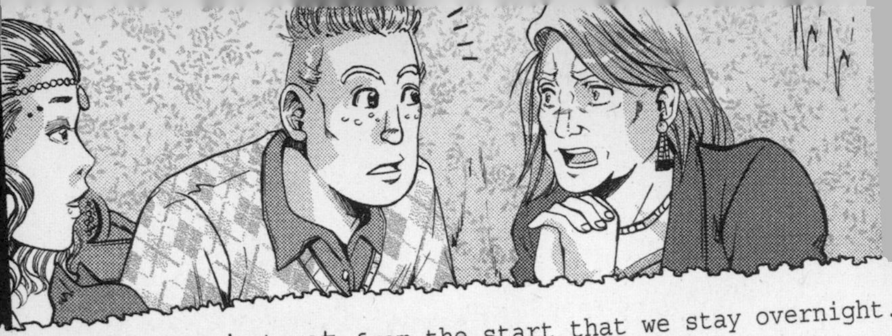

Nedra, insistent from the start that we stay overnight.

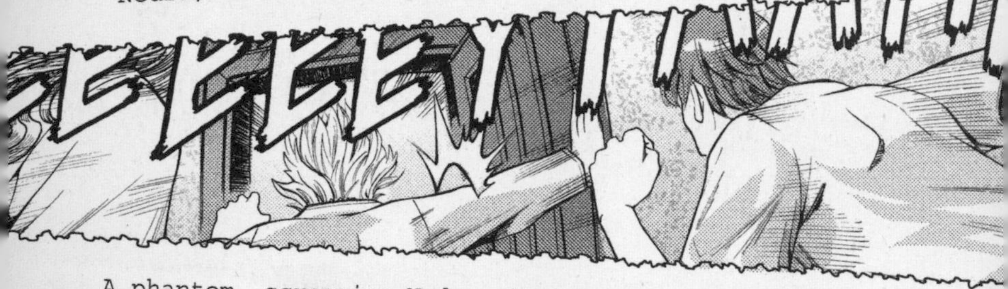

A phantom, screaming Nedra, locked in a room with no lock.

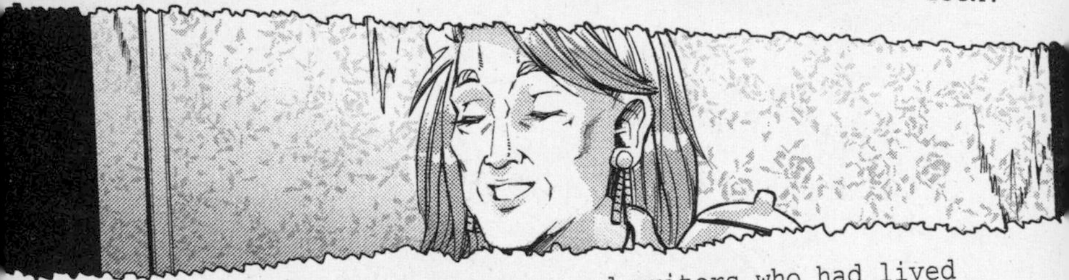

Nedra spoke of the artists and writers who had lived here. About their dreams. About their visions. She **wanted** to experience this for herself.

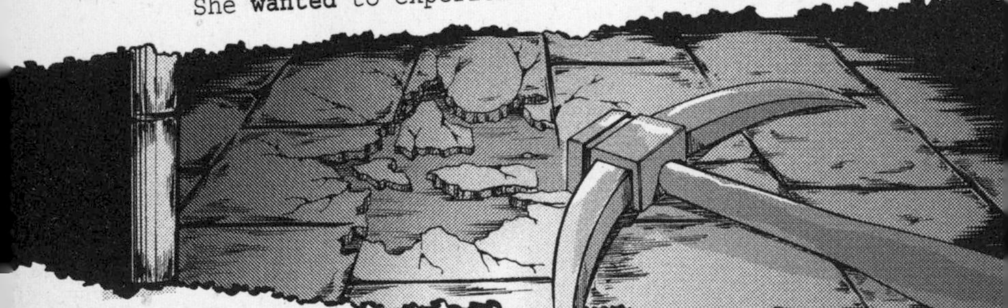

The contractors all quit. No one wanted to spend any time in this mansion...

...except Nedra.

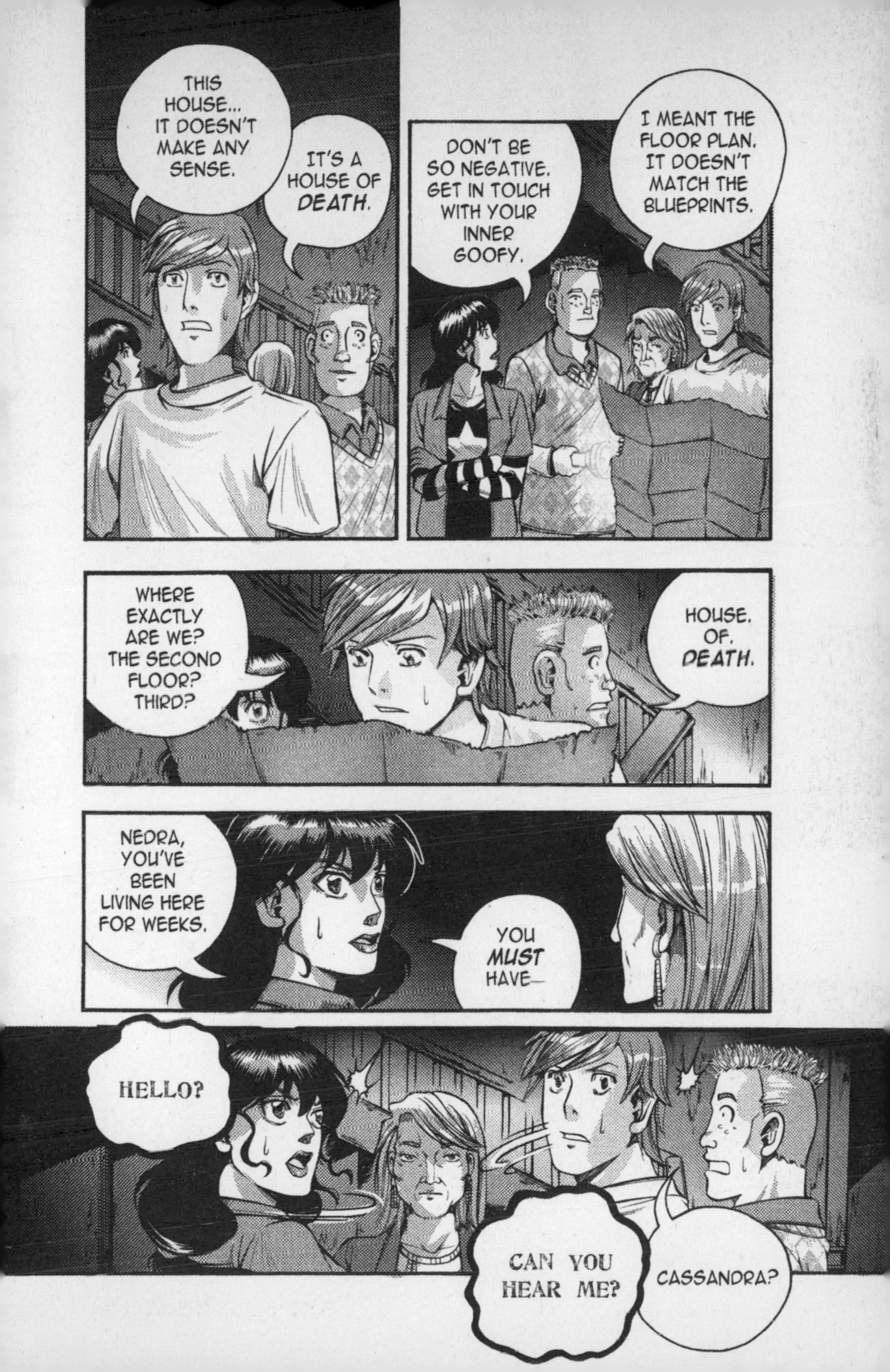
THIS HOUSE... IT DOESN'T MAKE ANY SENSE.
IT'S A HOUSE OF DEATH.
DON'T BE SO NEGATIVE. GET IN TOUCH WITH YOUR INNER GOOFY.
I MEANT THE FLOOR PLAN. IT DOESN'T MATCH THE BLUEPRINTS.
WHERE EXACTLY ARE WE? THE SECOND FLOOR? THIRD?
HOUSE. OF. DEATH.
NEDRA, YOU'VE BEEN LIVING HERE FOR WEEKS.
YOU MUST HAVE—
HELLO?
CAN YOU HEAR ME?
CASSANDRA?

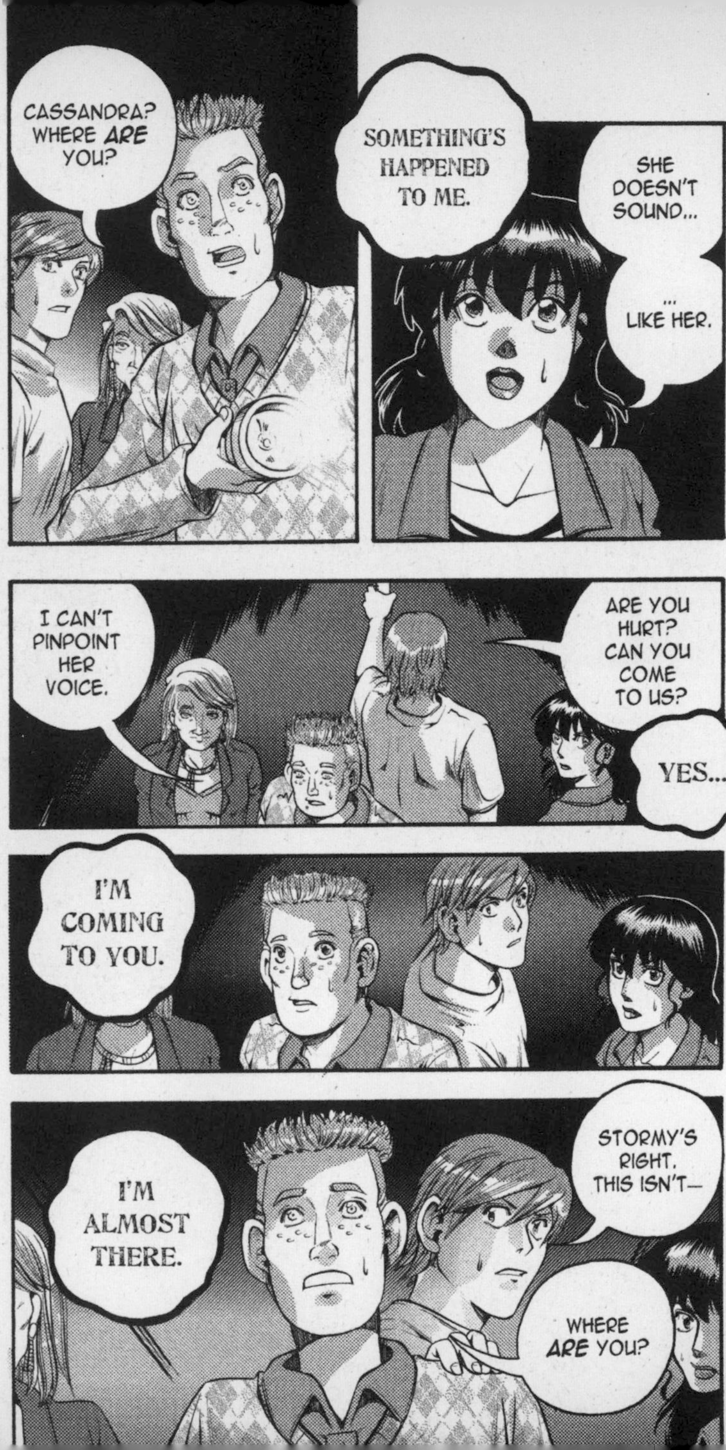
CASSANDRA? WHERE ARE YOU?
SOMETHING'S HAPPENED TO ME.
SHE DOESN'T SOUND...
... LIKE HER.
I CAN'T PINPOINT HER VOICE.
ARE YOU HURT? CAN YOU COME TO US?
YES...
I'M COMING TO YOU.
I'M ALMOST THERE.
STORMY'S RIGHT. THIS ISN'T—
WHERE ARE YOU?

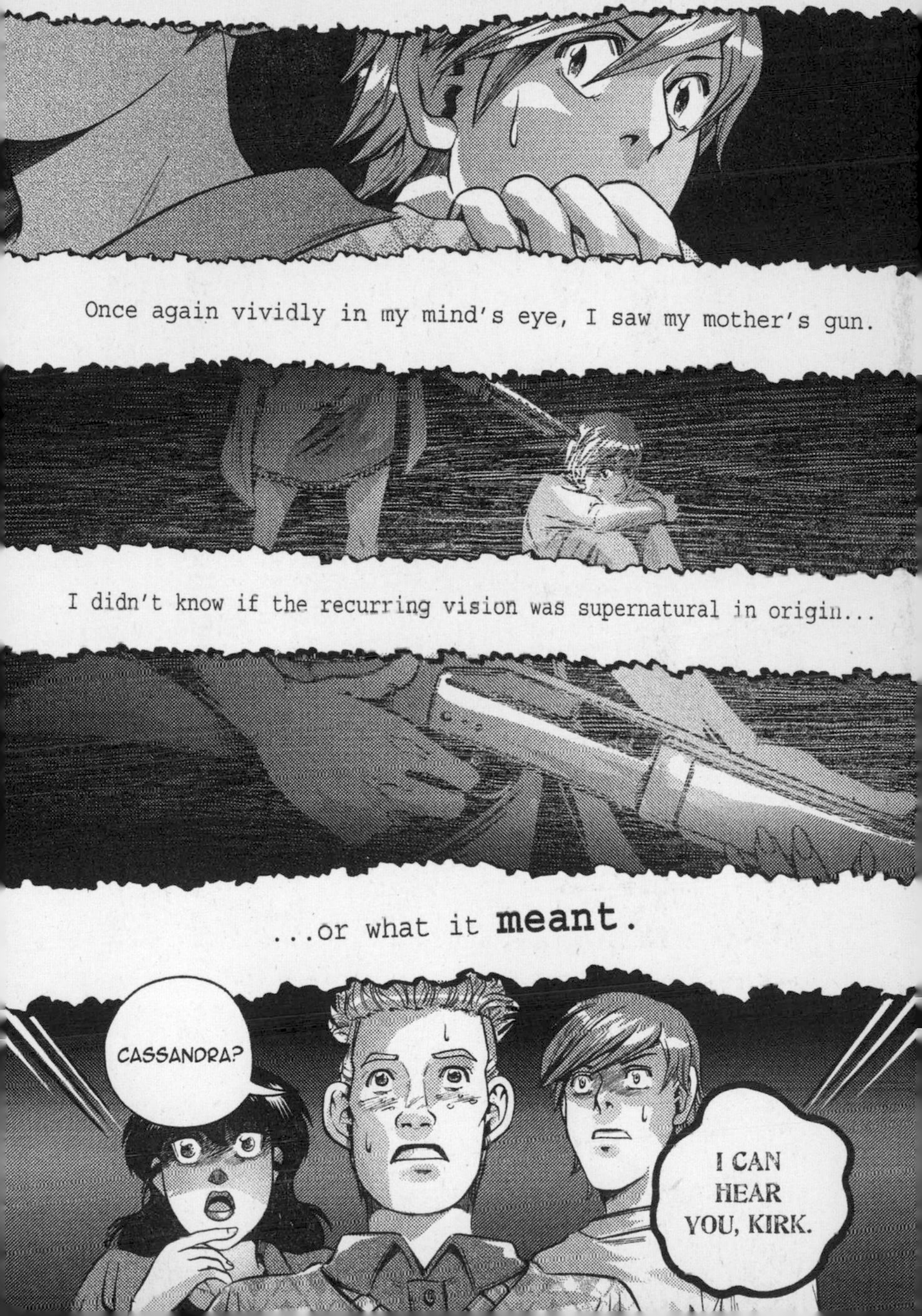
Once again vividly in my mind's eye, I saw my mother's gun.
I didn't know if the recurring vision was supernatural in origin...
...or what it **meant**.
CASSANDRA?
I CAN HEAR YOU, KIRK.

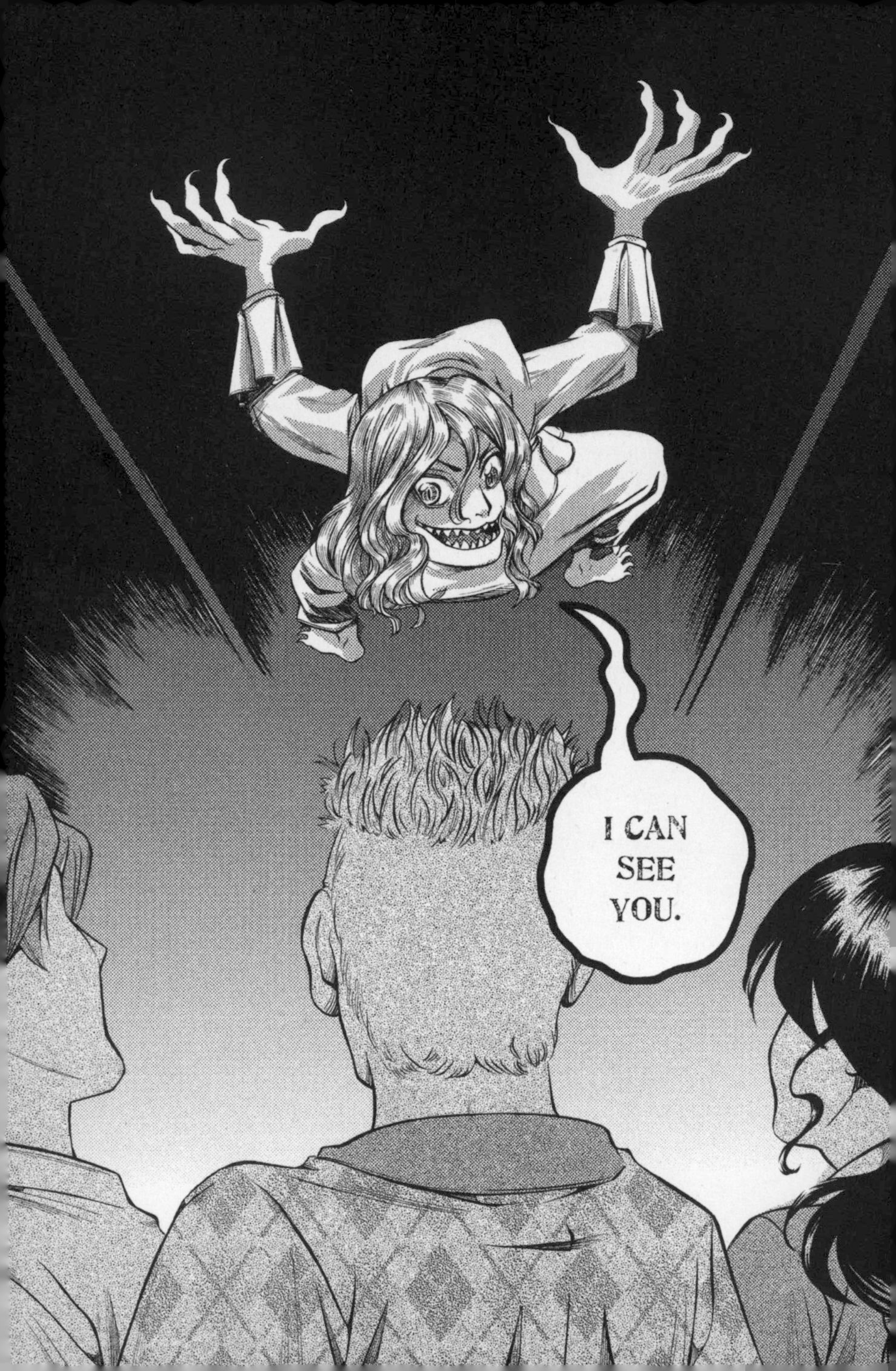
I CAN SEE YOU.

Chapter 11

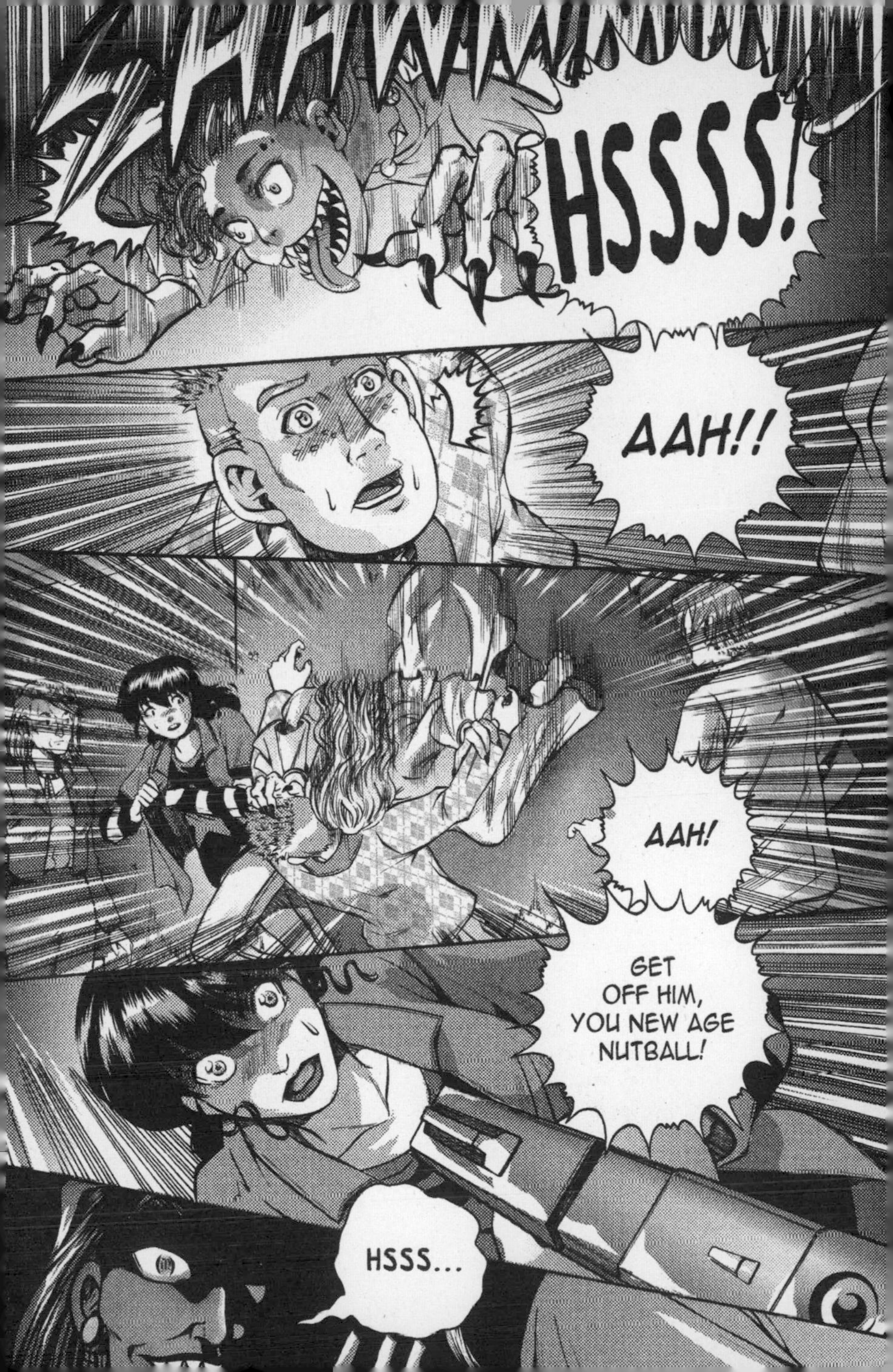
HSSSS!
AAH!!
AAH!
GET OFF HIM, YOU NEW AGE NUTBALL!
HSSS...

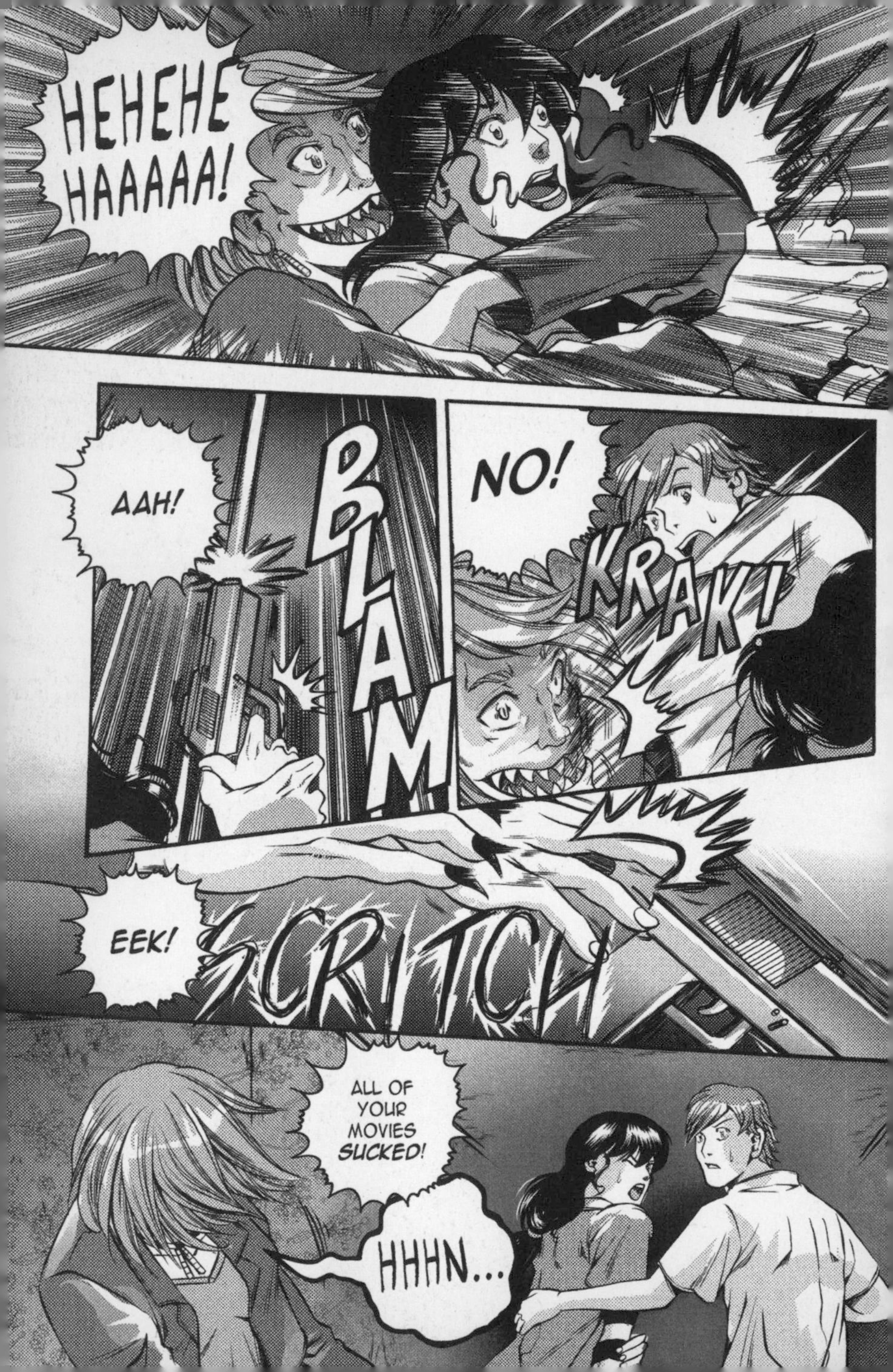
HEHEHE HAAAAA!
AAH!
BLAM
NO!
KRAK!
EEK!
SCRITCH
ALL OF YOUR MOVIES SUCKED!
HHHN...

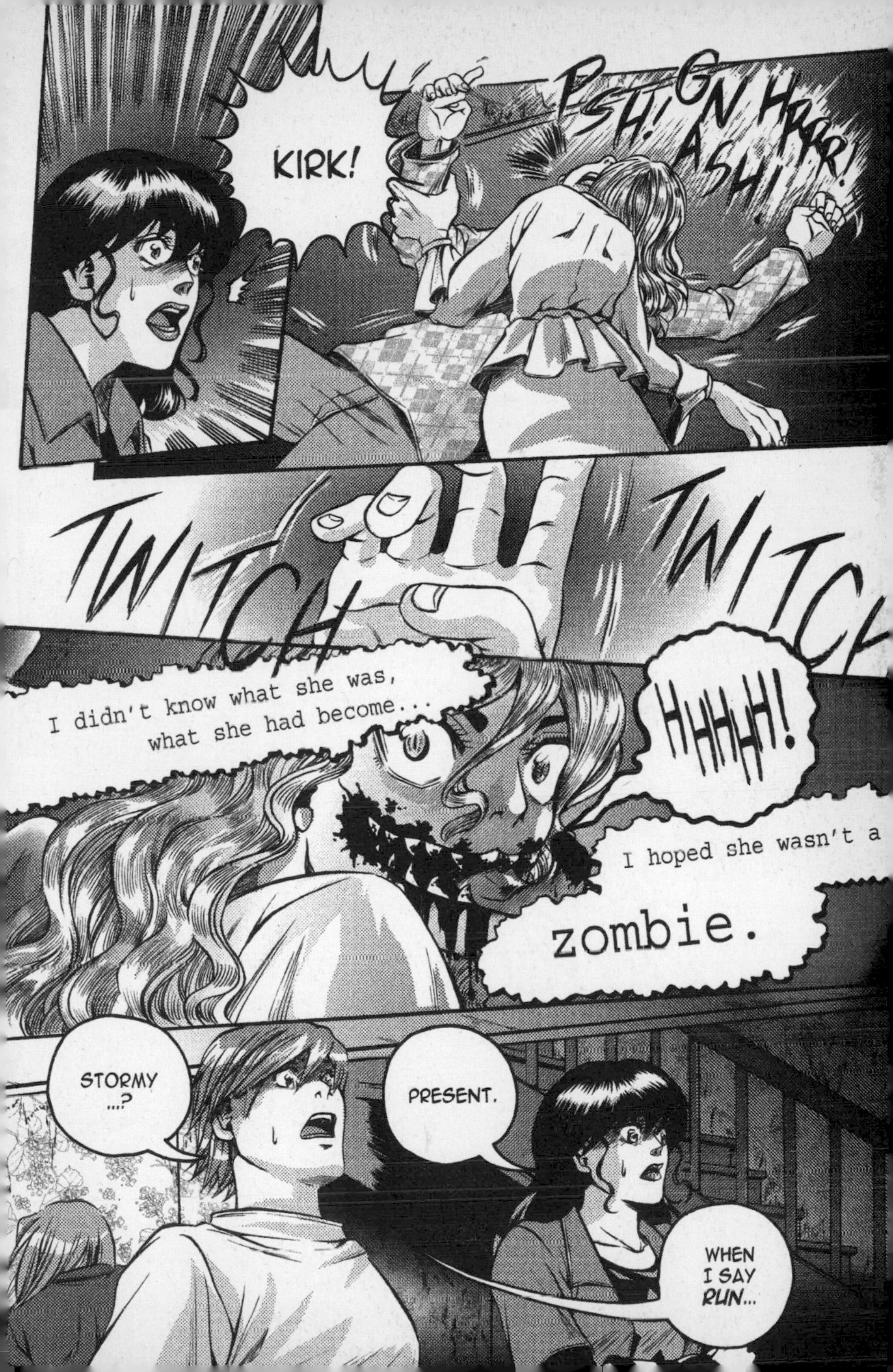
KIRK!
PSH! GNASH! HRRRR!
TWITCH TWITCH
I didn't know what she was, what she had become...
HHHHH!
I hoped she wasn't a
zombie.
STORMY ...?
PRESENT.
WHEN I SAY RUN...

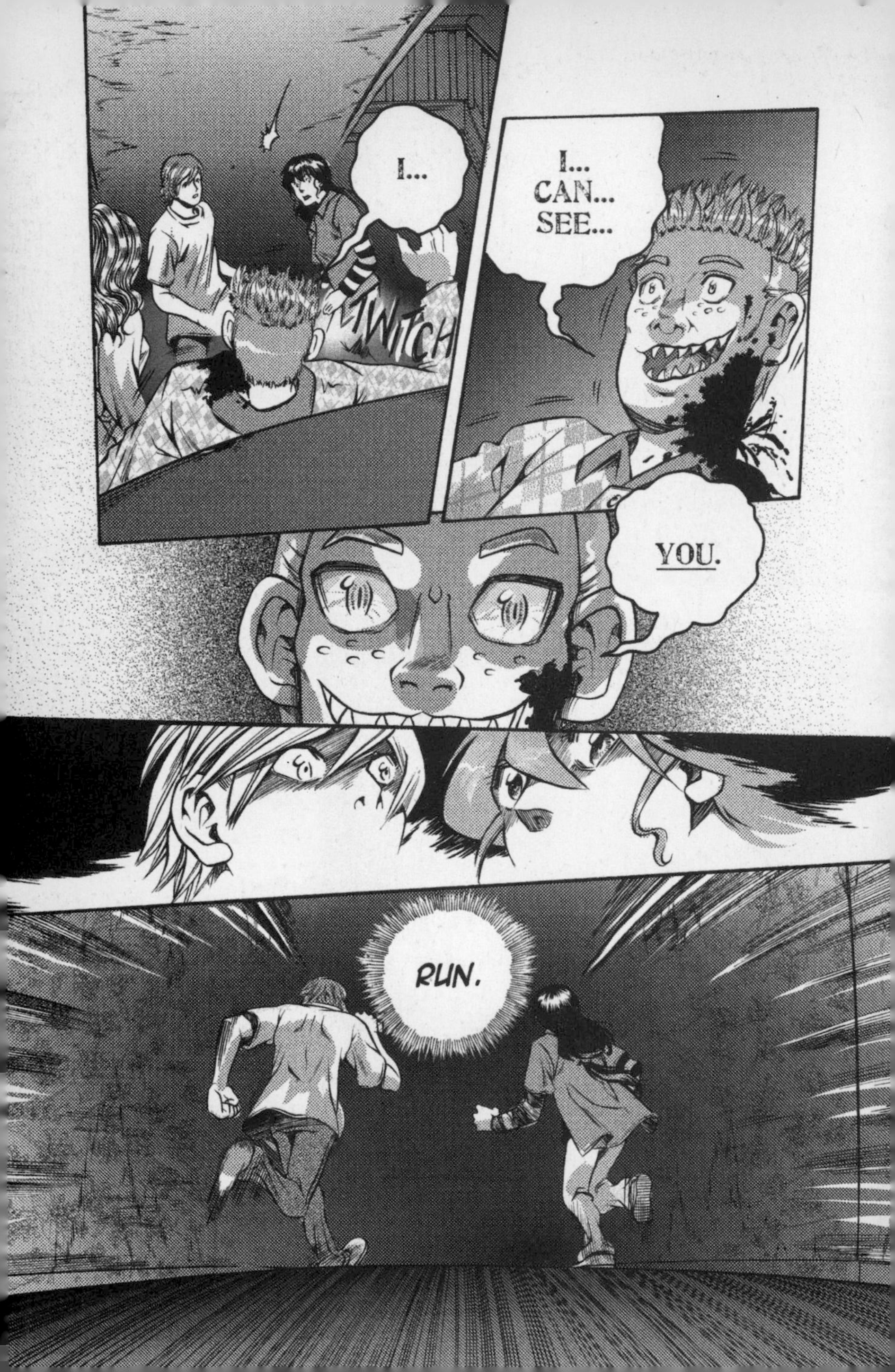
I...
TWITCH
I... CAN... SEE...
YOU.
RUN.

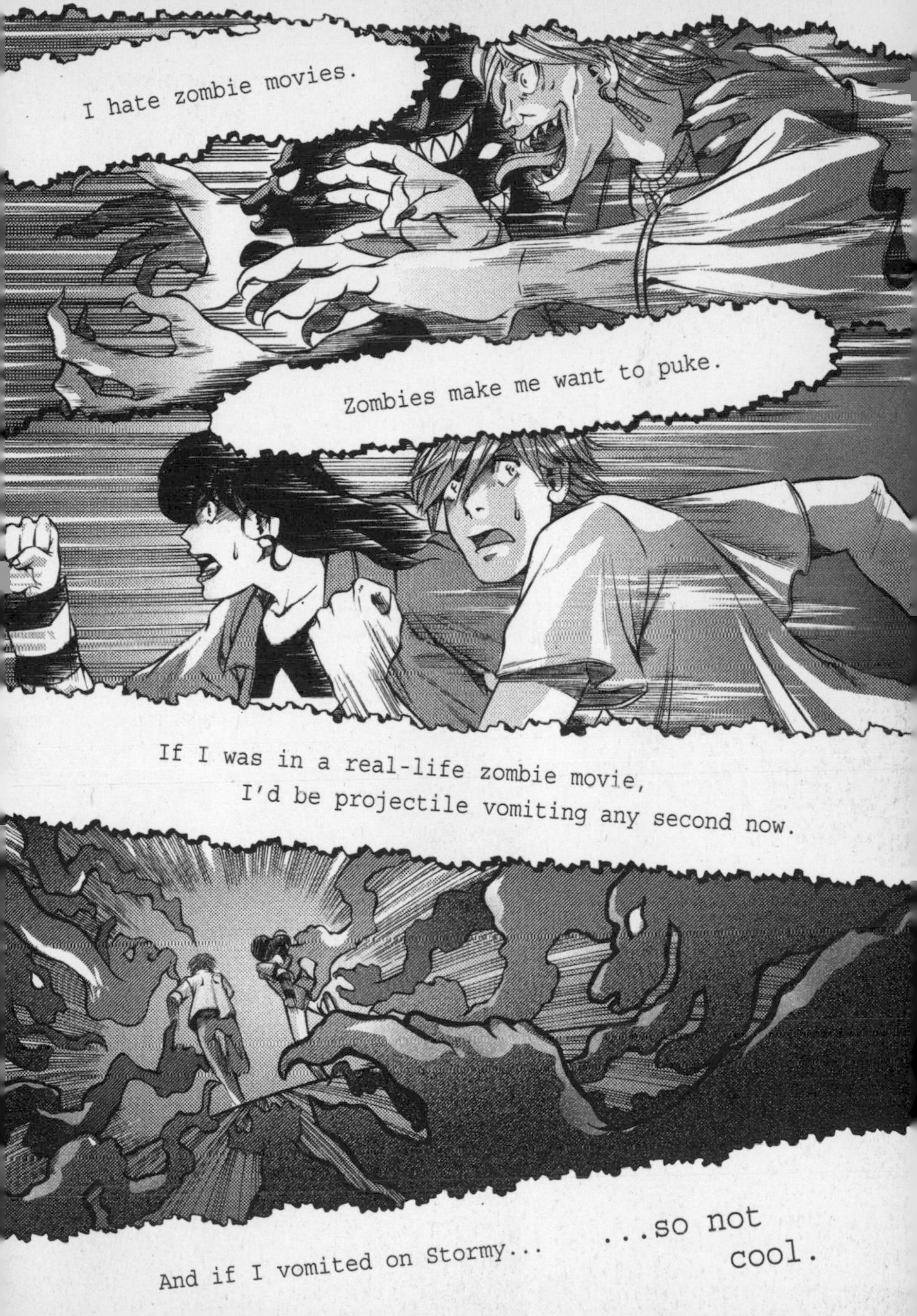
I hate zombie movies.
Zombies make me want to puke.
If I was in a real-life zombie movie,
I'd be projectile vomiting any second now.
And if I vomited on Stormy...
...so not cool.

The mazelike passageways of the mansion...

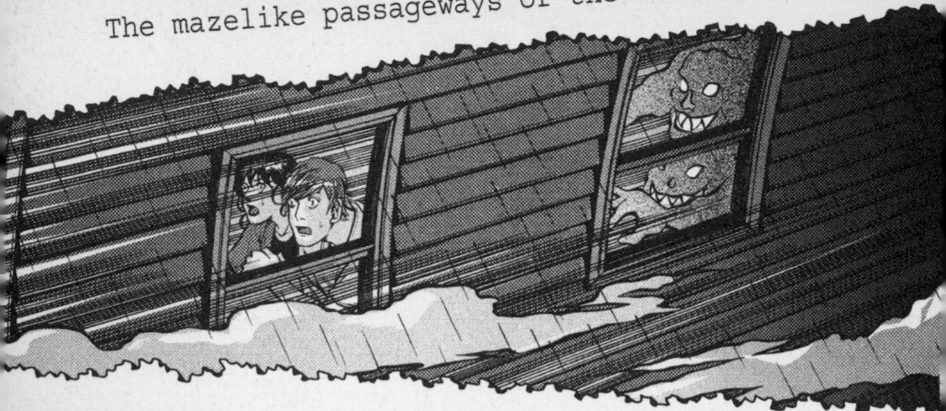

...they grew increasingly unnatural with each twist and every turn.

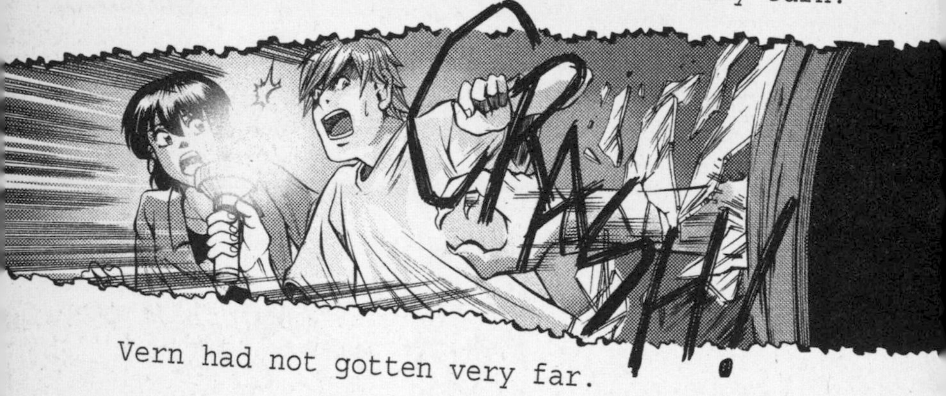
CRASH!

Vern had not gotten very far.

Only to Hell and back.

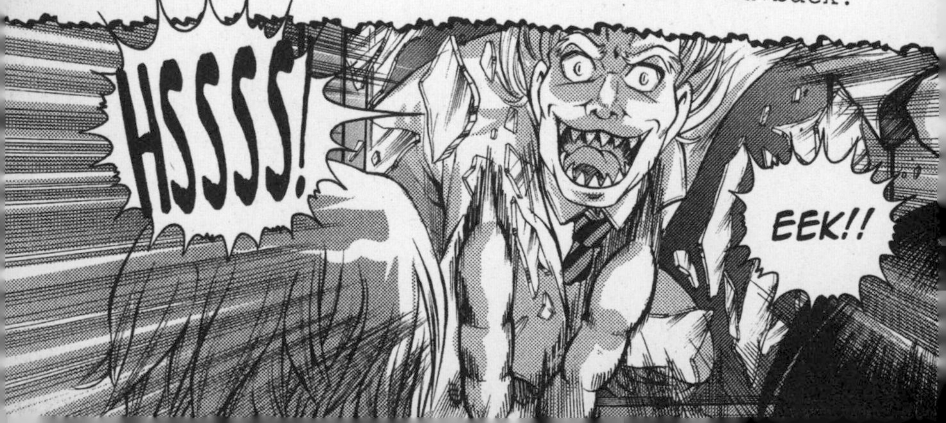
HSSSS!
EEK!!

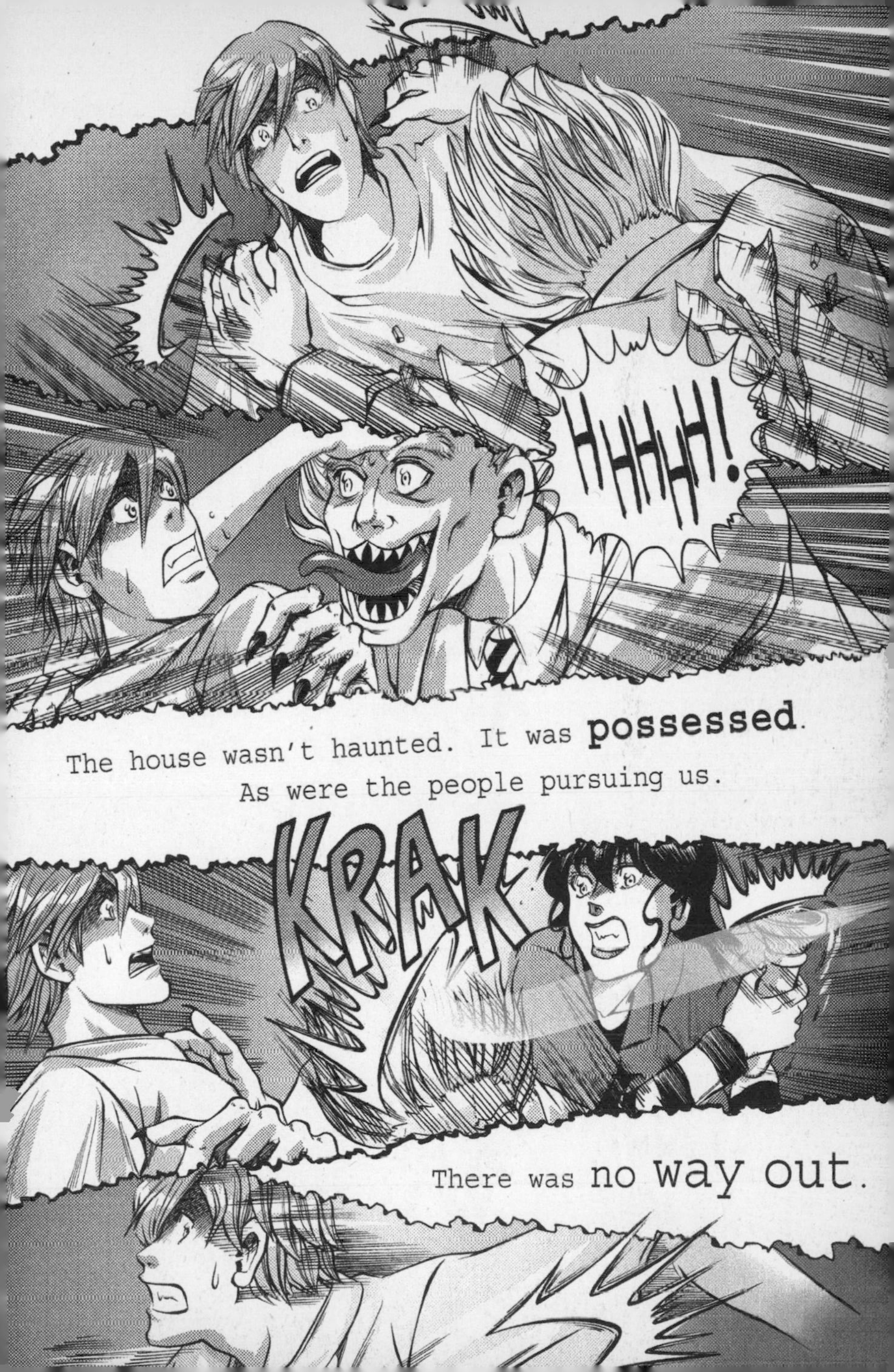
HHHHH!
The house wasn't haunted. It was possessed.
As were the people pursuing us.
KRAK
There was no way out.

Earlier in the evening, I had walked this house,
guided by psychic magnetism.

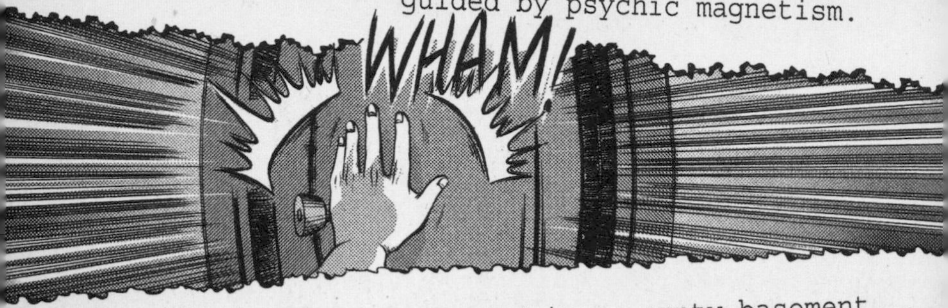
WHAM!

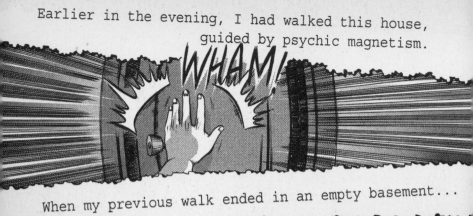

When my previous walk ended in an empty basement...

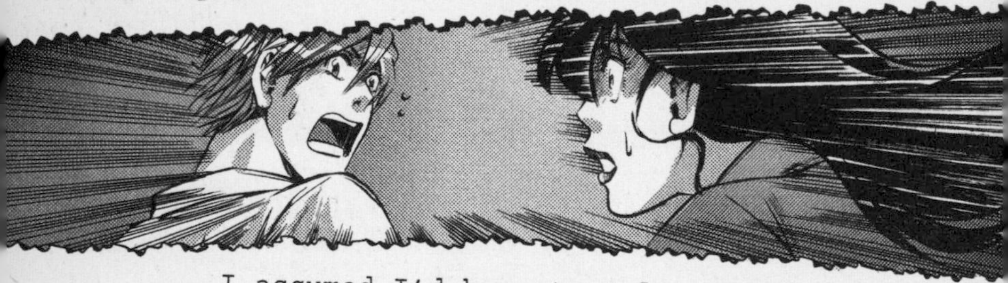

...I assumed I'd have to rely on more
conventional methods of investigation.

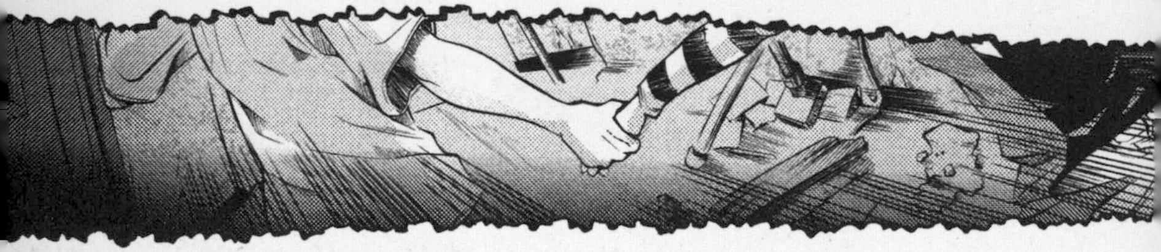

There were **no ghosts** in this haunted house.

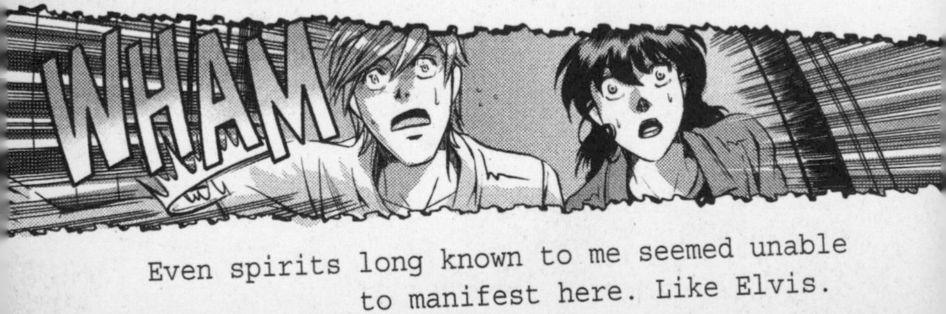
WHAM

Even spirits long known to me seemed unable
to manifest here. Like Elvis.

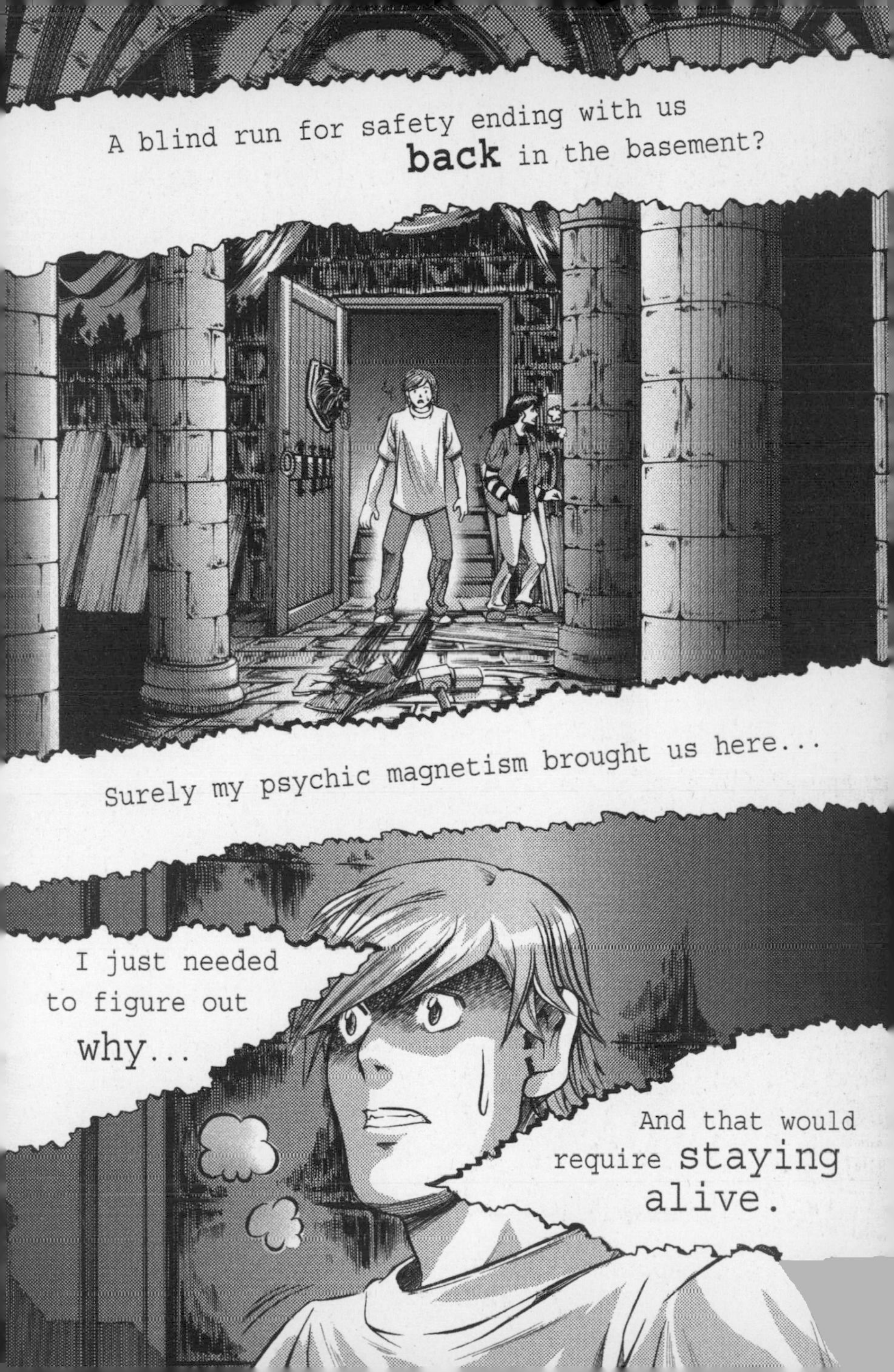
A blind run for safety ending with us **back** in the basement?
Surely my psychic magnetism brought us here...
I just needed to figure out why...
And that would require staying alive.

Chapter 12

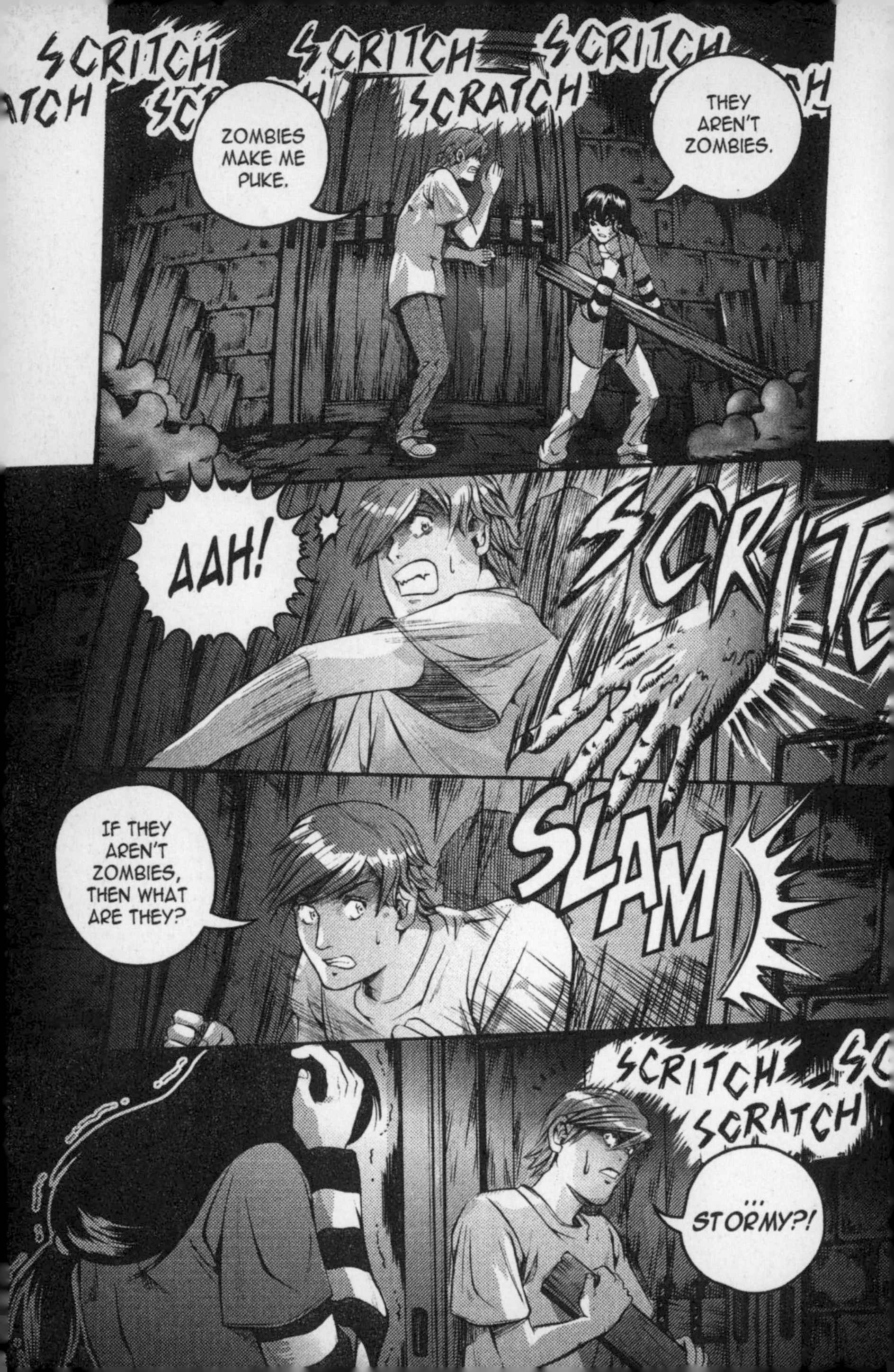
SCRITCH SCRITCH SCRITCH
SCRATCH SCRATCH
ZOMBIES MAKE ME PUKE.
THEY AREN'T ZOMBIES.
AAH!
IF THEY AREN'T ZOMBIES, THEN WHAT ARE THEY?
SLAM
SCRITCH
SCRATCH
...STORMY?!

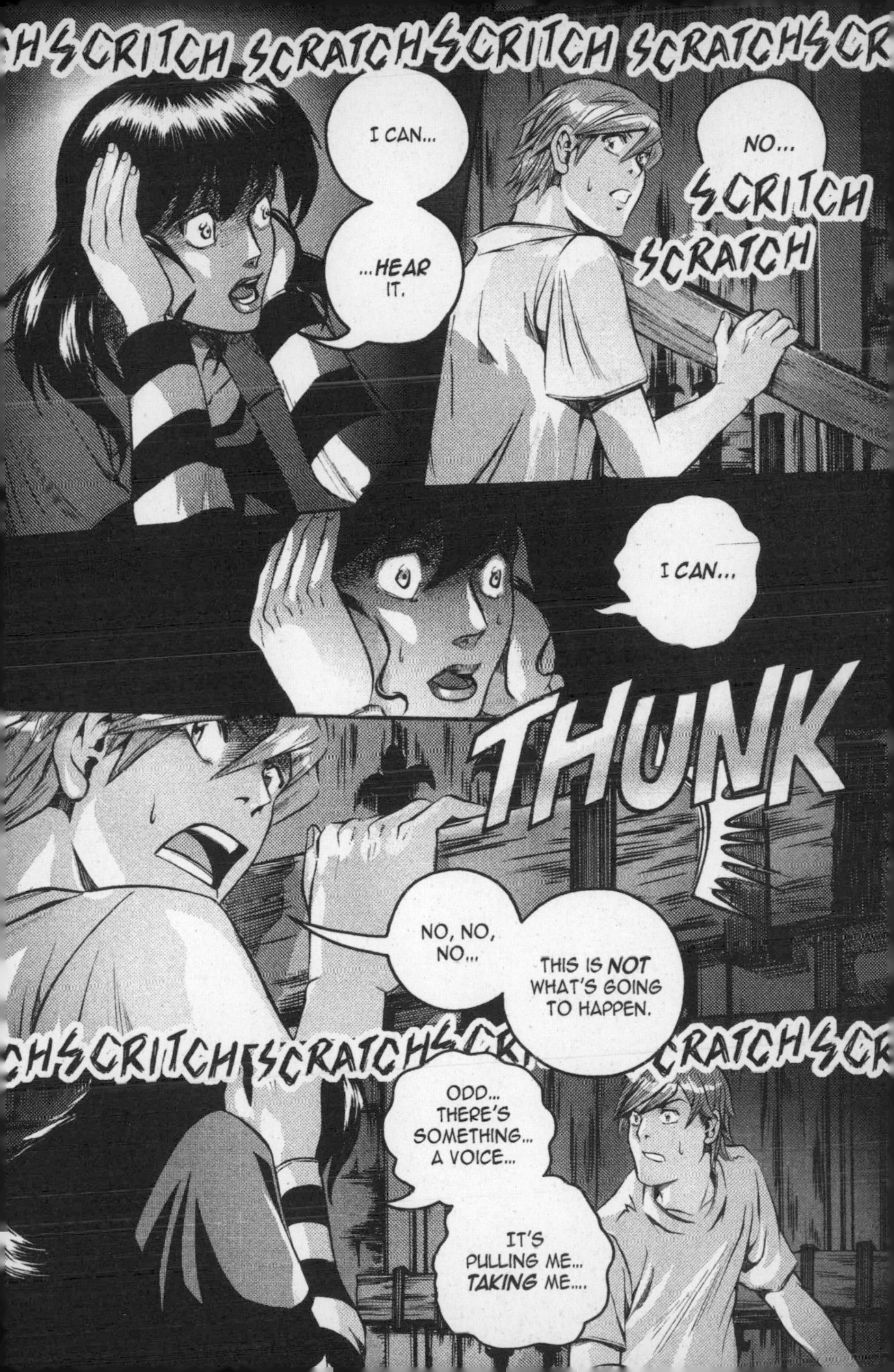
SCRITCH SCRATCH SCRITCH SCRATCH
I CAN...
...HEAR IT.
NO...
SCRITCH SCRATCH
I CAN...
THUNK
NO, NO, NO...
THIS IS NOT WHAT'S GOING TO HAPPEN.
SCRITCH SCRATCH SCRATCH
ODD... THERE'S SOMETHING... A VOICE...
IT'S PULLING ME... TAKING ME....

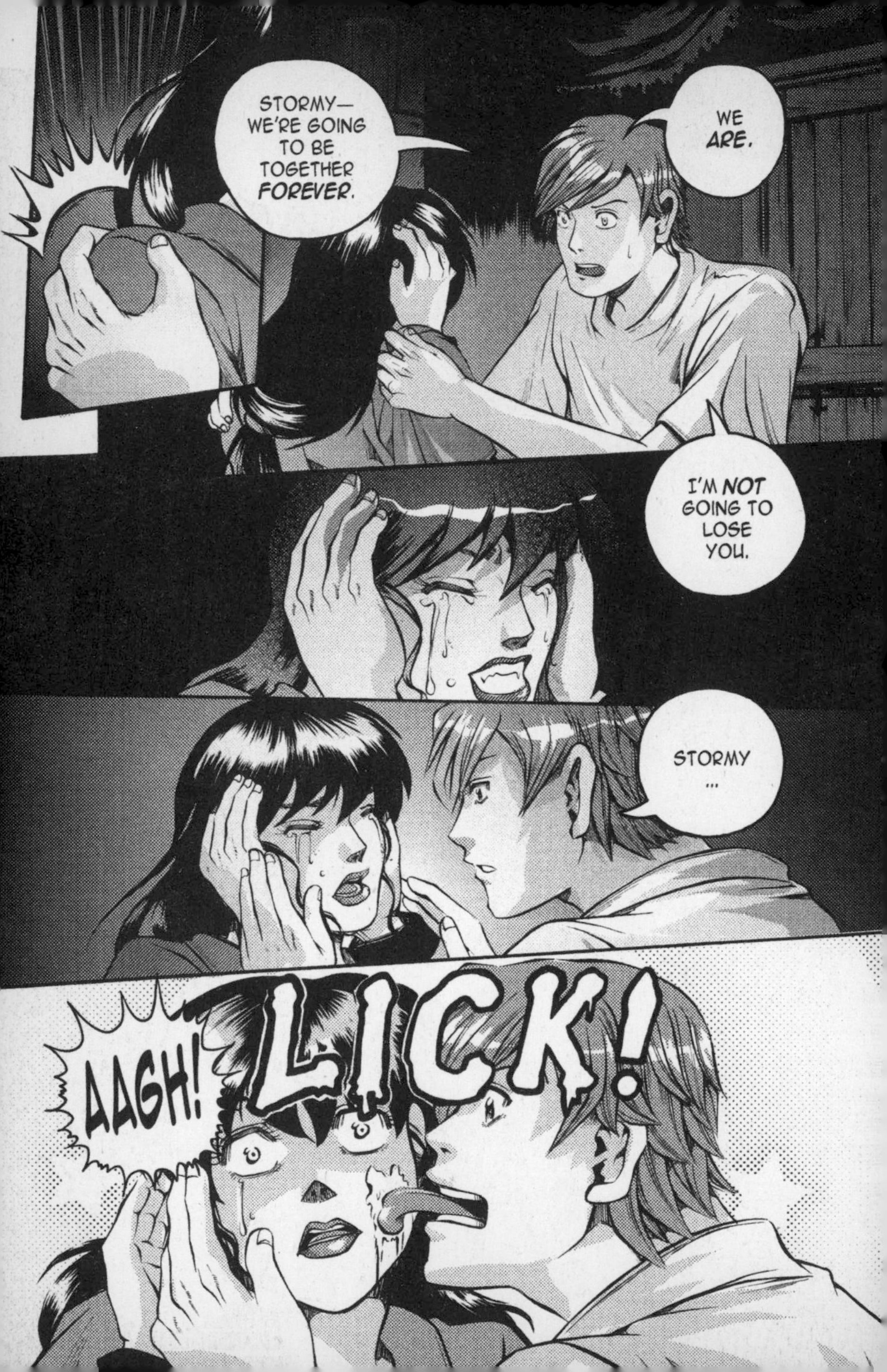
STORMY— WE'RE GOING TO BE TOGETHER *FOREVER*.
WE *ARE*.
I'M *NOT* GOING TO LOSE YOU.
STORMY ...
AAGH!
LICK!

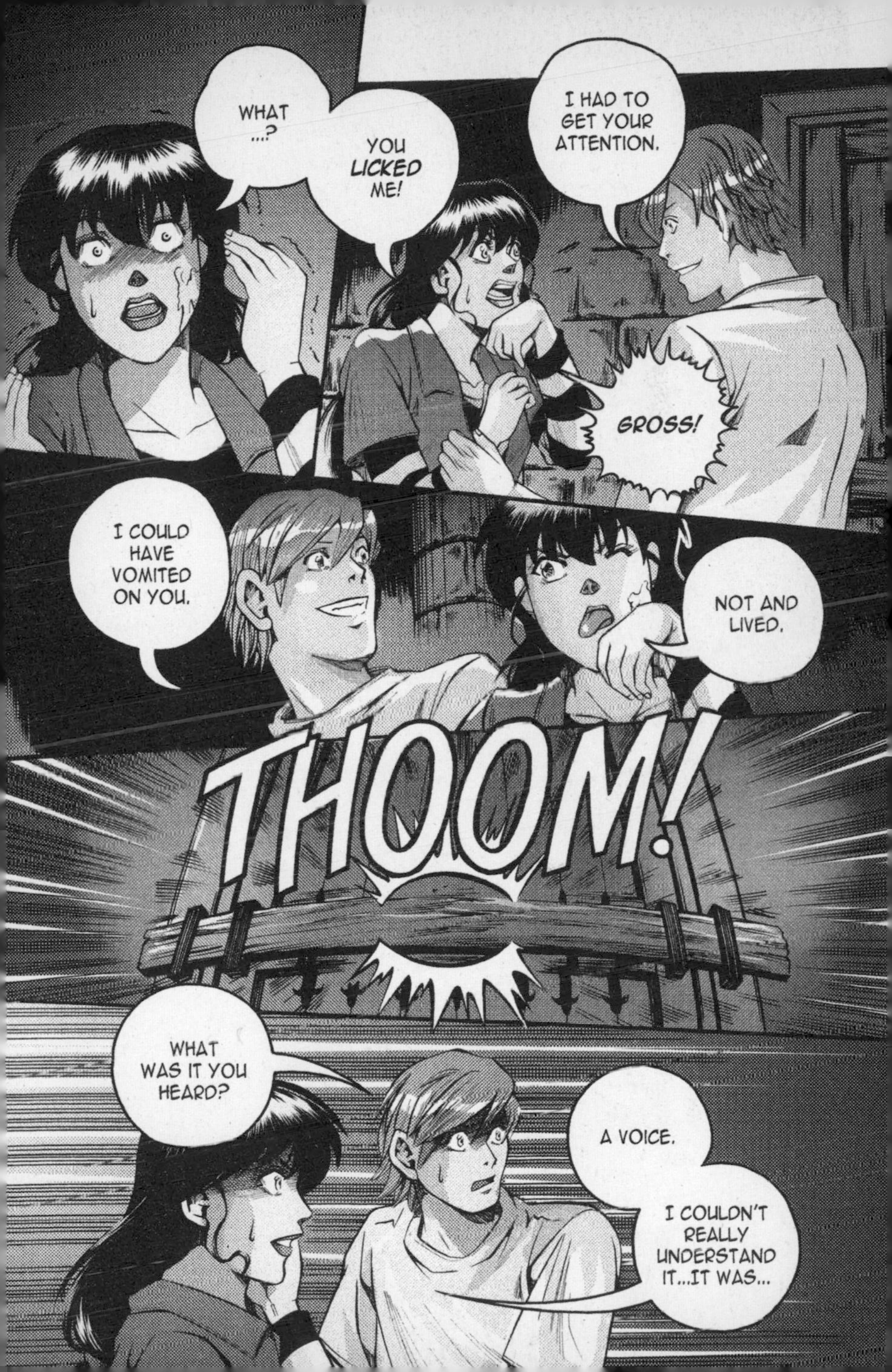
WHAT ...?
YOU LICKED ME!
I HAD TO GET YOUR ATTENTION.
GROSS!
I COULD HAVE VOMITED ON YOU.
NOT AND LIVED.
THOOM!
WHAT WAS IT YOU HEARD?
A VOICE.
I COULDN'T REALLY UNDERSTAND IT...IT WAS...

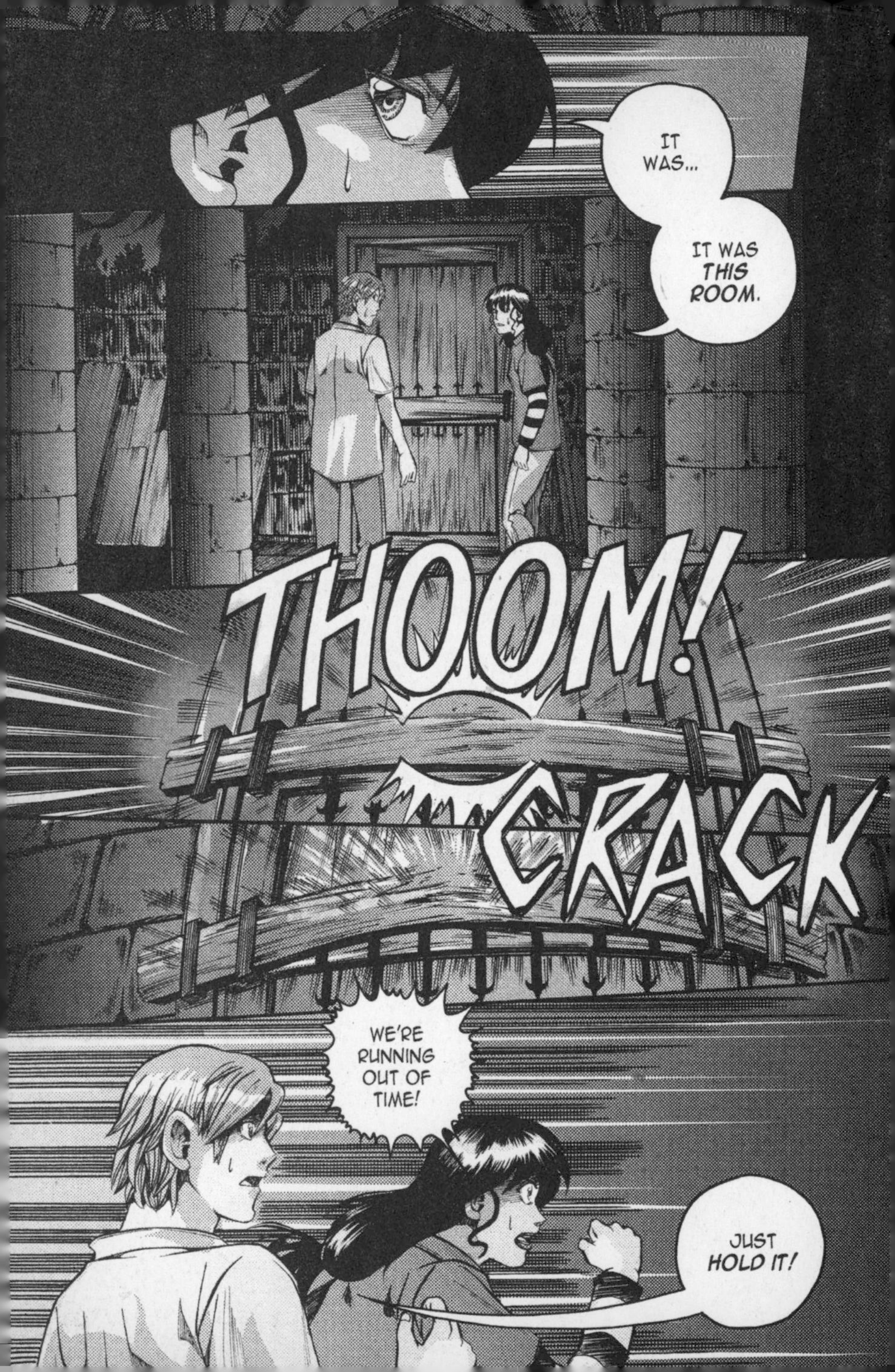
IT WAS...
IT WAS THIS ROOM.
THOOM!
CRACK
WE'RE RUNNING OUT OF TIME!
JUST HOLD IT!

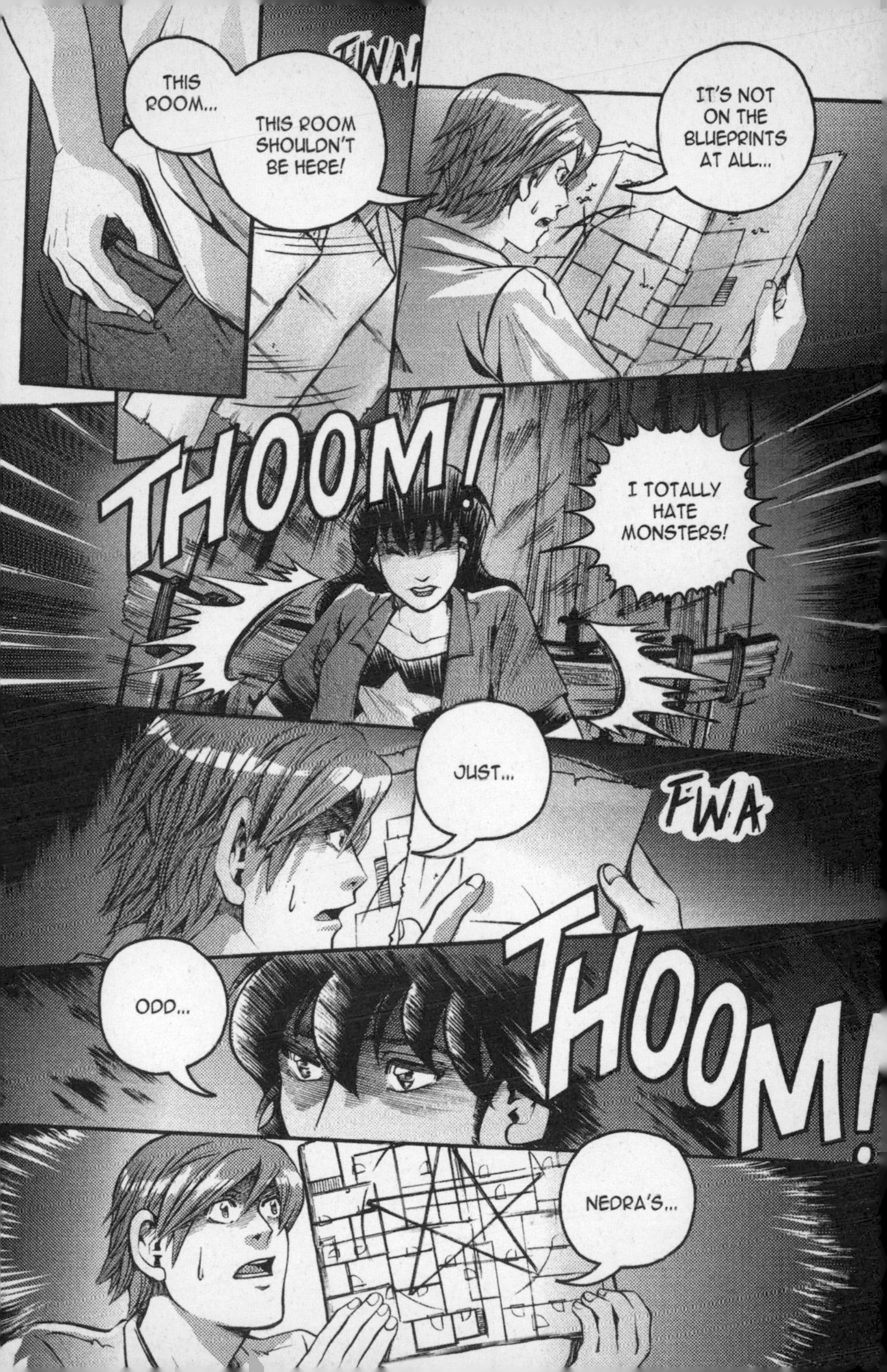
FWA
THIS ROOM...
THIS ROOM SHOULDN'T BE HERE!
IT'S NOT ON THE BLUEPRINTS AT ALL...
THOOM!
I TOTALLY HATE MONSTERS!
JUST...
FWA
ODD...
THOOM!
NEDRA'S...

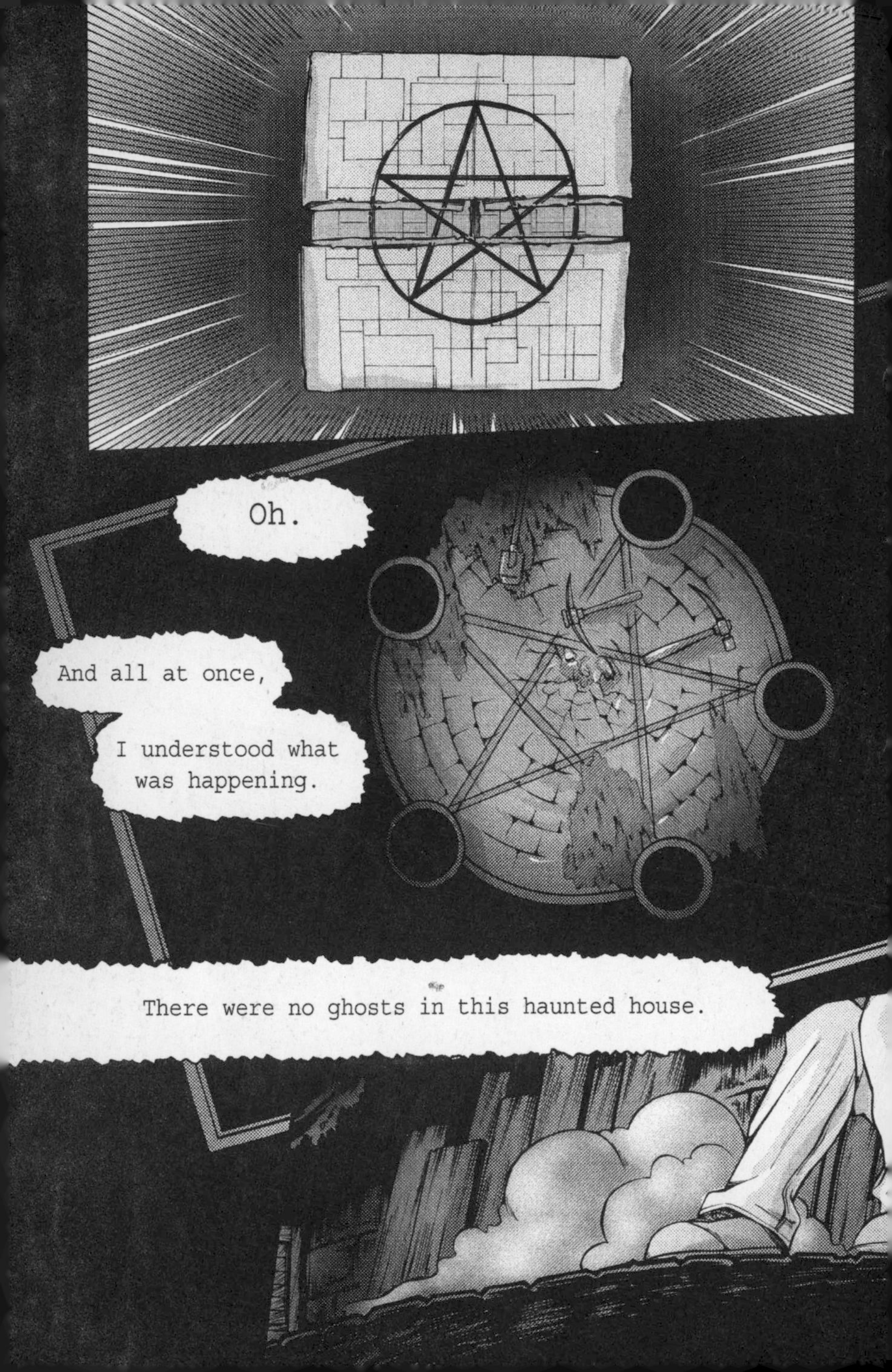
Oh.
And all at once,
I understood what was happening.
There were no ghosts in this haunted house.

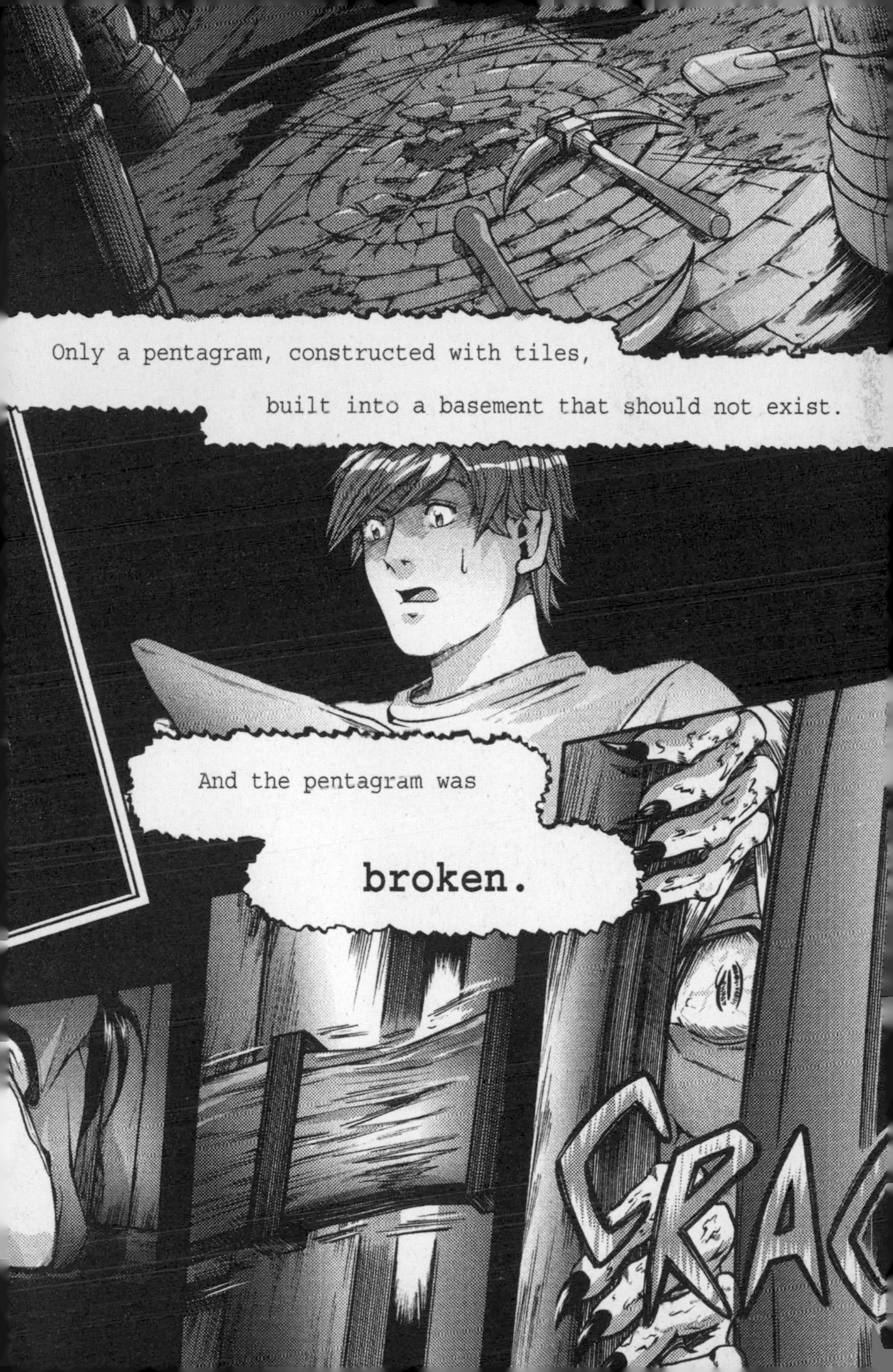
Only a pentagram, constructed with tiles,
built into a basement that should not exist.
And the pentagram was
broken.
CRAC

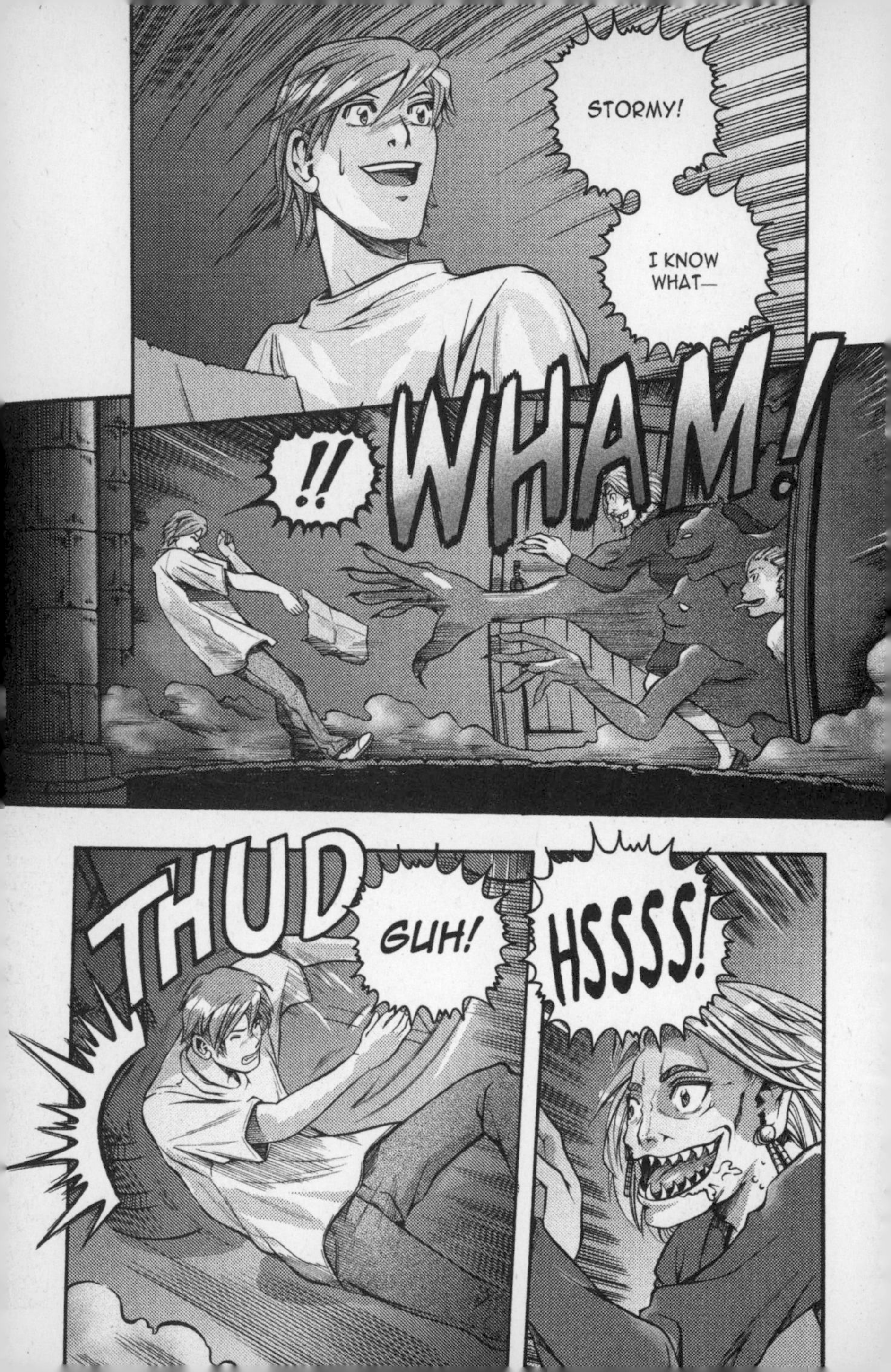
STORMY!
I KNOW WHAT—
!!
WHAM!
THUD
GUH!
HSSSS!

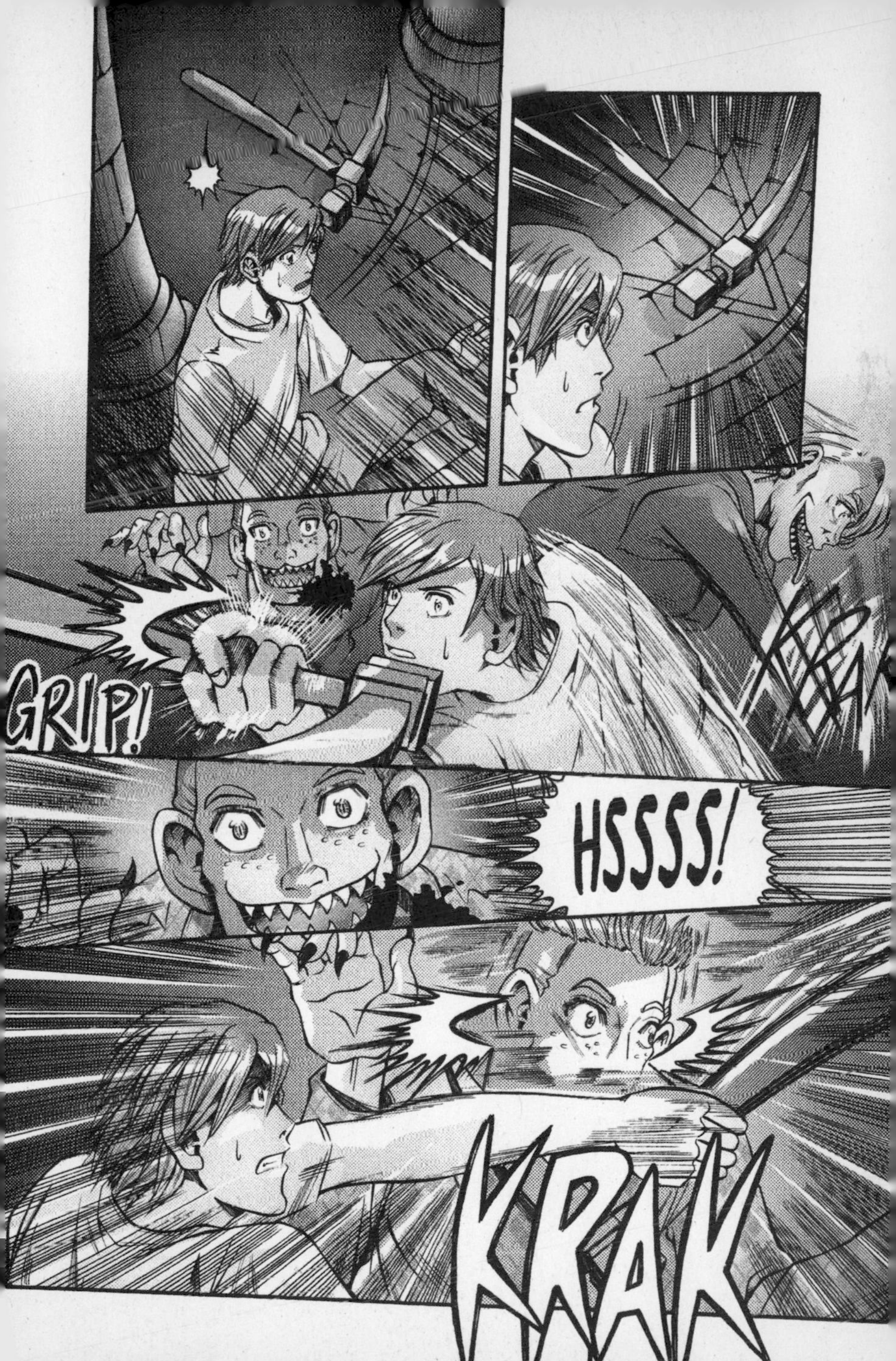
GRIP!
HSSSS!
KRAK

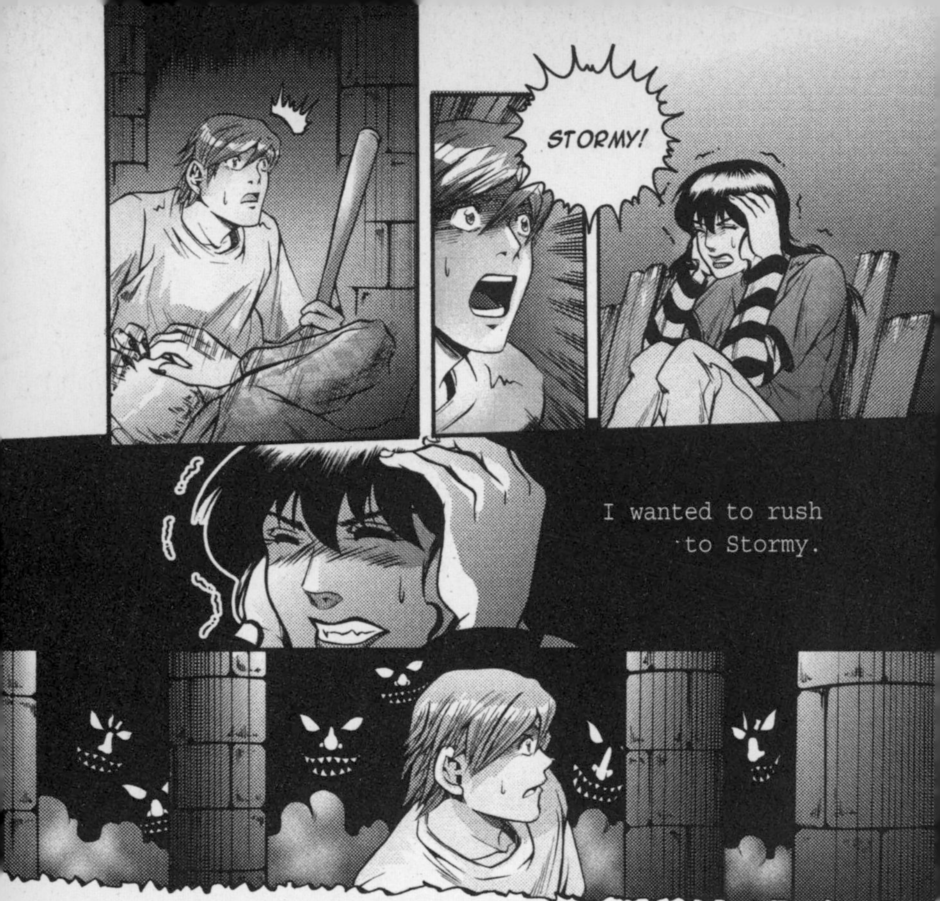
STORMY!
I wanted to rush to Stormy.

Not zombies. We were facing people possessed by a demon or demons. And they wanted me, not Stormy.

Because I held the key.

And I knew what to do with it.

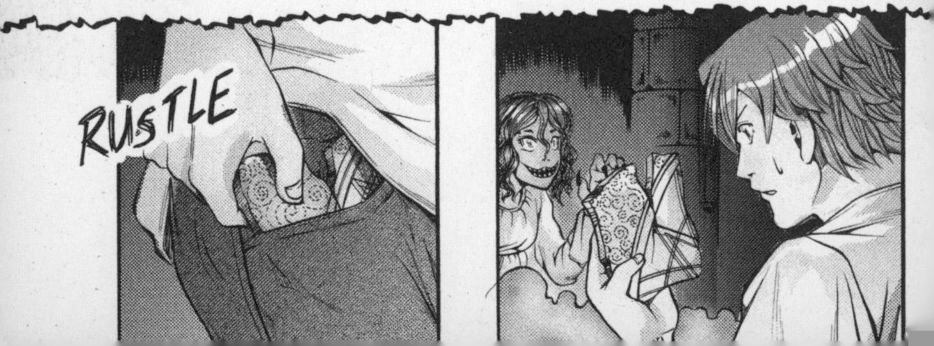
RUSTLE

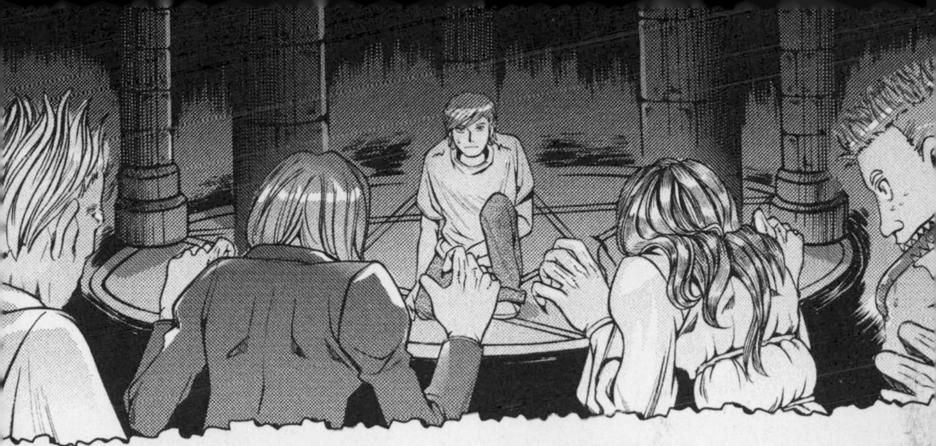

The **things** that were once **people** slipped in and out of the shadows.

But they didn't attack.

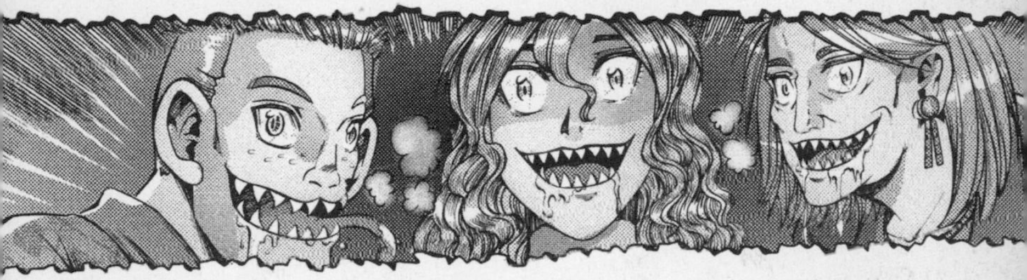

I suspected that they were wary to cross the threshold of the pentagram.

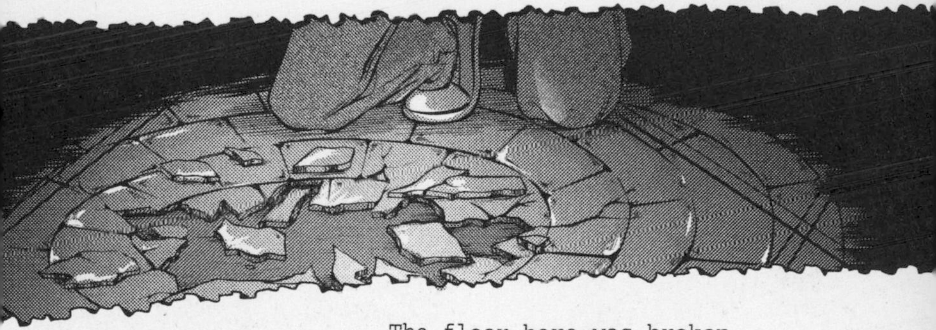

The floor here was broken.

But the tiles **could** be placed back in the correct order.

The pattern **could** be **restored.**

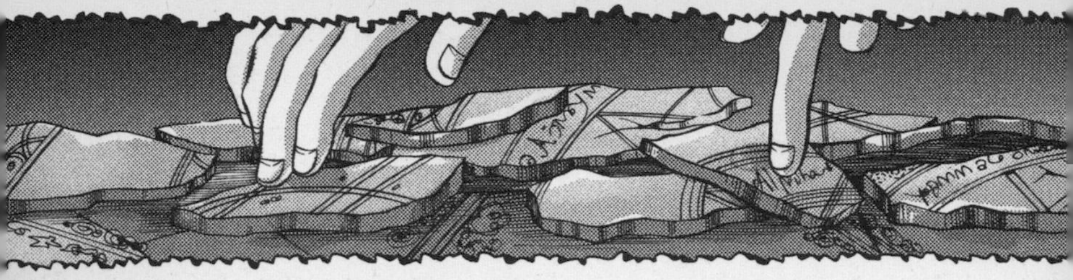

The job of any good fry cook is to
transform chaos into order.

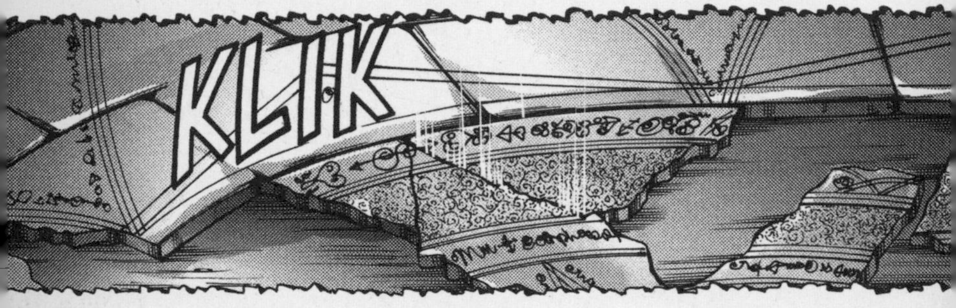
KLIK

At times it can be a challenge.
At times the chaos can threaten to pull you under.

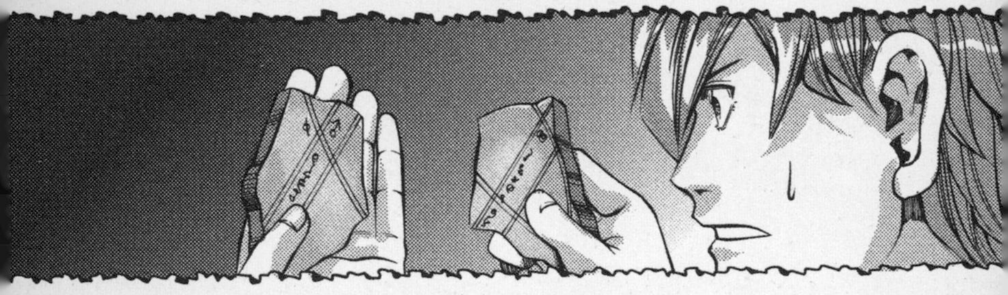

Absolute focus is the key.
You live only for the moment.

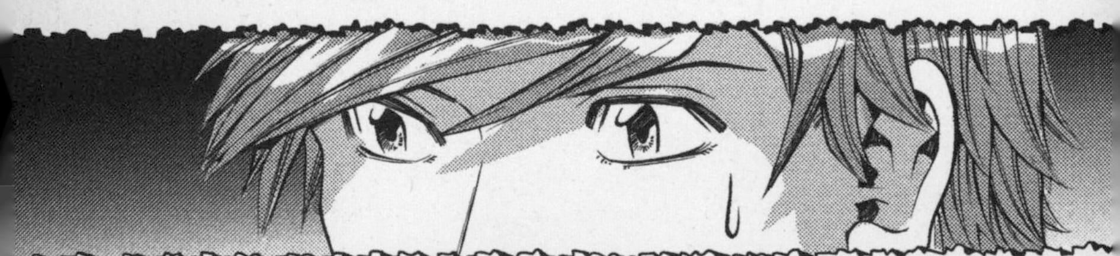

Concentration is one of the greatest and most undervalued skills.

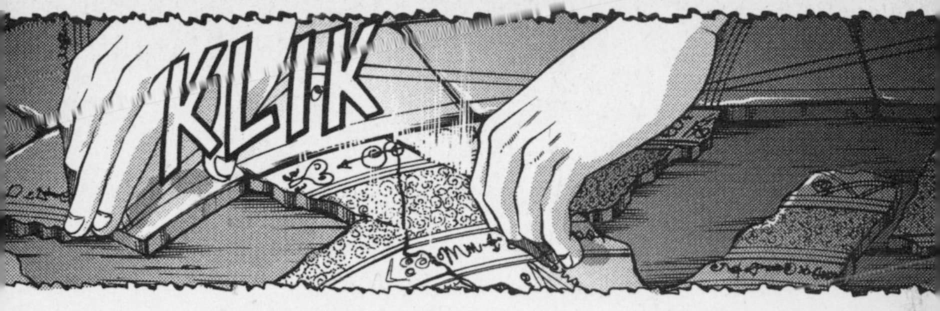
KLIK

I was standing in the center of an ornate **pentagram**, built into the floor of the hidden basement of a **haunted mansion**, surrounded by demonically possessed **ghost-busters**, while the love of my life struggled against the **psychic assault** of a **supernatural entity**.

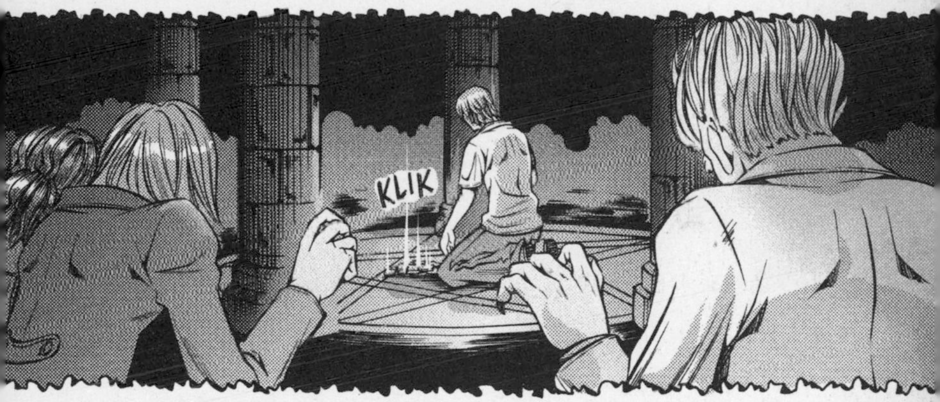
KLIK

I'm not going to lie to you. I'm not going to say that maintaining focus was easy.

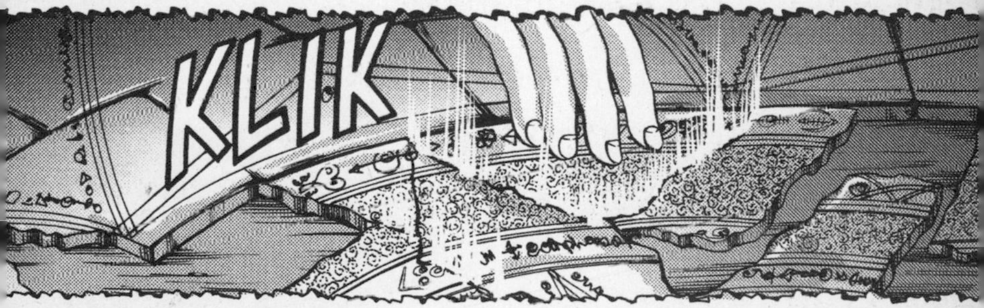
KLIK

But it wasn't as bad as the breakfast rush at the Pico Mundo Grille, either.

It's said that the pentagram acts like a gateway;
a conduit between our world and...somewhere else.

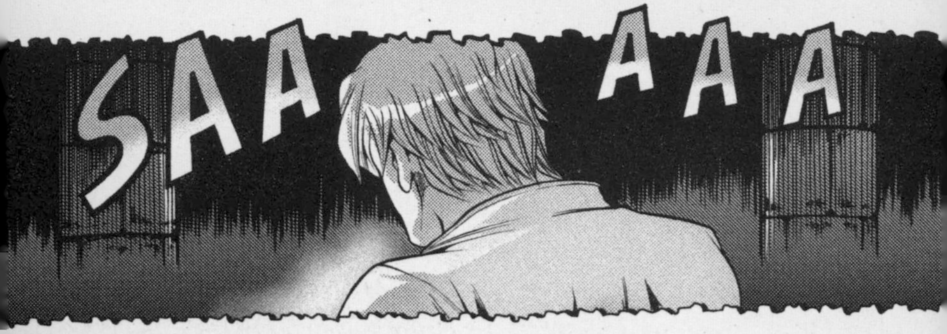
SAAAAA

As long as the design remains intact,
nothing within the pentagram can escape.

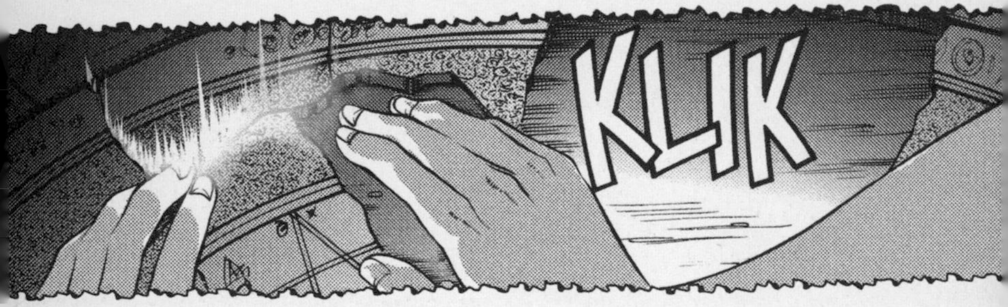
KLIK

The history of the basement pentagram was a mystery.

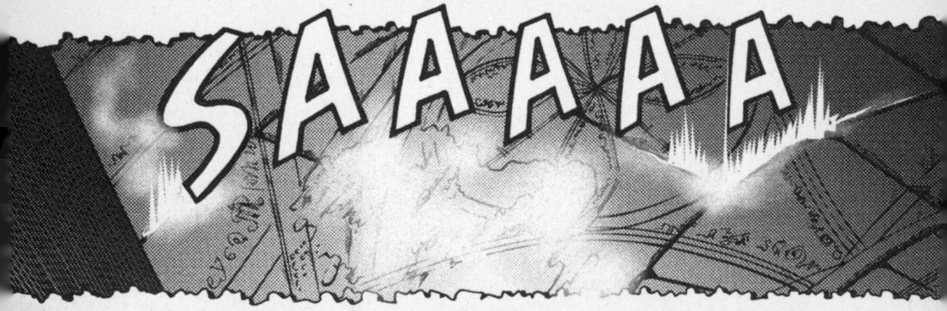
SAAAAA

Maybe the demon had been called forth
long ago by one of these "delightfully colorful"
groups that had occupied the house in the '60s.

Maybe the demon was trapped in the pentagram
until it had been broken by one of Nedra's workmen.

It had to be repaired. I knew that without knowing *how* I knew.

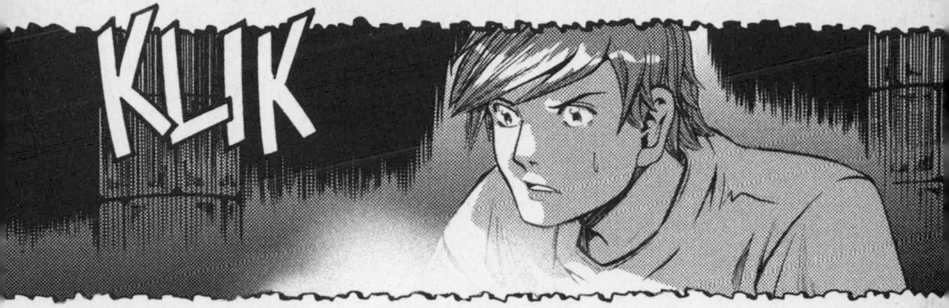
KLIK

Maybe I had gleaned the knowledge during one of
my many late-night conversations with Ozzie Boone.

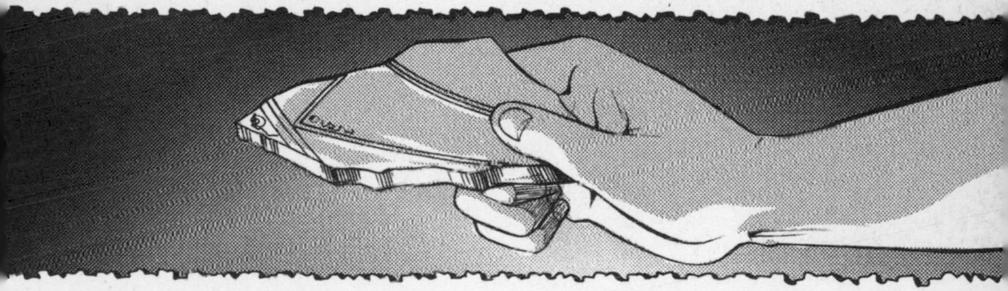

Or maybe I saw it in a movie once,
late at night, while channel surfing.

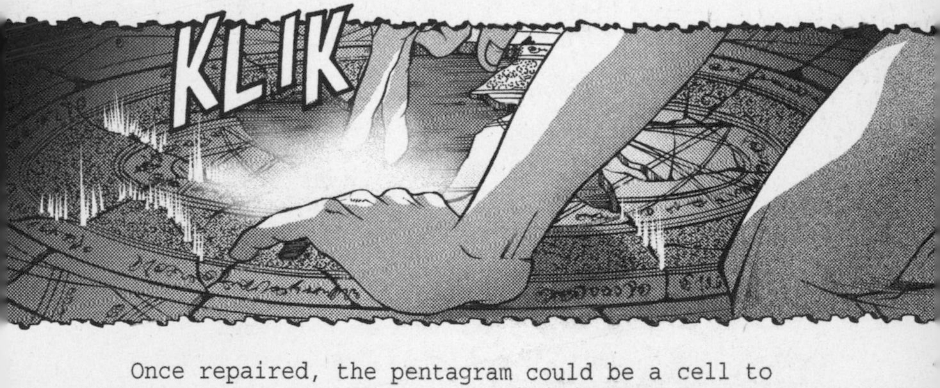
KLIK

Once repaired, the pentagram could be a cell to
imprison the demon. Maybe even a door to send it back.

Unfortunately, because of the size of the pentagram and the location of the damage...

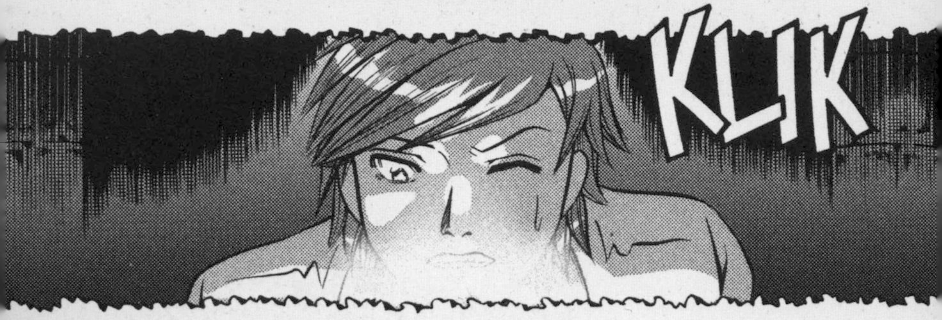
KLIK

This could only be done from the **inside**.

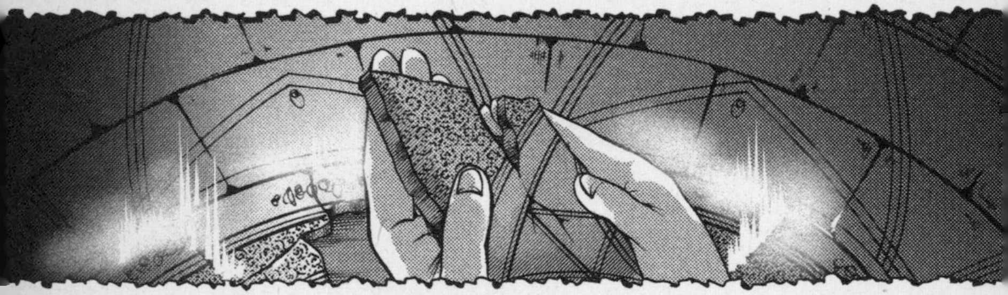

I thought of **Stormy**. Of our past, and the promised future offered by the cheap carnival machine...

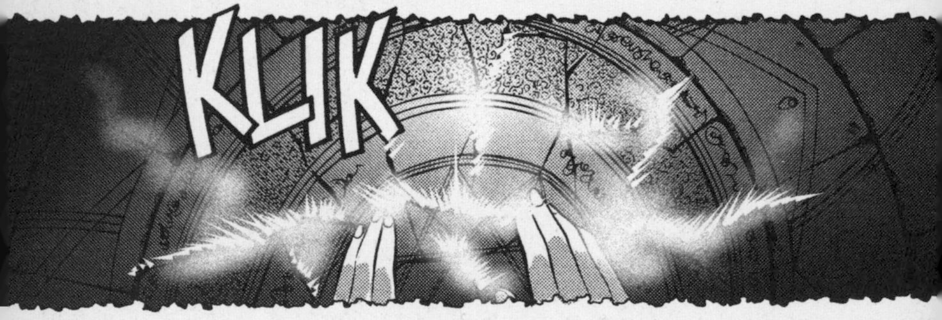
KLIK

...and I did what I **must**.

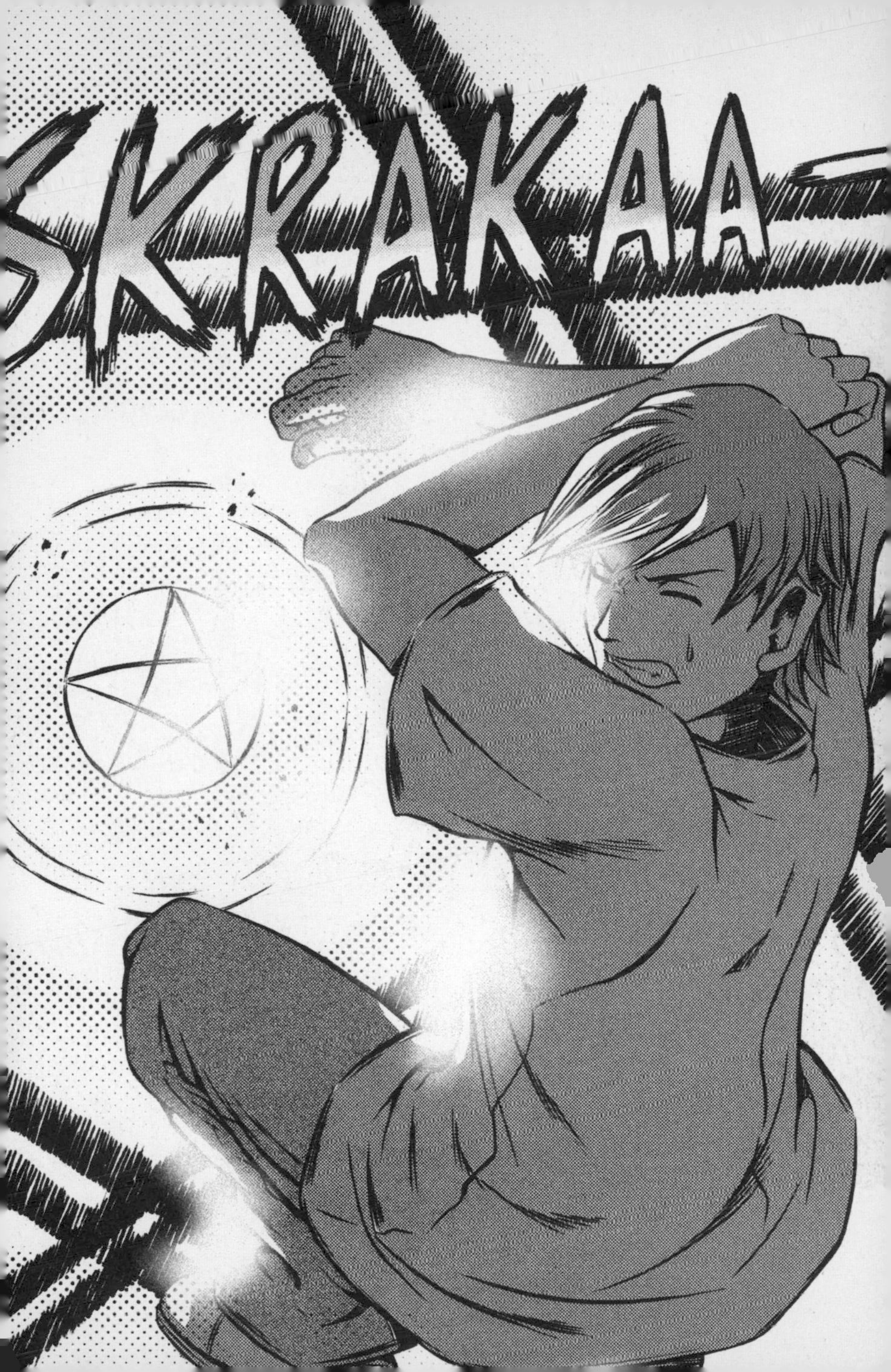
SKRAKAA

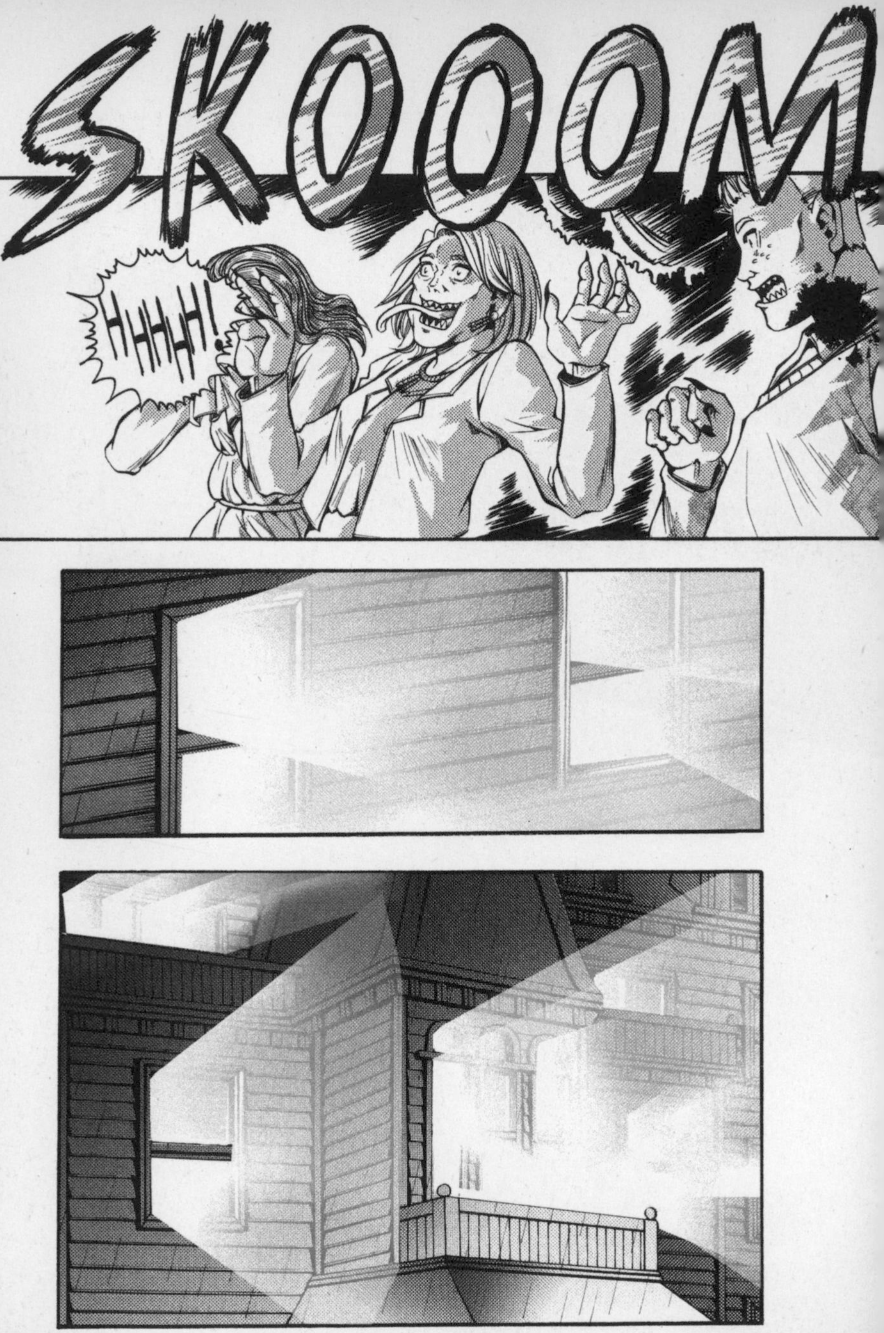

SKOOOM
HHHHH!

SKA-THOOM

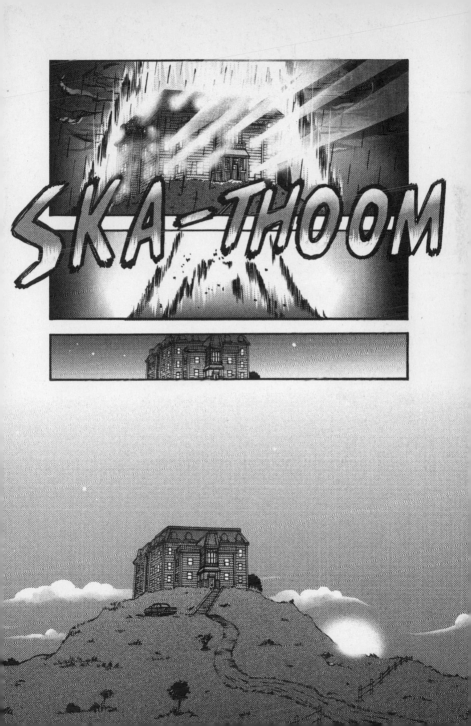

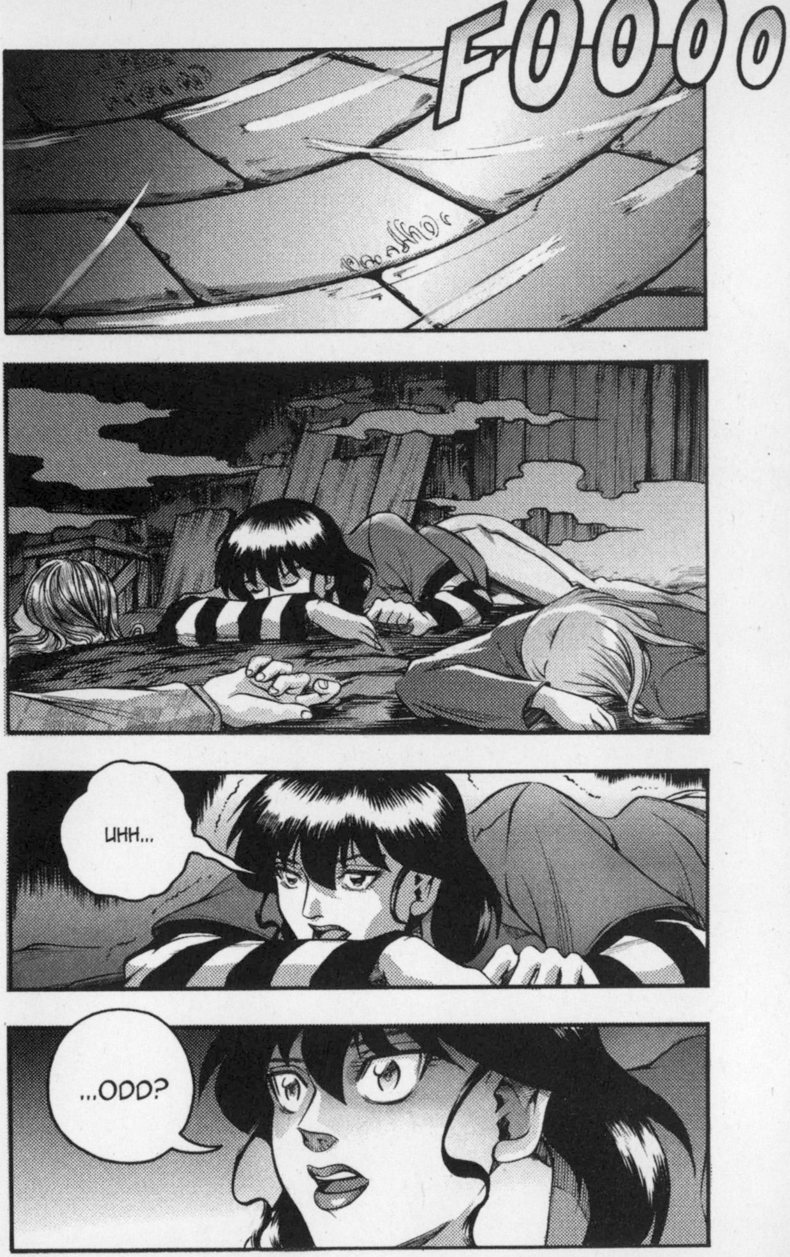
FOOOO
UHH...
...ODD?

Chapter 13

I was **nowhere.**

Surrounded by
nothing.

...But I **wasn't** dead.

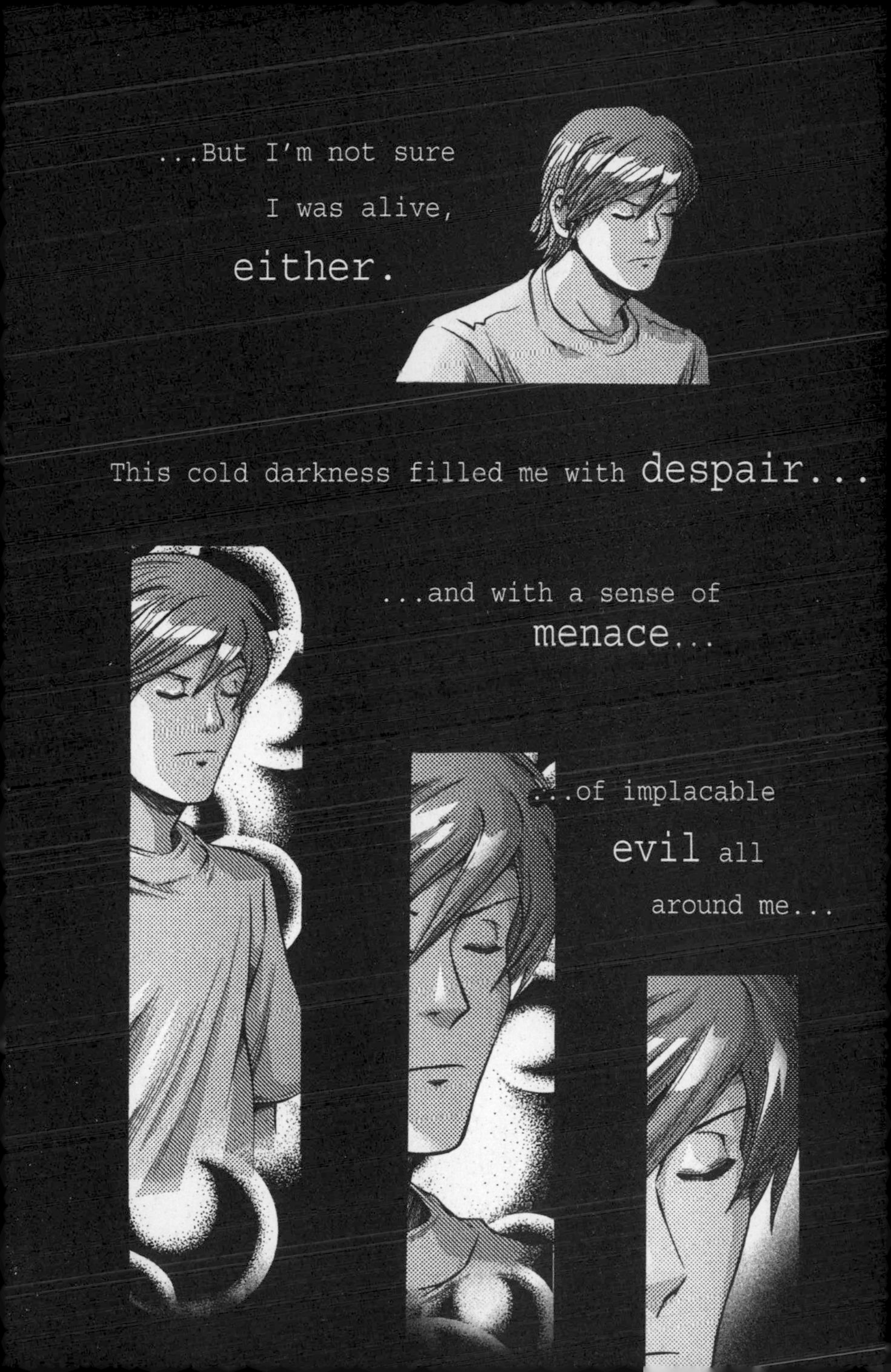
...But I'm not sure
I was alive,
either.
This cold darkness filled me with despair...
...and with a sense of
menace...
...of implacable
evil all
around me...

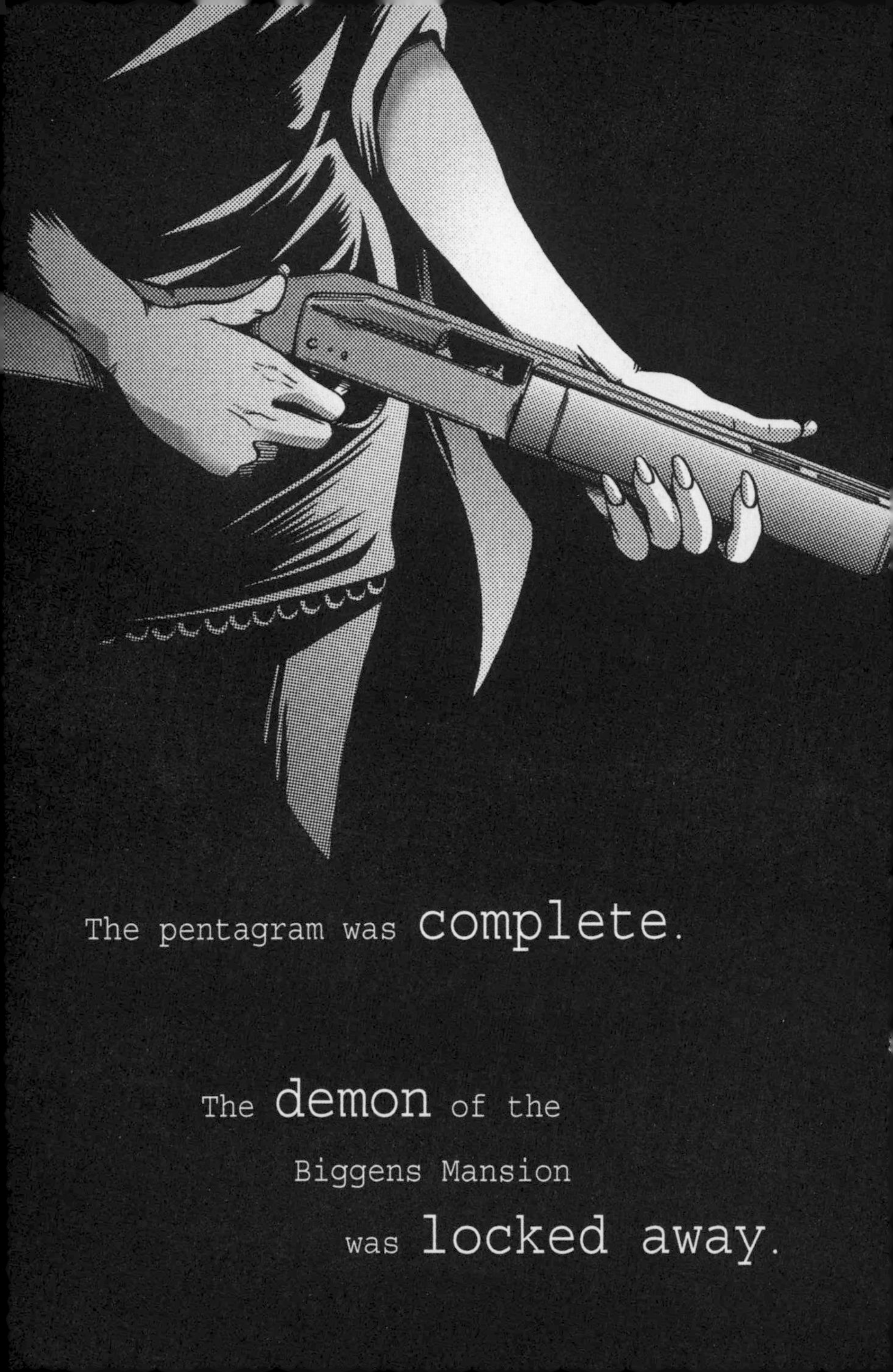
The pentagram was complete.
The demon of the
Biggens Mansion
was locked away.

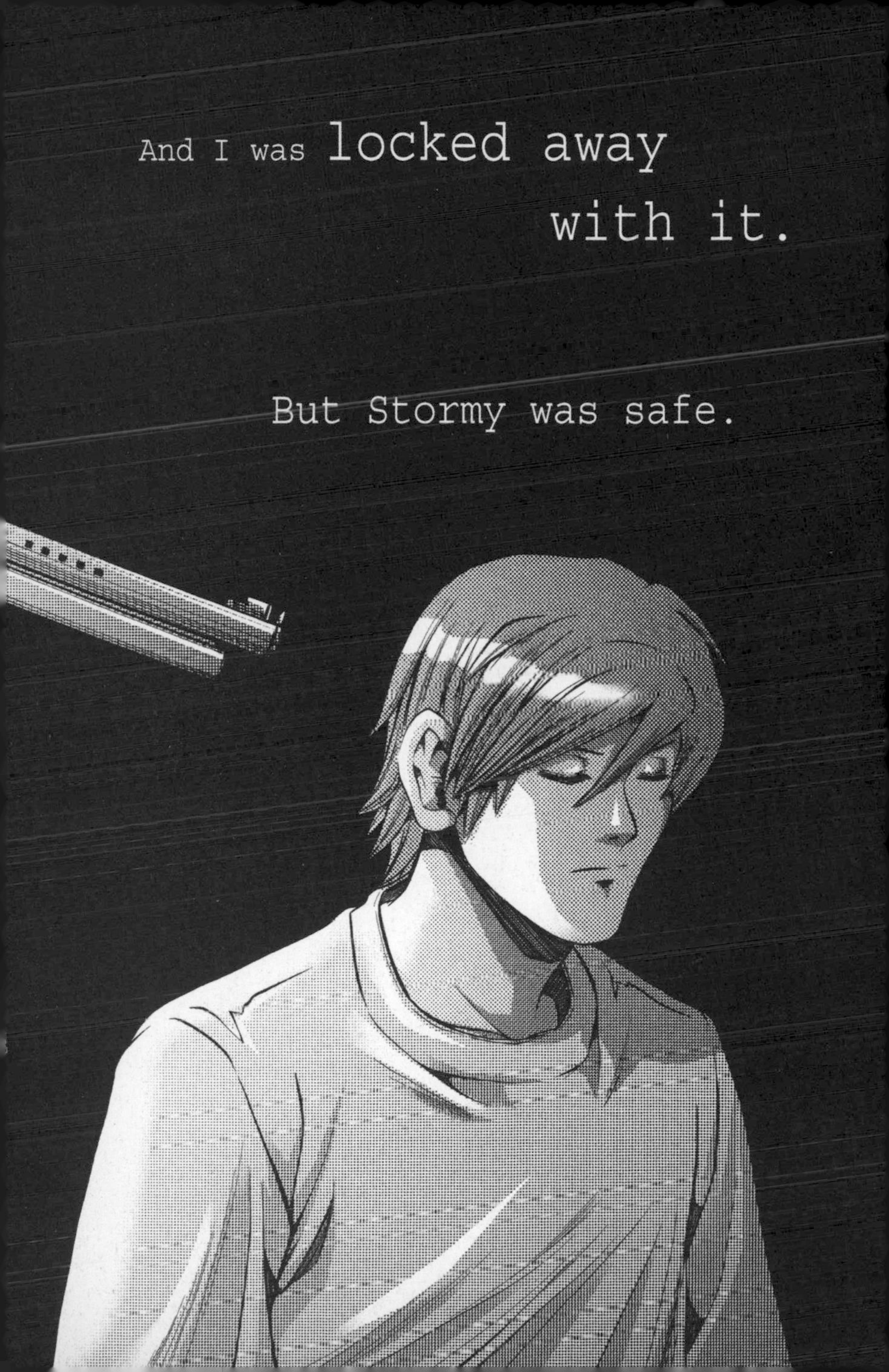
And I was locked away with it.
But Stormy was safe.

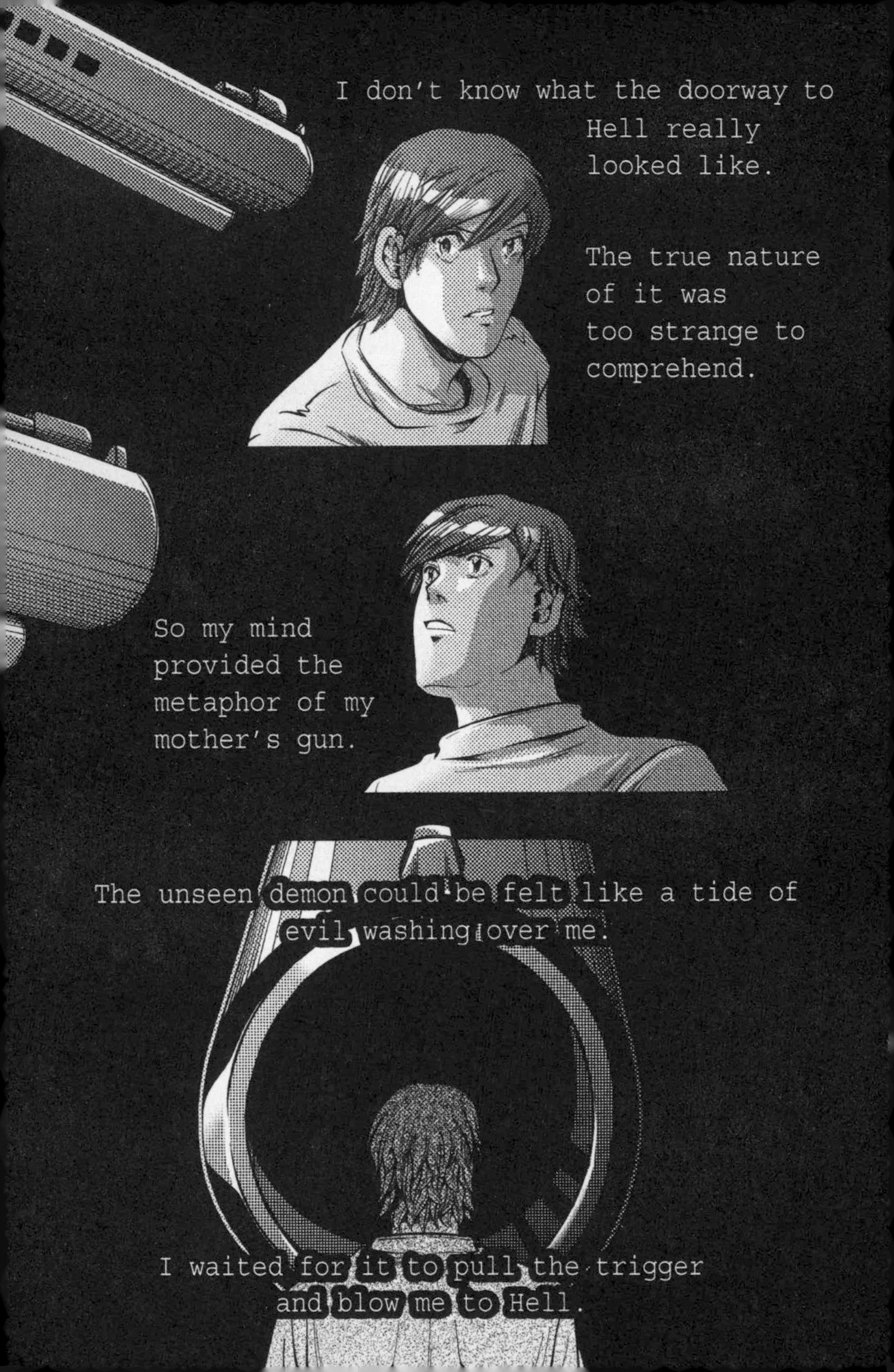
I don't know what the doorway to Hell really looked like.
The true nature of it was too strange to comprehend.
So my mind provided the metaphor of my mother's gun.
The unseen demon could be felt like a tide of evil washing over me.
I waited for it to pull the trigger and blow me to Hell.

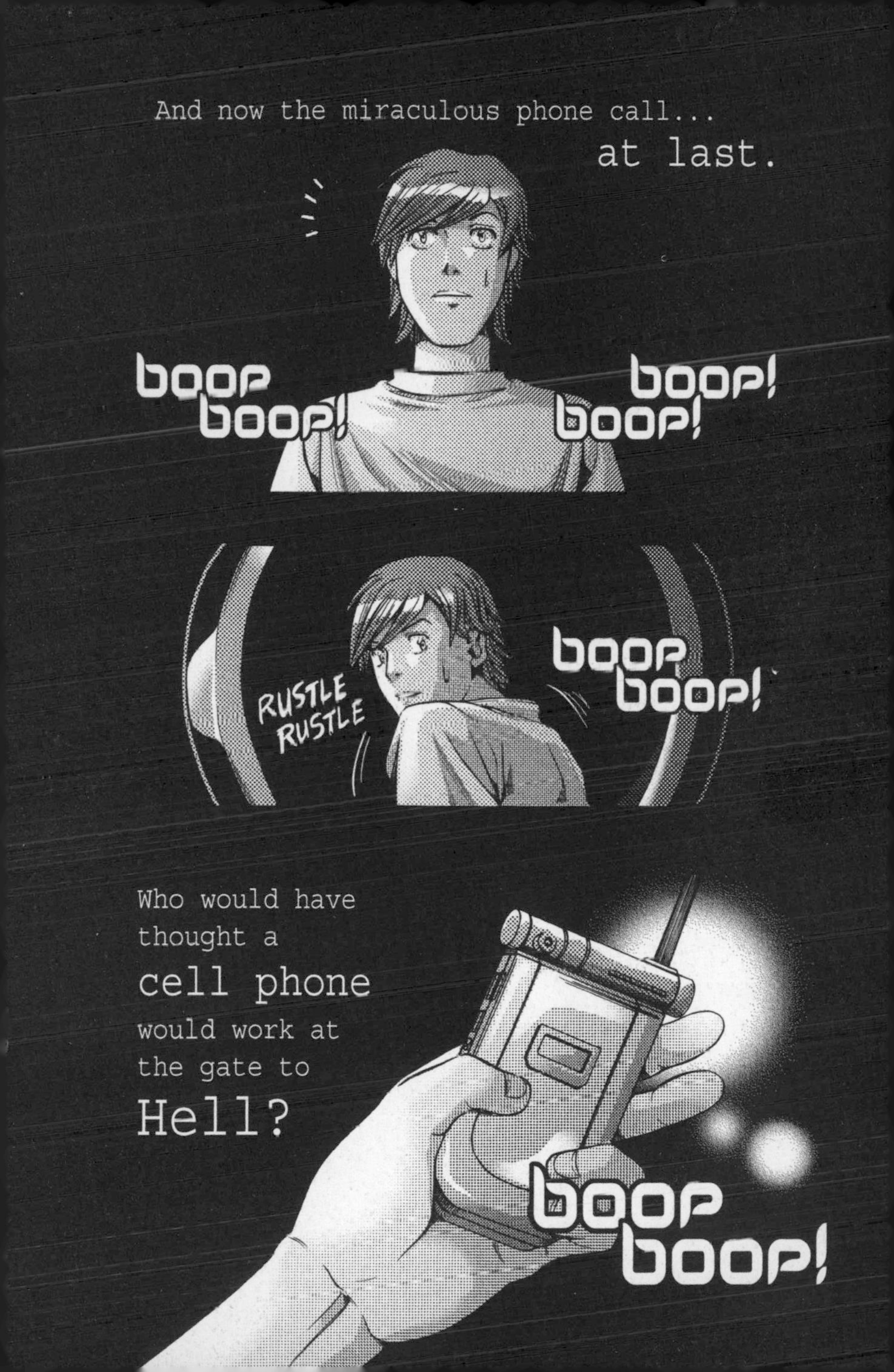
And now the miraculous phone call...
at last.
boop boop!
boop! boop!
RUSTLE RUSTLE
boop boop!
Who would have thought a cell phone would work at the gate to Hell?
boop boop!

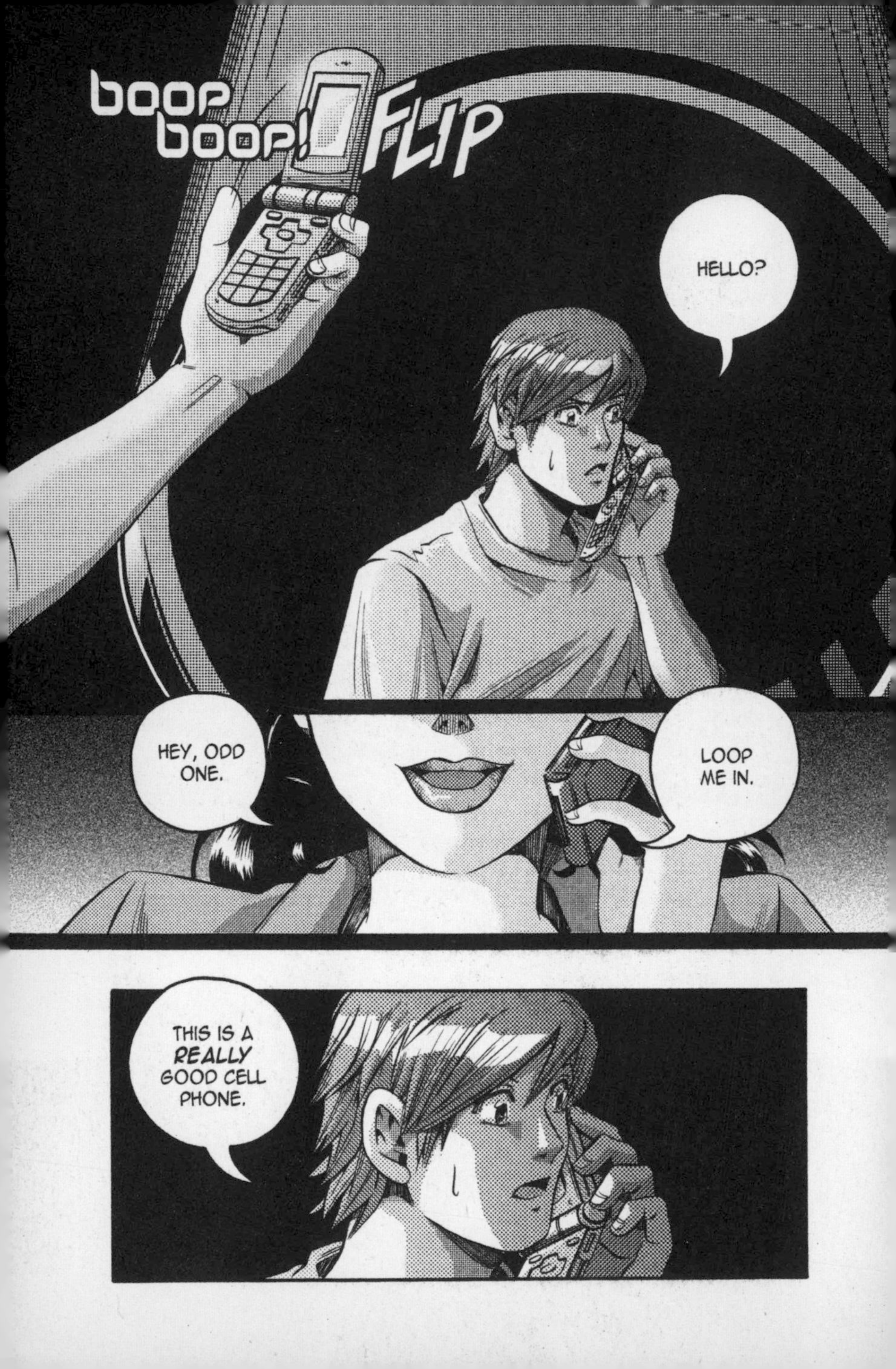
boop boop!
FLIP
HELLO?
HEY, ODD ONE.
LOOP ME IN.
THIS IS A REALLY GOOD CELL PHONE.

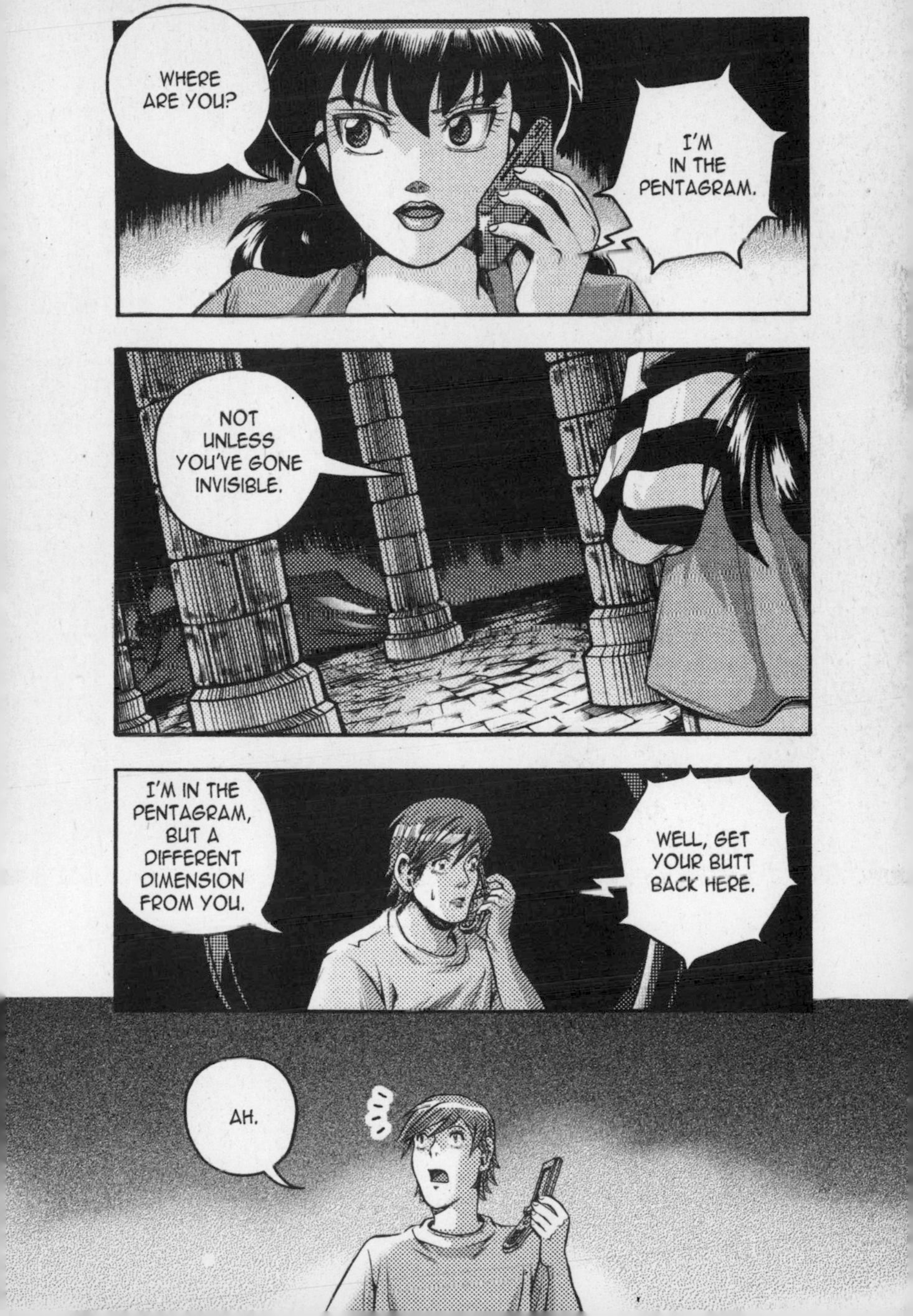
WHERE ARE YOU?
I'M IN THE PENTAGRAM.
NOT UNLESS YOU'VE GONE INVISIBLE.
I'M IN THE PENTAGRAM, BUT A DIFFERENT DIMENSION FROM YOU.
WELL, GET YOUR BUTT BACK HERE.
AH.

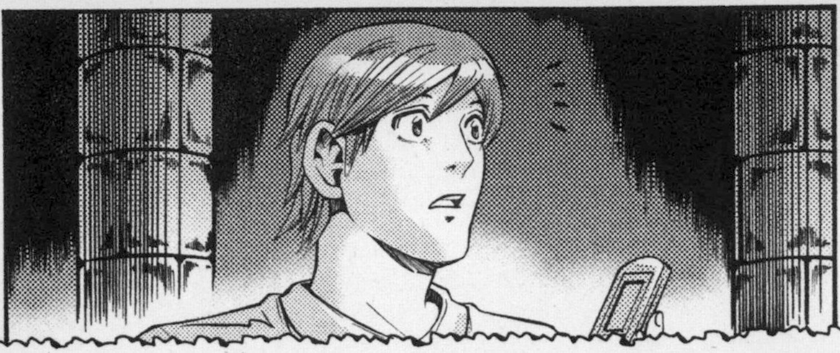

Stormy had called me back.

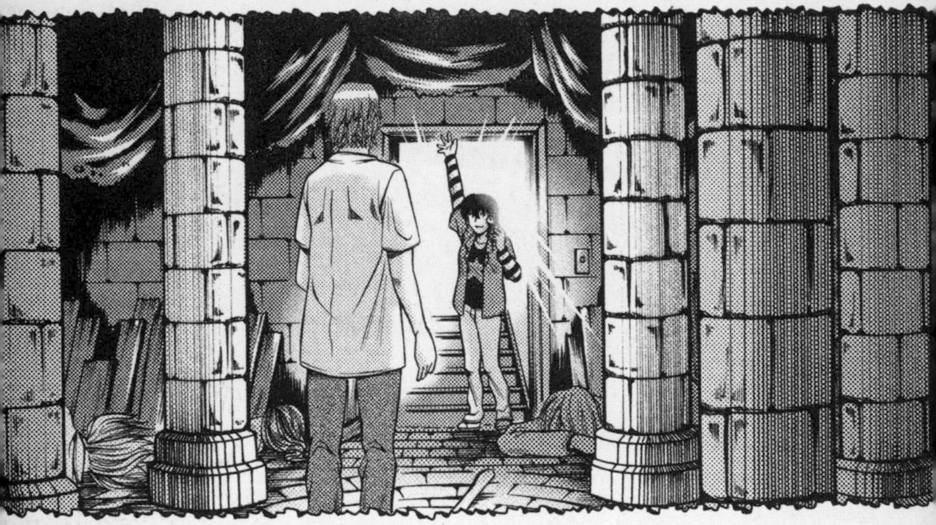

She was my lifeline, reaching through multiple planes of existence with nothing more than a cell phone. It's just further evidence of the depth of our connection.

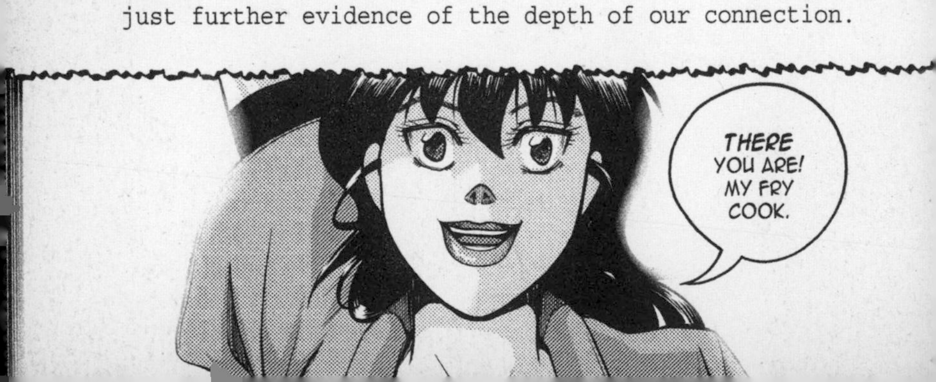
THERE YOU ARE! MY FRY COOK.

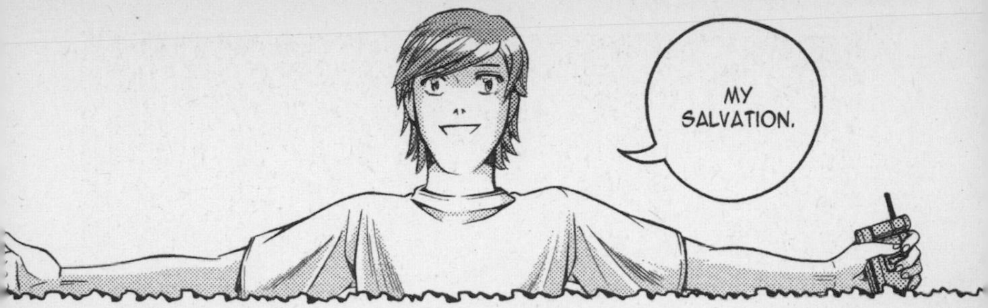
MY SALVATION.

Neither Nedra nor the Sissies were possessed anymore. Everyone had returned to normal—well, as normal as they had ever been.

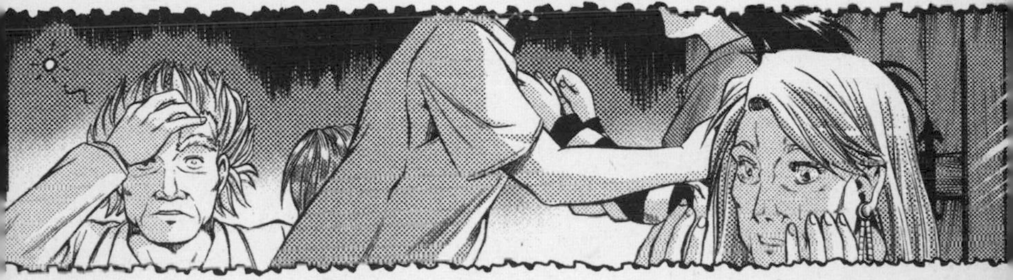

The architecture of the house made sense again.

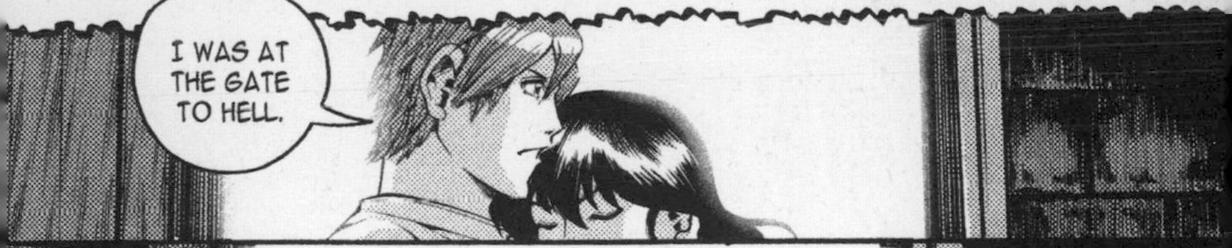
I WAS AT THE GATE TO HELL.

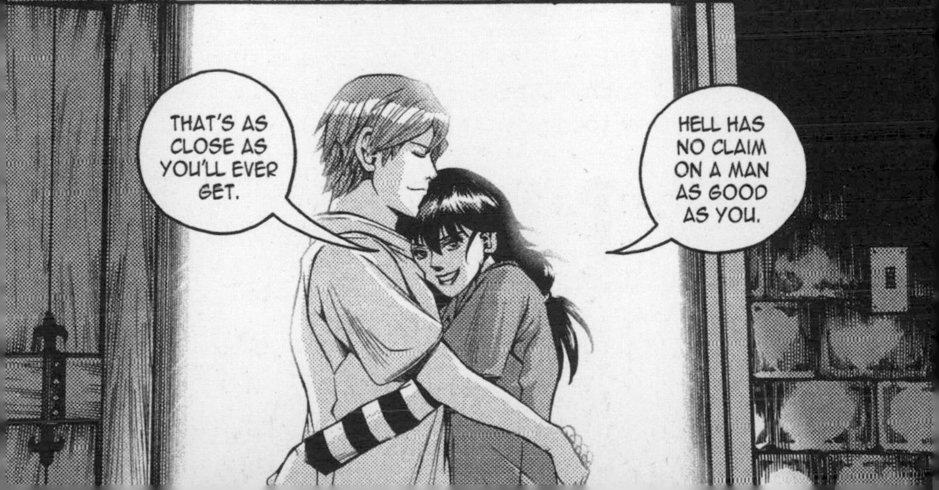
THAT'S AS CLOSE AS YOU'LL EVER GET.
HELL HAS NO CLAIM ON A MAN AS GOOD AS YOU.

Chapter 14

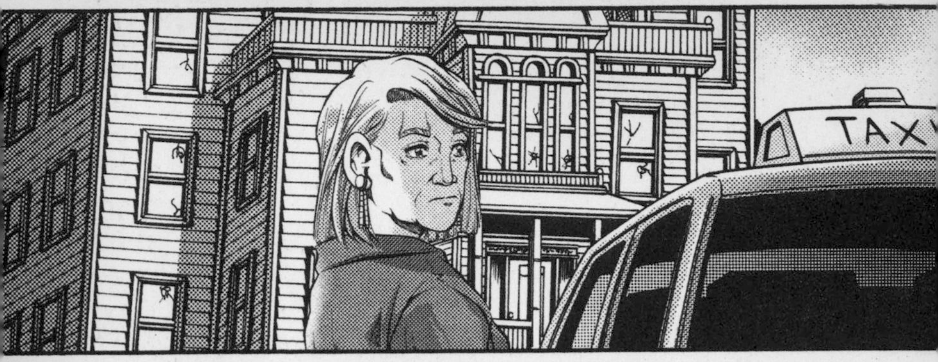
TAX

Nedra decided to quit retirement and make more movies.

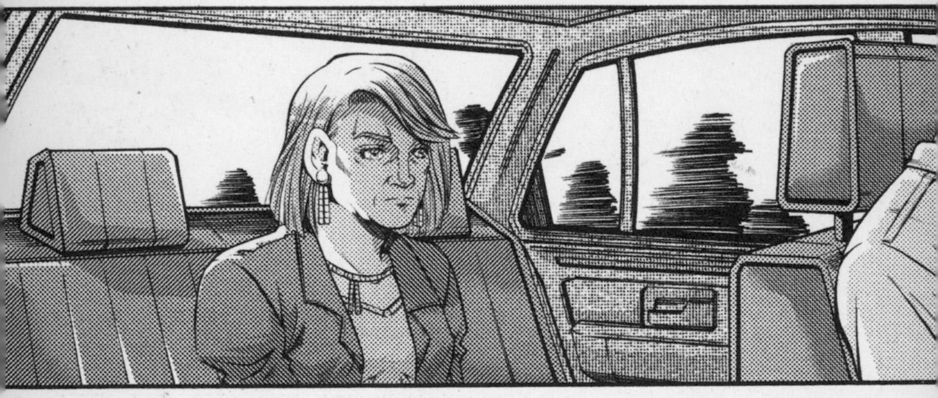

She said all the monsters here scared her.
She knew how to deal with the monsters in Hollywood.

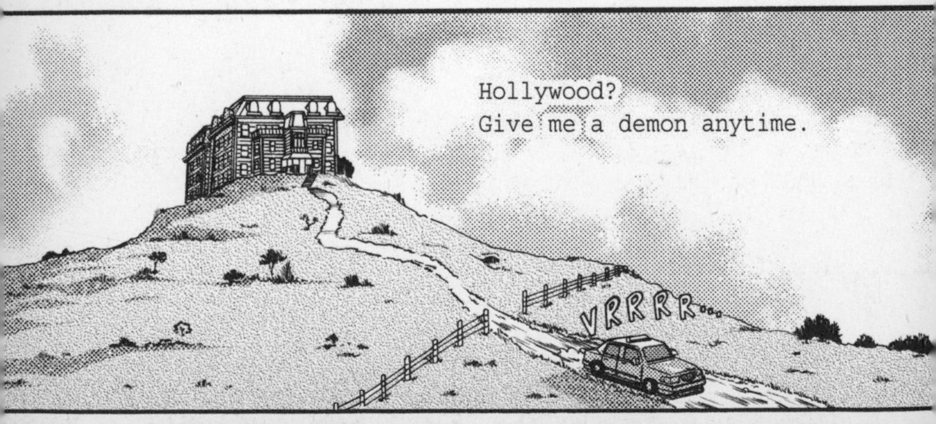
Hollywood?
Give me a demon anytime.
VRRRR...

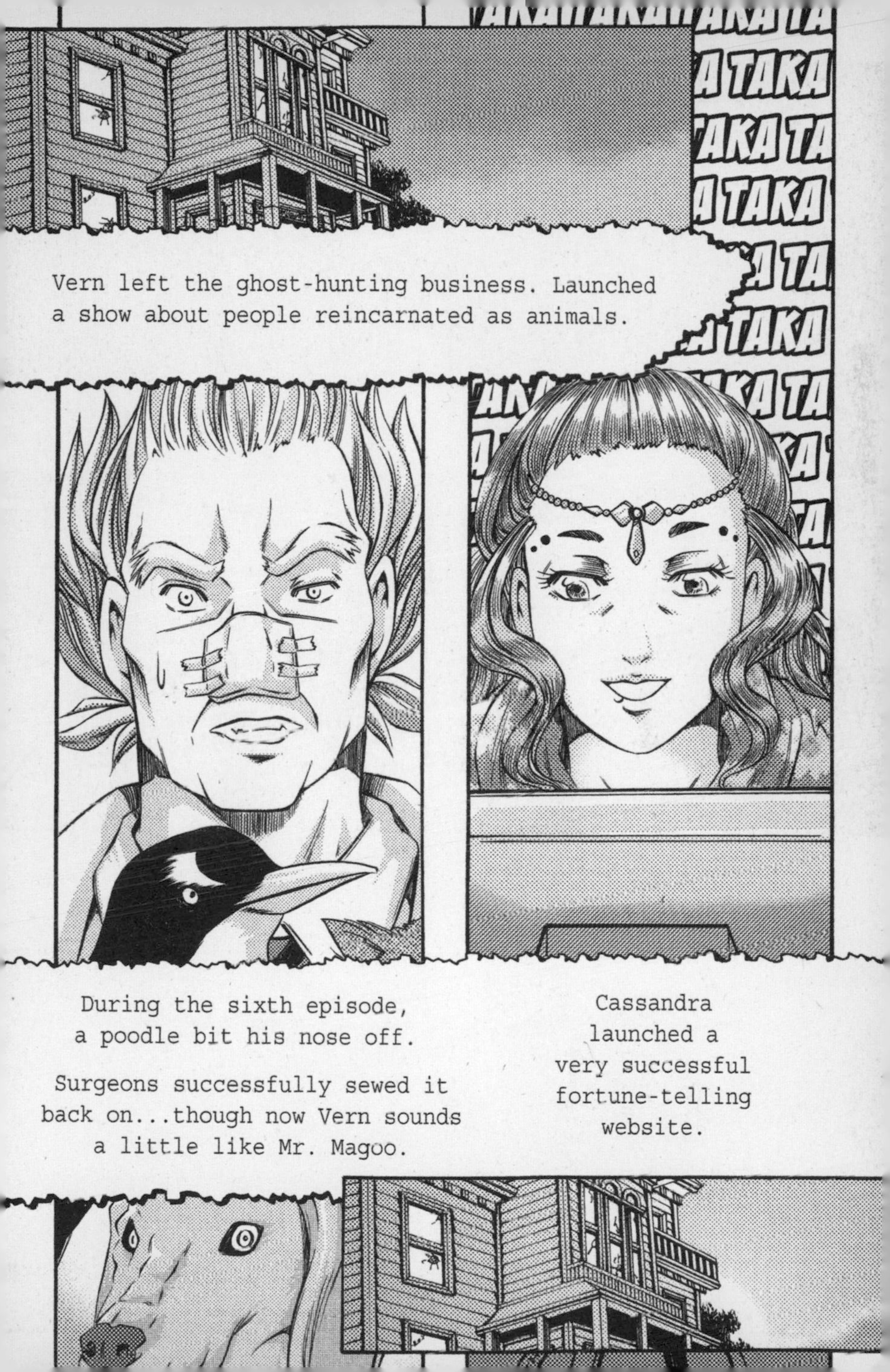
TAKA TAKA TAKA TAKA TAKA TAKA
Vern left the ghost-hunting business. Launched a show about people reincarnated as animals.
During the sixth episode, a poodle bit his nose off.
Surgeons successfully sewed it back on...though now Vern sounds a little like Mr. Magoo.
Cassandra launched a very successful fortune-telling website.

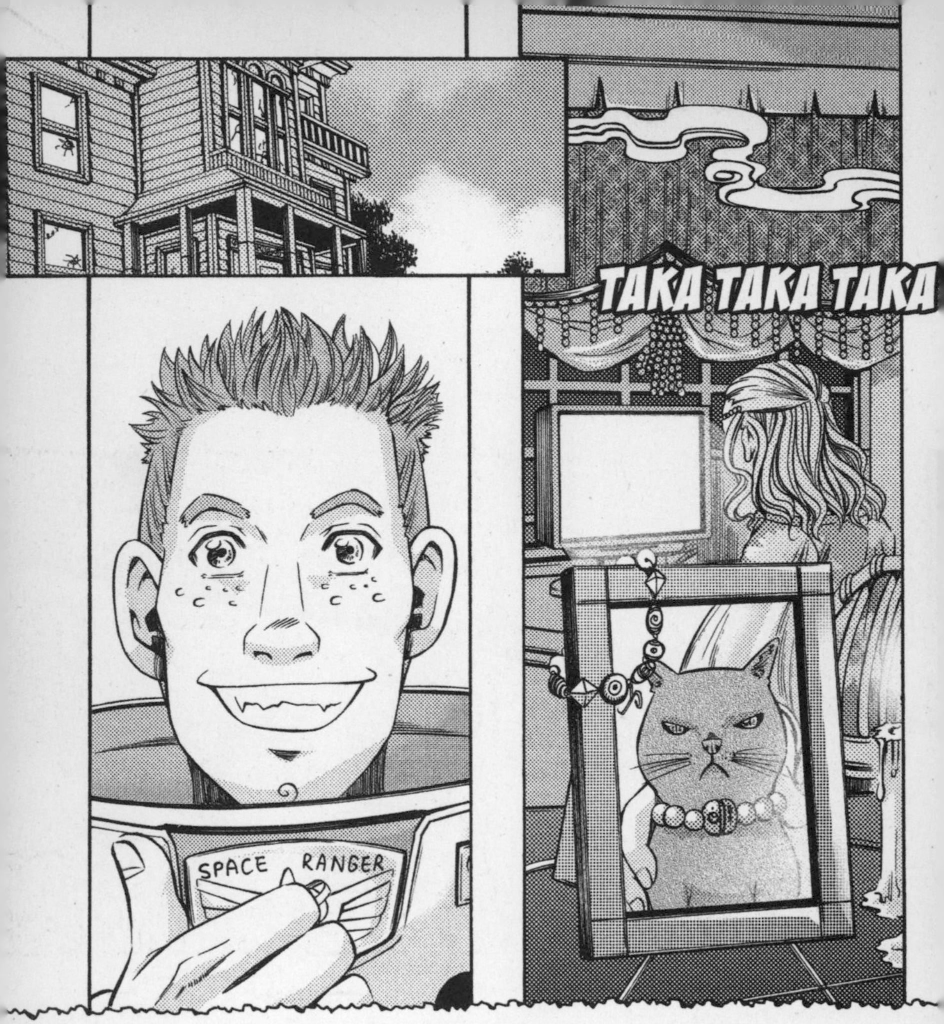
TAKA TAKA TAKA
SPACE RANGER

Kirk went back to Disneyland. They didn't need a Goofy, but he loves being Buzz Lightyear. I can respect that.

Houdini was never seen again.

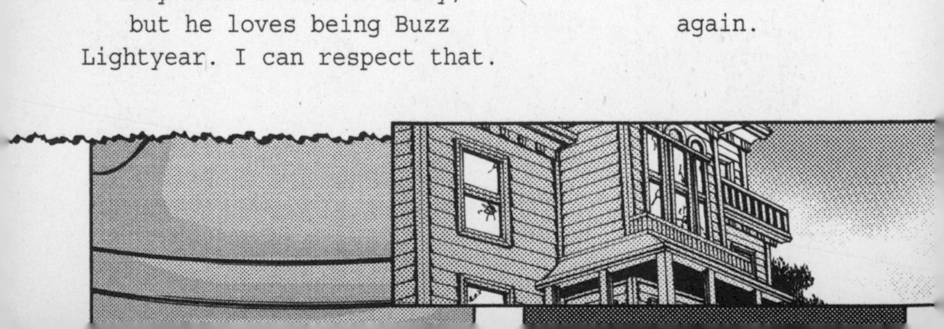

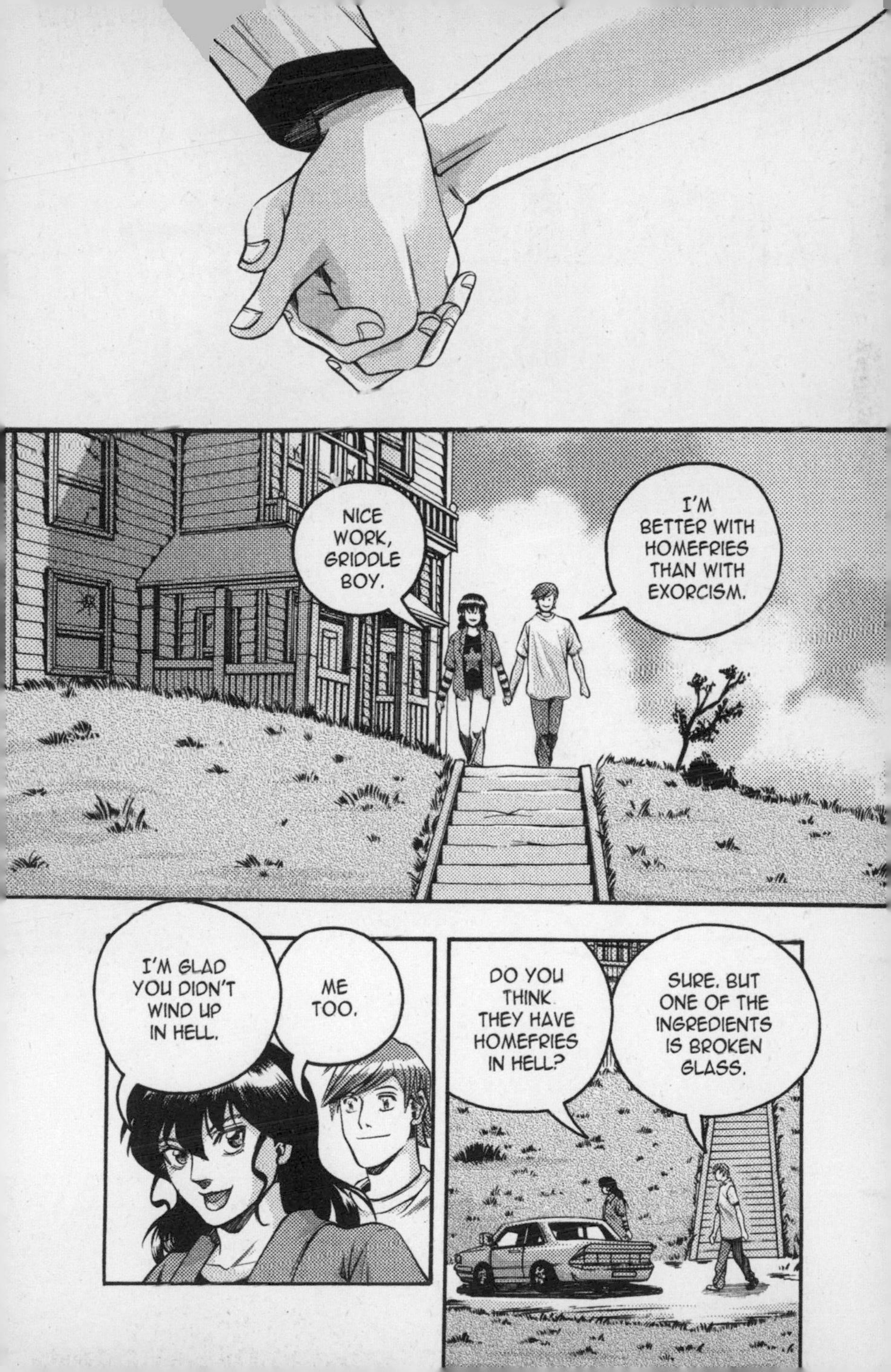
NICE WORK, GRIDDLE BOY.
I'M BETTER WITH HOMEFRIES THAN WITH EXORCISM.
I'M GLAD YOU DIDN'T WIND UP IN HELL.
ME TOO.
DO YOU THINK THEY HAVE HOMEFRIES IN HELL?
SURE. BUT ONE OF THE INGREDIENTS IS BROKEN GLASS.

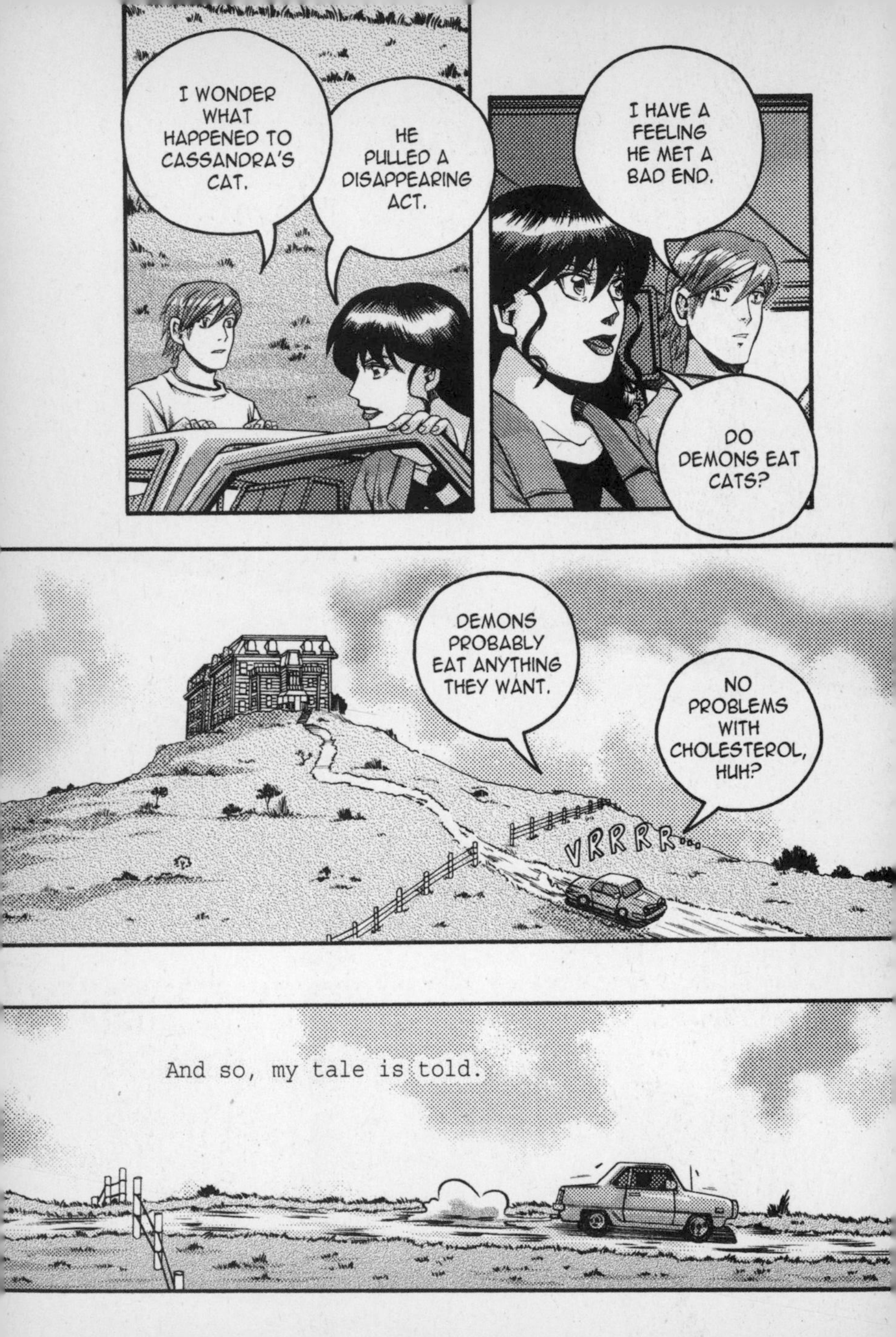
I WONDER WHAT HAPPENED TO CASSANDRA'S CAT.
HE PULLED A DISAPPEARING ACT.
I HAVE A FEELING HE MET A BAD END.
DO DEMONS EAT CATS?
DEMONS PROBABLY EAT ANYTHING THEY WANT.
NO PROBLEMS WITH CHOLESTEROL, HUH?
VRRRR...
And so, my tale is told.

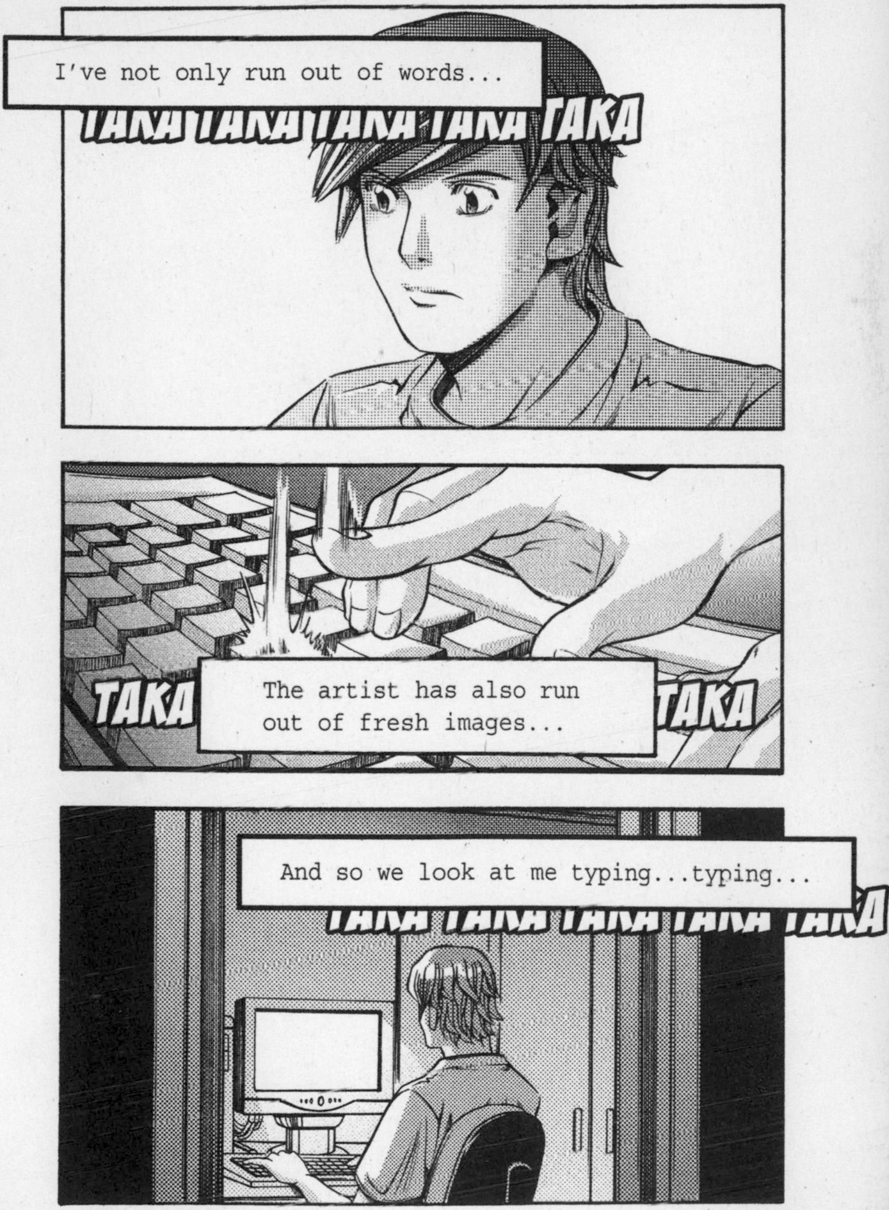

I've not only run out of words...
TAKA
TAKA
The artist has also run out of fresh images...
And so we look at me typing...typing...

This latest
walk on the Odd side
has come to an end.

SLAM

The mystery
of the
haunted mansion
is solved.

And once more,
all was right with the world.

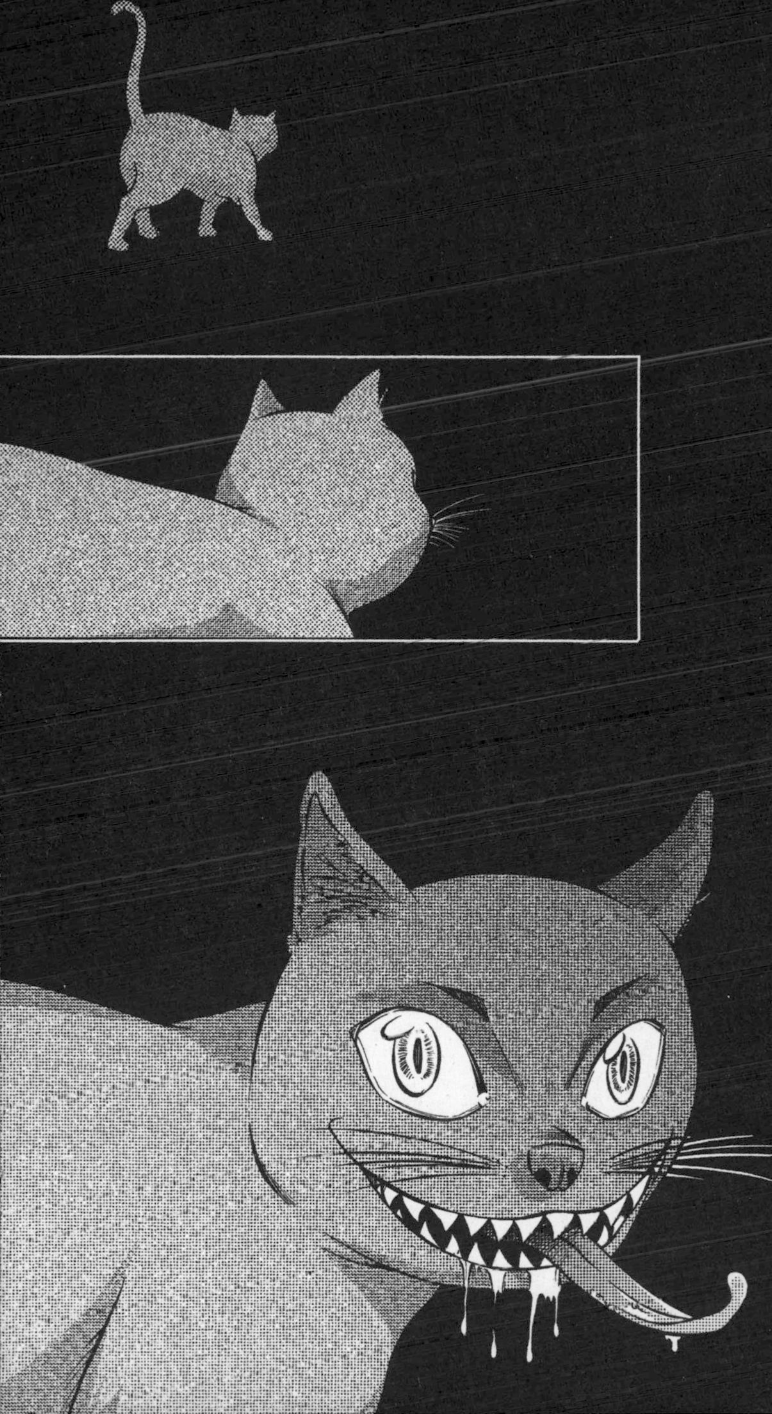

ABOUT THE CREATORS

DEAN KOONTZ is the author of many #1 *New York Times* bestsellers. He lives with his wife, Gerda, in Southern California.

QUEENIE CHAN was born in Hong Kong and emigrated to Australia when she was six years old. She is the creator of the mystery-horror graphic novel series *The Dreaming* and has illustrated three graphic novels based on Dean Koontz's character Odd Thomas. She provided art for the *Boy's Book of Positive Quotations* by Steve Deger and draws a number of online comic strips on her personal website: www.queeniechan.com/

LANDRY Q. WALKER has been writing comics for twenty years, and is the co-creator of *Kid Gravity* and *Little Gloomy*—two comics that were featured prominently in *Disney Adventures Magazine*. He is best known for his 2008 reinvention of the DC Comics character *Supergirl* and is currently looking forward to seeing his comic series *The Super Scary Monster Show* adapted into animation. landrywalker.blogspot.com

ARTIST'S SKETCHBOOK

This is the third graphic novel to star Odd Thomas, following *In Odd We Trust* and *Odd Is on Our Side*. In the first book, artist Queenie Chan established the appearance of Odd and Stormy. In *House of Odd,* her challenge was to come up with the look of Hollywood producer Nedra Nolan and the members of the CISI team whose investigations would form the center of the plot. On the following pages are Dean Koontz's descriptions of each character, plus Queenie's sketches and comments as she sent them in for Dean's approval.

NEDRA NOLAN

"A successful film producer among whose hits were two films based on Ozzie's novels. She should resemble Helen Mirren."

NEDRA

NEDRA IS BASED ON
HELEN MIRREN,
WHICH I GUESS
MEANS THAT SHE'S
A DISTINGUISHED-
LOOKING,
NO-NONSENSE
OLDER LADY.

VERN

"A forty-something guy with Finsteinian hair, who talks about ghost chasing as if it's as refined a science as quantum mechanics, but it's really just idiot jargon."

VERN

ACTION-HERO SCIENTIST,
A ROLE MADE
FOR TELEVISION.
VERN IS A SQUARE-JAWED
MAN WITH AN UNFRIENDLY
MOUTH, BECAUSE HE'S
A VERY STERN, SERIOUS
FELLOW.

CASSANDRA

"A thirty-something true believer who comes with her cat, Houdini, which she sometimes holds and points like a dowsing rod to lead her to the haunting spirit." Queenie argued that Cassandra should have dark hair, saying, "Honestly, few psychic ladies are blonde. It doesn't seem to fit the image." But Dean liked this first sketch, asking only that Cassandra's "gypsy shawl" be deleted.

CASSANDRA

CASSANDRA IS A
TRUE-BELIEVER WITH
LOTS OF EYE-MAKEUP.
SHE IS A FULL-ON
MOON-WORSHIPPING,
CRYSTAL-BALL-READING,
TAROT-CARD-WAVING
PAGAN. SHE IS
CURRENTLY LOOKING
AT THE DEAD PERSON
STANDING RIGHT
BEHIND YOU.

KIRK

"Kirk was so traumatized by seeing on DVD *The Ghost and Mr. Chicken* with Don Knotts when he was only eight years old that he sees supernatural threats everywhere and feels that he must 'stand up to Disembodied Evil wherever it is found or be doomed to live in a world ruled by capricious ghosts dedicated to a reign of terror because they can no longer eat Rocky Road ice cream and drink good beer.' "

KIRK

KIRK IS A
YOUNG MAN WITH
A GOOFY SMILE,
A LONG FACE AND
EARS THAT STICK OUT.
HE SEEMS LIKE
A NICE KID.
HE ALSO LOOKS
LIKE HE SHOULD
BE A REDHEAD.

HOUDINI

Oddly enough, Houdini was the only sketch Dean rejected, saying he too closely resembled Terrible Chester, Ozzie Boone's cat seen in *Odd Is on Our Side.*

HOUDINI

HOUDINI IS A
SMALL COMPACT
CAT, WHO IS
PERMANENTLY
SLEEPY OR
LOOKING BORED.
HIS ROLE IS MOSTLY
COMIC-RELIEF
ANYWAY (UNTIL
THE VERY END).

HOUDINI

Queenie dashed off a quick revised sketch and Dean approved it right away.

An excerpt from

ODD HOURS

by Dean Koontz

Odd's adventures continue in a series of full-length novels by Dean Koontz. The first novel is *Odd Thomas*, which was excerpted in the graphic novel *In Odd We Trust*. The second is *Forever Odd*, excerpted in the graphic novel *Odd Is on Our Side*. Here you can read an excerpt from *Odd Hours*, the fourth in the series, which begins when Odd meets a young woman he has seen in a troubling dream—and ends with Odd facing dangers he could never have imagined. The story will continue in *Odd Apocalypse*, on sale Summer 2012.

ONE

IT'S ONLY LIFE. WE ALL GET THROUGH IT.

Not all of us complete the journey in the same condition. Along the way, some lose their legs or eyes in accidents or altercations, while others skate through the years with nothing worse to worry about than an occasional bad-hair day.

I still possessed both legs and both eyes, and even my hair looked all right when I rose that Wednesday morning in late January. If I returned to bed sixteen hours later, having lost all of my hair but nothing else, I would consider the day a triumph. Even minus a few teeth, I'd call it a triumph.

When I raised the window shades in my bedroom, the cocooned sky was gray and swollen, windless and still, but pregnant with a promise of change.

Overnight, according to the radio, an airliner had crashed in Ohio. Hundreds perished. The sole survivor, a ten-month-old child, had been found upright and unscathed in a battered seat that stood in a field of scorched and twisted debris.

Throughout the morning, under the expectant sky, low sluggish waves exhausted themselves on the shore. The Pacific was gray and awash with inky shadows, as if sinuous sea beasts of fantastical form swam just below the surface.

During the night, I had twice awakened from a dream in which the tide flowed red and the sea throbbed with a terrible light.

As nightmares go, I'm sure you've had worse. The problem is that a few of my dreams have come true, and people have died.

While I prepared breakfast for my employer, the kitchen radio brought news that the jihadists who had the previous day seized an ocean liner in the Mediterranean were now beheading passengers.

Years ago I stopped watching news programs on television. I can tolerate words and the knowledge they impart, but the images undo me.

Because he was an insomniac who went to bed at dawn, Hutch ate breakfast at noon. He paid me well, and he was kind, so I cooked to his schedule without complaint.

Hutch took his meals in the dining room, where the draperies were always closed. Not one bright sliver of any windowpane remained exposed.

He often enjoyed a film while he ate, lingering over coffee until the credits rolled. That day, rather than cable news, he watched Carole Lombard and John Barrymore in *Twentieth Century*.

Eighty-eight years old, born in the era of silent films, when Lillian Gish and Rudolph Valentino were stars, and having later been a successful actor, Hutch thought less in words than in images, and he dwelt in fantasy.

Beside his plate stood a bottle of Purell sanitizing gel. He lavished it on his hands not only before and after eating, but also at least twice during a meal.

Like most Americans in the first decade of the new century, Hutch feared everything except what he ought to fear.

When TV-news programs ran out of stories about drunk, drug-addled, murderous, and otherwise crazed celebrities—which happened perhaps twice a year—they sometimes filled the brief gap with a sensationalistic piece on that rare flesh-eating bacteria.

Consequently, Hutch feared contracting the ravenous germ. From time to time, like a dour character in a tale by Poe, he huddled in his lamplit study, brooding about his fate, about the fragility of his flesh, about the insatiable appetite of his microscopic foe.

He especially dreaded that his nose might be eaten away.

Long ago, his face had been famous. Although time had disguised him, he still took pride in his appearance.

I had seen a few of Lawrence Hutchison's movies from the 1940s and '50s. I liked them. He'd been a commanding presence on screen.

Because he had not appeared on camera for five decades, Hutch was less known for his acting than for his children's books about a swashbuckling rabbit named Nibbles. Unlike his creator, Nibbles was fearless.

Film money, book royalties, and a habit of regarding investment opportunities with paranoid suspicion had left Hutch financially secure in his old age. Nevertheless, he worried that an explosive rise in the price of oil or a total collapse in the price of oil would lead to a worldwide financial crisis that would leave him penniless.

His house faced the boardwalk, the beach, the ocean. Surf broke less than a minute's stroll from his front door.

Over the years, he had come to fear the sea. He could not bear to sleep on the west side of the house, where he might hear the waves crawling along the shore.

Therefore, I was quartered in the ocean-facing master suite

at the front of the house. He slept in a guest room at the back.

Within a day of arriving in Magic Beach, more than a month previous to the red-tide dream, I had taken a job as Hutch's cook, doubling as his chauffeur on those infrequent occasions when he wanted to go out.

My experience at the Pico Mundo Grill served me well. If you can make hash browns that wring a flood from salivary glands, fry bacon to the crispness of a cracker without parching it, and make pancakes as rich as pudding yet so fluffy they seem to be at risk of floating off the plate, you will always find work.

At four-thirty that afternoon in late January, when I stepped into the parlor with Boo, my dog, Hutch was in his favorite armchair, scowling at the television, which he had muted.

"Bad news, sir?"

His deep and rounded voice rolled an ominous note into every syllable: "Mars is warming."

"We don't live on Mars."

"It's warming at the same rate as the earth."

"Were you planning to move to Mars to escape global warming?"

He indicated the silenced anchorman on the TV. "This means the sun is the cause of both, and nothing can be done about it. Nothing."

"Well, sir, there's always Jupiter or whatever planet lies beyond Mars."

He fixed me with that luminous gray-eyed stare that conveyed implacable determination when he had played crusading district attorneys and courageous military officers.

"Sometimes, young man, I think you may be from beyond Mars."

"Nowhere more exotic than Pico Mundo, California. If you

won't need me for a while, sir, I thought I'd go out for a walk."

Hutch rose to his feet. He was tall and lean. He kept his chin lifted but craned his head forward as does a man squinting to sharpen his vision, which might have been a habit that he developed in the years before he had his cataracts removed.

"Go out?" He frowned as he approached. "Dressed like that?"

I was wearing sneakers, jeans, and a sweatshirt.

He was not troubled by arthritis and remained graceful for his age. Yet he moved with precision and caution, as though expecting to fracture something.

Not for the first time, he reminded me of a great blue heron stalking tide pools.

"You should put on a jacket. You'll get pneumonia."

"It's not that chilly today," I assured him.

"You young people think you're invulnerable."

"Not this young person, sir. I've got every reason to be astonished that I'm not already permanently horizontal."

Indicating the words MYSTERY TRAIN on my sweatshirt, he asked, "What's that supposed to mean?"

"I don't know. I found it in a thrift shop."

"I have never been in a thrift shop."

"You haven't missed much."

"Do only very poor people shop there or is the criteria merely thriftiness?"

"They welcome all economic classes, sir."

"Then I should go one day soon. Make an adventure of it."

"You won't find a genie in a bottle," I said, referring to his film *The Antique Shop.*

"No doubt you're too modern to believe in genies and such. How do you get through life when you've nothing to believe in?"

"Oh, I have beliefs."

Lawrence Hutchison was less interested in my beliefs than in the sound of his well-trained voice. "I keep an open mind regarding all things supernatural."

I found his self-absorption endearing. Besides, if he were to have been curious about me, I would have had a more difficult time keeping all my secrets.

He said, "My friend Adrian White was married to a fortune-teller who called herself Portentia."

I traded anecdotes with him: "This girl I used to know, Stormy Llewellyn—at the carnival, we got a card from a fortune-telling machine called Gypsy Mummy."

"Portentia used a crystal ball and prattled a lot of mumbo jumbo, but she was the real thing. Adrian adored her."

"The card said Stormy and I would be together forever. But it didn't turn out that way."

"Portentia could predict the day and very hour of a person's death."

"Did she predict yours, sir?"

"Not mine. But she predicted Adrian's. And two days later, at the hour Portentia had foretold, she shot him."

"Incredible."

"But true, I assure you." He glanced toward a window that did not face the sea and that, therefore, was not covered by draperies. "Does it feel like tsunami weather to you, son?"

"I don't think tsunamis have anything to do with the weather."

"I feel it. Keep one eye on the ocean during your walk."

Like a stork, he stilted out of the parlor and along the hallway toward the kitchen at the back of the house.

I left by the front door, through which Boo had already passed. The dog waited for me in the fenced yard.

An arched trellis framed the gate. Through white lattice twined purple bougainvillea that produced a few flowers even in winter.

I closed the gate behind me, and Boo passed through it as for a moment I stood drawing deep breaths of the crisp salted air.

After spending a few months in a guest room at St. Bartholomew's Abbey, high in the Sierra, trying to come to terms with my strange life and my losses, I had expected to return home to Pico Mundo for Christmas. Instead, I had been called here, to what purpose I didn't know at the time and still had not deduced.

My gift—or curse—involves more than a rare prophetic dream. For one thing, irresistible intuition sometimes takes me places to which I would not go by choice. And then I wait to find out why.

Boo and I headed north. Over three miles long, the board-walk serving Magic Beach was not made of wood but of concrete. The town called it a boardwalk anyway.

Words are plastic these days. Small loans made to desperate people at exorbitant interest rates are called payday advances. A cheesy hotel paired with a seedy casino is called a resort. Any assemblage of frenetic images, bad music, and incoherent plot is called a major motion picture.

Boo and I followed the concrete boardwalk. He was a German shepherd mix, entirely white. The moon traveling horizon to horizon moved no more quietly than did Boo.

Only I was aware of him, because he was a ghost dog.

I see the spirits of dead people who are reluctant to move on from this world. In my experience, however, animals are always eager to proceed to what comes next. Boo was unique.

His failure to depart was a mystery. The dead don't talk, and neither do dogs, so my canine companion obeyed two vows of silence.

Perhaps he remained in this world because he knew I would need him in some crisis. He might not have to linger much longer, as I frequently found myself up to my neck in trouble.

On our right, after four blocks of beachfront houses came shops, restaurants, and the three-story Magic Beach Hotel with its white walls and striped green awnings.

To our left, the beach relented to a park. In the sunless late afternoon, palm trees cast no shadows on the greensward.

The lowering sky and the cool air had discouraged beach-goers. No one sat on the park benches.

Nevertheless, intuition told me that she would be here, not in the park but sitting far out above the sea. She had been in my red dream.

Except for the lapping of the lazy surf, the day was silent. Cascades of palm fronds waited for a breeze to set them whispering.

Broad stairs led up to the pier. By virtue of being a ghost, Boo made no sound on the weathered planks, and as a ghost in the making, I was silent in my sneakers.

At the end of the pier, the deck widened into an observation platform. Coin-operated telescopes offered views of ships in transit, the coastline, and the marina in the harbor two miles north.

The Lady of the Bell sat on the last bench, facing the horizon, where the moth-case sky met the sullen sea in seamless fusion.

Leaning on the railing, I pretended to meditate on the time-less march of waves. In my peripheral vision, I saw that she seemed to be unaware of my arrival, which allowed me to study her profile.

She was neither beautiful nor ugly, but neither was she plain. Her features were unremarkable, her skin clear but too pale, yet she had a compelling presence.

My interest in her was not romantic. An air of mystery veiled her, and I suspected that her secrets were extraordinary. Curiosity drew me to her, as did a feeling that she might need a friend.

Although she had appeared in my dream of a red tide, perhaps it would not prove to be prophetic. She might not die.

I had seen her here on several occasions. We had exchanged a few words in passing, mostly comments about the weather.

Because she talked, I knew she wasn't dead. Sometimes I realize an apparition is a ghost only when it fades or walks through a wall.

On other occasions, when they have been murdered and want me to bring their killers to justice, they may choose to materialize with their wounds revealed. Confronted by a man whose face has imploded from the impact of a bullet or by a woman carrying her severed head, I am as quick as the next guy to realize I'm in the company of a spook.

In the recent dream, I had been standing on a beach, snakes of apocalyptic light squirming across the sand. The sea had throbbed as some bright leviathan rose out of the deep, and the heavens had been choked with clouds as red and orange as flames.

In the west, the Lady of the Bell, suspended in the air above the sea, had floated toward me, arms folded across her breast, her eyes closed. As she drew near, her eyes opened, and I glimpsed in them a reflection of what lay behind me.

I had twice recoiled from the vision that I beheld in her eyes, and I had both times awakened with no memory of it.

Now I walked away from the pier railing, and sat beside her.

The bench accommodated four, and we occupied opposite ends.

Boo curled up on the deck and rested his chin on my shoes. I could feel the weight of his head on my feet.

When I touch a spirit, whether dog or human, it feels solid to me, and warm. No chill or scent of death clings to it.

Still gazing out to sea, the Lady of the Bell said nothing.

She wore white athletic shoes, dark-gray pants, and a baggy pink sweater with sleeves so long her hands were hidden in them.

Because she was petite, her condition was more apparent than it would have been with a larger woman. A roomy sweater couldn't conceal that she was about seven months pregnant.

I had never seen her with a companion.

From her neck hung the pendant for which I had named her. On a silver chain hung a polished silver bell the size of a thimble. In the sunless day, this simple jewelry was the only shiny object.

She might have been eighteen, three years younger than I was. Her slightness made her seem more like a girl than like a woman.

Nevertheless, I had not considered calling her the Girl of the Bell. Her self-possession and calm demeanor required *lady*.

"Have you ever heard such stillness?" I asked.

"There's a storm coming." Her voice floated the words as softly as a breath of summer sets dandelion seeds adrift. "The pressure in advance weighs down the wind and flattens the waves."

"Are you a meteorologist?"

Her smile was lovely, free of judgment and artifice. "I'm just a girl who thinks too much."

"My name's Odd Thomas."

"Yes," she said.

Prepared to explain the dysfunctional nature of my family that had resulted in my name, as I had done countless times before, I was surprised and disappointed that she had none of the usual questions.

"You knew my name?" I asked.

"As you know mine."

"But I don't."

"I'm Annamaria," she said. "One word. It would have come to you."

Confused, I said, "We've spoken before, but I'm sure we've never exchanged names."

She only smiled and shook her head.

A white flare arced across the dismal sky: a gull fleeing to land as the afternoon faded.

Annamaria pulled back the long sleeves of her sweater, revealing her graceful hands. In the right she held a translucent green stone the size of a fat grape.

"Is that a jewel?" I asked.

"Sea glass. A fragment of a bottle that washed around the world and back, until it has no sharp edges. I found it on the beach." She turned it between her slender fingers. "What do you think it means?"

"Does it need to mean anything?"

"The tide washed the sand as smooth as a baby's skin, and as the water winked away, the glass seemed to open like a green eye."

The shrieking of birds shattered the stillness, and I looked up to see three agitated sea gulls sailing landward.

Their cries announced company: footfalls on the pier behind us.

Three men in their late twenties walked to the north end of

the observation platform. They stared up the coast toward the distant harbor and marina.

The two in khakis and quilted jackets appeared to be brothers. Red hair, freckles. Ears as prominent as handles on beer mugs.

The redheads glanced at us. Their faces were so hard, their eyes so cold, I might have thought they were evil spirits if I hadn't heard their footsteps.

One of them favored Annamaria with a razor-slash smile. He had the dark and broken teeth of a heavy methamphetamine user.

The freckled pair made me uneasy, but the third man was the most disturbing of the group. At six four, he towered half a foot above the others, and had that muscled massiveness only steroid injections can produce.

Unfazed by the cool air, he wore athletic shoes without socks, white shorts, and a yellow-and-blue, orchid-pattern Hawaiian shirt.

The brothers said something to him, and the giant looked at us. He might be called handsome in an early Cro-Magnon way, but his eyes seemed to be as yellow as his small chin beard.

We did not deserve the scrutiny we received from him. Annamaria was an ordinary-looking pregnant woman, and I was just a fry cook who had been fortunate enough to reach twenty-one years of age without losing a leg or an eye, or my hair.

Malevolence and paranoia cohabit in a twisted mind. Bad men trust no one because they know the treachery of which they themselves are capable.

After a long suspicious stare, the giant turned his attention once more to the northern coast and the marina, as did his cohorts, but I didn't think they were done with us.

Half an hour of daylight remained. Because of the overcast,

however, twilight seemed to be already upon us. The lamp-posts lining the pier brightened automatically, but a thin veil of fog had risen out of nowhere to aid and abet the coming dusk.

Boo's behavior confirmed my instincts. He had gotten to his feet. Hackles raised, ears flattened, he focused intently on the giant.

To Annamaria, I said, "I think we better go."

"Do you know them?"

"I've seen their kind before."

As she rose from the bench, she closed the green orb in her right fist. Both hands shrank back into the sleeves of her sweater.

I sensed strength in her, yet she also had an aura of inno-cence, an almost waiflike air of vulnerability. The three men were the kind to whom vulnerability had a scent as surely as rabbits hidden in tall grass have a smell easily detected by wolves.

Bad men wound and destroy one another, although as tar-gets they prefer those who are innocent and as pure as this world allows anyone to be. They feed on violence, but they *feast* on the despoiling of what is good.

As Annamaria and I walked off the observation deck and toward the shore, I was dismayed that no one had come onto the pier. Usually a few evening fishermen would already have arrived with rods and tackle boxes.

I glanced back and saw Boo moving closer to the three men, who were oblivious of him. The hulk with the chin beard looked over the heads of the other two, again staring at An-namaria and me.

The shore was still distant. The shrouded sun slowly sank behind a thousand fathoms of clouds, toward the drowning horizon, and rising mist damped the lamplight.

When I looked back again, the freckled pair were approaching at a brisk walk.

"Keep going," I told Annamaria. "Off the pier, among people."

She remained calm. "I'll stay with you."

"*No.* I can handle this."

Gently, I pushed her ahead of me, made sure that she kept moving, and then turned toward the redheads. Instead of standing my ground or backing away, I walked toward them, smiling, which surprised them enough to bring them to a halt.

As the one with the bad teeth looked past me at Annamaria, and as number two reached inside his unzipped jacket, I said, "You guys know about the tsunami warning?"

Number two kept his hand in his jacket, and the poster boy for dental hygiene shifted his attention to me. "Tsunami?"

"They estimate twenty to thirty feet."

"They who?"

"Even thirty feet," I said, "won't wash over the pier. She got scared, didn't want to stay, but I want to ride it out, see it. We must be—what?—forty feet off the water. It could be cool."

Throughout all this, the big guy had been approaching. As he joined us, number two asked him, "You hear about a tsunami?"

I said with some excitement, "The break slope on the shore here is twenty feet, but the other ten feet of the wave, man, it's gonna wipe out the front row of buildings."

Glancing back, as if to assess the potential for destruction, I was relieved to see Annamaria reaching the end of the pier.

"But the pier has deep pilings," I said. "The pier will ride it out. I'm pretty sure. It's solid. Don't you think the pier will ride it out?"

The big guy's mother had probably told him that he had

hazel eyes. Hazel is a light golden-brown. He did not have hazel eyes. They were yellow rather than golden, and they were more yellow than brown.

If his pupils had been elliptical instead of round, I could almost have believed that he was a humanoid puppet and that an intelligent mutant cat was curled up in his skull, peering at me through the empty sockets. And not a *nice* intelligent mutant cat.

His voice dispelled the feline image, for it had a timbre more suited to a bear. "Who're you?"

Instead of answering, I pretended excitement about the coming tsunami and looked at my wristwatch. "It could hit shore in like a few minutes. I gotta be on the observation deck when it comes."

"Who're you?" the hulk repeated, and he put his big right paw on my left shoulder.

The instant he touched me, reality flipped out of sight as if it were a discarded flashcard. I found myself not on the pier but on the shore instead, on a beach across which squirmed reflections of fire. A hideous bright something rose in a sea that pulsed with hellish light under an apocalyptic sky.

The nightmare.

Reality flipped into view again.

The hulk had snatched his hand back from my shoulder. With his wide eyes focused on his spread fingers, he looked as if he had been stung—or had seen the red tide of my dream.

Never before had I passed a dream or a vision, or a thought, or anything but a head cold, to someone else by a touch. Surprises like this spare me from a dull life.

Like the cold-jewel stare of a stone-temple god, the yellow gaze fixed on me again, and he said, "Who the hell are you?"

The tone of his voice alerted the redheads that an extraordinary event had occurred. The one with his hand inside his jacket withdrew a pistol, and the one with bad teeth reached into his jacket, most likely not for dental floss.

I ran three steps to the side of the pier, vaulted the railing, and dropped like a fry cook through mist and fading light.

Cold, dark, the Pacific swallowed me, my eyes burned in the brine, and as I swam beneath the surface, I fought the buoyant effect of the salt water, determined that the sea would not spit me up into a bullet-riddled twilight.